# Hotel Sales & Operations

# Hotel Sales & Operations

## Ahmed Ismail

Delmar Publishers

an International Thomson Publishing company

Albany • Bonn • Boston • Cincinnati • Detroit • London • Madrid
Melbourne • Mexico City • New York • Pacific Grove • Paris • San Francisco
Singapore • Tokyo • Toronto • Washington

## NOTICE TO THE READER

Publisher does not warrant or guarantee any of the products described herein or perform any independent analysis in connection with any of the product information contained herein. Publisher does not assume, and expressly disclaims, any obligation to obtain and include information other than that provided to it by the manufacturer.

The reader is expressly warned to consider and adopt all safety precautions that might be indicated by the activities herein and to avoid all potential hazards. By following the instructions contained herein, the reader willingly assumes all risks in connection with such instructions.

The publisher makes no representation or warranties of any kind including, but not limited to, the warranties of fitness for particular purpose or merchantability, nor are any such representations implied with respect to the material set forth herein, and the publisher takes no responsibility with respect to such material. The publisher shall not be liable for any special, consequential, or exemplary damages resulting, in whole or in part, from the readers' use of, or reliance upon, this material.

Cover Design: Elaine Scull
Cover Art: © Don Bishop for Artville

*Delmar Staff*
Publisher: Susan Simpfenderfer
Acquisitions Editor: Jeff Burnham
Developmental Editor: Andrea Edwards Myers
Production Manager: Wendy Troeger
Production Editor: Elaine Scull
Marketing Manager: Katherine M. Hans


Printed in Canada

For more information contact:

**Delmar Publishers**
3 Columbia Circle, Box 15015
Albany, New York 12212-5015

**International Thomson Publishing Europe**
Berkshire House
168–173 High Holborn
London, WC1V7AA
United Kingdom

**Nelson ITP, Australia**
102 Dodds Street
South Melbourne,
Victoria, 3205 Australia

**International Thomson Publishing France**
Tour Maine-Montparnasse
33 Avenue du Maine
73755 Paris Cedex 15, France

**Nelson Canada**
1120 Birchmont Road
Scarborough, Ontario
5G4 M1K Canada

**International Thomson Editores**
Seneca 53
Colonia Polanco
11560 Mexico D. F. Mexico

**International Thomson Publishing Gmbh**
Königswinterer Strasse 418
53227 Bonn
Germany

**International Thomson Publishing Asia**
60 Albert Street
#15-01 Albert Complex
Singapore 189969

**International Thomson Publishing Japan**
Hirakawa-cho Kyowa Building, 3F
2–2–1 Hirakawa-cho, Chiyoda-ku,
102 Tokyo, Japan

**ITE Spain/Paraninfo**
Calle Magallanes, 25
28015-Madrid, Espana



2 3 4 5 6 7 8 9 10 XXX 04 03 02 01 00 99 98

Library of Congress Cataloging-in-Publication Data
Ismail, Ahmed.
Hotel sales & operations / Ahmed Ismail.
p. cm.
Includes index.
ISBN 0-8273-8647-8
1. Hotels—Marketing. I. Title.
TX911.3.M3I86 1999
647.94'068'8—dc21 98-20547
CIP

Printed in Canada

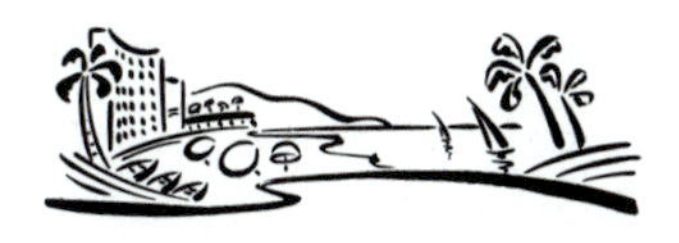

*Delmar Publishers is pleased to offer the following books on*

# HOSPITALITY, TRAVEL AND TOURISM

- **Catering & Convention Services**
  Ahmed Ismail
- **Conducting Tours, 2E**
  Marc Mancini
- **Destination: North America**
  Dawne M. Flammger
- **Dining Room and Banquet Management, 2E**
  Anthony Strianese
- **Domestic Ticketing and Airfare**
  Linda Hood
- **Geography of Travel & Toursim, 3E**
  Lloyd Hudman and Richard Jackson
- **Hospitality and Travel Marketing, 2E**
  Alastair Morrison
- **Hosting the Disabled: Crossing Communications Barriers Group Travel, 2E**
  Martha Sarbey deSouto
- **Hotel, Restaurant and Travel Law, 5E**
  Norman Cournoyer, Anthony G. Marshall and Karen Morris
- **Hotel Sales & Operations**
  Ahmed Ismail
- **International Air Fares Construction and Ticketing**
  Helle Sorensen
- **International Travel and Tourism**
  Helle Sorensen
- **Introduction to Corporate Travel**
  Annette Reiff
- **Learning Apollo: Basic and Advanced Training**
  Talula Austine Gunter
- **Marketing & Selling the Travel Product, 2E**
  James Burke and Barry Resnick
- **Math for Food Service, 3E**
  Robert Haines
- **Passport: An Introduction to Travel & Tourism, 2E**
  David Howell
- **Practical Food & Beverage Cost Control**
  Clement Ojugo
- **Practical Guide to Fares and Ticketing, 2E**
  Jeanne Semer-Purzycki
- **Sabre Reservations: Basic and Advanced Training**
  Gerald Capwell and Barry Resnick
- **Selling Destinations: Geography for the Travel Professional**
  Marc Mancini
- **Travel Agency Management**
  Gerald Fuller
- **Travel Perspectives: A Guide to Becoming a Travel Agent, 2E**
  Susan Rice and Ginger Todd
- **Welcome to Hospitality: An Introduction**
  Dr. Kye-Sung (Kaye) Chon and Dr. Ray Sparrowe

*an International Thomson Publishing company* ITP®

# Contents

# *Preface*

*Hotel Sales and Operations* approaches the intricate world of hospitality in a unique way. Various aspects of sales and marketing are covered to provide the student or inexperienced hotel sales professional with foundational concepts and keys to selling a hotel. While focused primarily on the room sales side of a hotel, *Hotel Sales and Operations* also ties the outlet/ancillary and catering sales sides together so that the interrelationship of all revenue-generating departments is understood.

The text is organized logically; each chapter builds on the previous one. Considerable effort was made to ensure that *Hotel Sales and Operations* was presented in such a way as to promote learning and discussion. Each chapter ends with a summary of key concepts and a series of review questions to provoke thought.

Throughout *Hotel Sales and Operations,* the reader will find examples that encourage creative thinking. An innovative component of this text, called "Industry Perspectives," was developed to give the reader a real-world view from industry professionals who address various relevant topics. Graphs and charts are presented in an easy-to-follow format.

# Acknowledgments

The author's thanks go to many people who assisted in the making of this text. The professionals who gave their support and input include Jim Craig, Lisa Darlington, Dawn Hill, Carolyn Morton, Ric Nicholson, John Pohl, Carolyn Porter, Scott Silvia, and John Sweetland. The support and patience of my wife Jamie ensured that this text would be completed. Most of all, I wish to thank my father. He provided the vision and encouragement that made me believe this book could be done.

# About the Author

**Ahmed Ismail** is an acknowledged authority in the hospitality industry. He received a B.A. from Gustavus Adolphus College, St. Peter, MN, in International Management. His professional experience spans over a decade in hotel sales and marketing with Marriott, Hyatt and Renaissance Corporations. Throughout his career, he has received numberous awards for sales leadership and marketing innovation. He is sought after by many hotel companies for sales and operations consulting as well as numerous speaking engagements. He has guided many to rewarding and successful careers in the hospitality industry.

CHAPTER 1

# The Foundation of Hotel Sales

*"Awareness of one's surroundings leads to awareness of oneself."*

ANONYMOUS

## INTRODUCTION

What exactly is *hotel sales*? What do hotel salespeople actually *sell*? The images that come to mind for those not familiar with the industry can vary greatly. In fact, it is not uncommon for hospitality professionals not engaged in sales to be unsure of exactly what the members of the hotel sales office do daily.

*Hotel sales* is defined for our purposes as the combination of room and catering sales. The members of a hotel's team who are engaged in these efforts are called salespeople. In hospitality, all the salespeople make up a **sales team**. The sales team is divided into two main parts that mirror the two main hotel revenue sources: the room sales division and the catering sales division. Each part of the sales team endeavors to maximize its potential to contribute to the hotel's success. This chapter provides the foundation as to what the sales team sells and why the sales team is important.

## REVENUE SOURCES

In the hospitality industry, as in any other industry, a successful and profitable operation is the ultimate goal. Hotel owners, managers, and employees all play roles in achieving this goal. What exactly is meant by *success* in hospitality? A successful hotel has maximized all its revenue sources. A **revenue source** is the result of a product or service a hotel makes available to guests for a price. The sizes and scopes of revenue sources can differ greatly from hotel to hotel. Most hotels use three main revenue sources:

1. Sleeping rooms
2. Meeting/function space
3. Outlets/ancillaries

### SLEEPING ROOMS

A **sleeping room** is traditionally the main product of any hotel, because a hotel's primary purpose is to provide accommodations. A sleeping room is defined as one accommodation unit. The price of each accommodation unit is called the room rate. The room rates from all used, or occupied, sleeping rooms are a significant revenue source for the hotel.

### MEETING/FUNCTION SPACE

In addition to the revenue source of sleeping room sales, many hotels incorporate the revenue source of nonsleeping room sales. Unlike sleeping rooms, **meeting/function space** is used for any type of group function. A group function can be a meeting, a meal, a dance, an exposition, or any other gathering of more than one person. One way in which hotels derive revenue from meeting/function space is by selling the space for a specified period. Function rooms are not sold as much as they are rented, however. The proceeds from the renting of meeting/function rooms is called room rental. Hotels also derive revenue from meeting/function rooms by providing food and beverage service in these rooms. This revenue is called banquet or catering revenue.

## OUTLETS/ANCILLARIES

An **outlet** is defined as a food and beverage point of sale. Restaurants, bars, lounges, room service, and other outlets can provide a hotel with significant revenue sources. An **ancillary** is a revenue source outside sleeping rooms or food and beverage. An ancillary revenue source can be a hotel's business center, golf course, tennis center, audiovisual services, or gift shop. The revenue from outlets and ancillary revenue sources is generally tied to the number of guests in the hotel. Therefore, the ability to fill sleeping and meeting rooms leads to better outlet/ancillary performance.

Thus, running a successful hotel entails:

1. Selling as many sleeping rooms as possible;
2. Selling meeting/function space to maximize its potential; and
3. Maximizing the capacity of the outlets and ancillary profit centers through the selling of sleeping and meeting rooms (Numbers 1 and 2).

The selling of the three main revenue sources in a hotel dictates the hotel's success (Figure 1–1). The room sales effort fills the sleeping rooms nightly. The catering sales effort endeavors to fill the meeting space. The combination of the two translates into sales in the outlet and ancillary

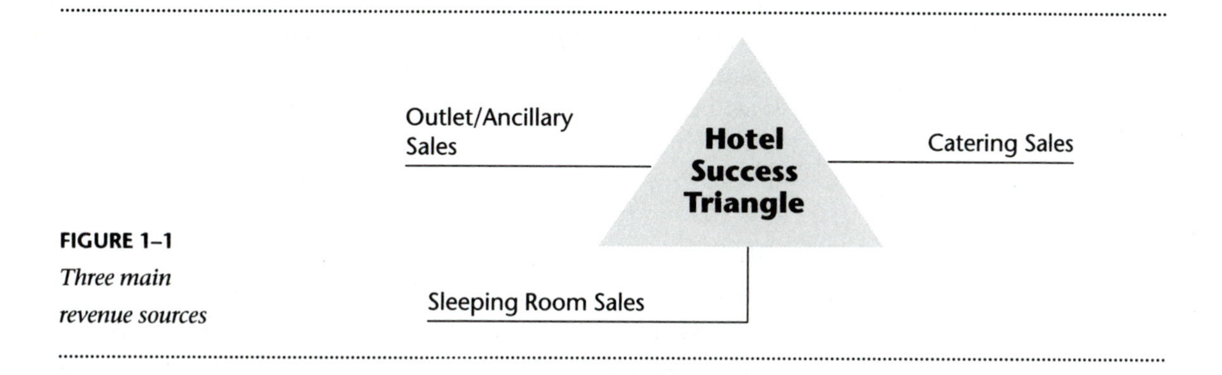


**FIGURE 1–1**
*Three main revenue sources*

revenue sources. This three-sided relationship can be viewed as a hotel's **successful sales triangle**.

## ROOM SALES DIFFERENTIATION

As Figure 1–1 shows, sleeping room sales make up the base of the hotel success triangle. The sleeping room sales effort is conducted by the room sales team with the ultimate goal of selling every available room in the hotel each night. **Occupancy** is the measurement of how many rooms are sold each night versus how many rooms the hotel has available to sell. This measurement is viewed by the industry as one of the most important to overall hotel performance.

The rooms that are sold fall into two types or categories: group and transient. The combination of group and transient rooms makes up the hotel's occupancy.

### GROUP ROOMS

**Group rooms** originate from reservations that are made to bring more than one guest into the hotel. A reservation is a booking made by a travel agent, some other intermediary, or the guest for one or more nights at a hotel. An **intermediary** is the person or entity that acts as a liaison between a guest and the hotel. Group rooms involve a series of bookings that correspond to specific functions. These functions can be conventions, meetings, or other events held at the hotel or nearby. Most hotels consider a booking of ten or more rooms per night a group booking.

The purpose of the group room sales effort is to seek group bookings and to bring them to the hotel. A relatively recent development in the hospitality industry, group sales is counted on to fill a certain number of hotel rooms a night. The group base is the measurement of how many group rooms are "on the books" on a given night. The group reserving this base is contractually obligated to arrive on a certain day and to fill a specific number of rooms. Therefore, a hotel can look to future group bookings as good indications of its upcoming occupancy levels.

Groups, because they can be booked far in advance, are sought after. The group sales team may reduce the room rate offered to a group in exchange for the group's contribution to the hotel's overall base. The specific tools for booking groups are addressed later, but is crucial to note here that group rooms are often offered at lower rates.

### TRANSIENT ROOMS

**Transient rooms** are rooms that originate from individual reservations. Transient rooms are generally filled by business and pleasure guests who stay at the hotel for reasons unrelated to functions being held there or nearby. Transient rooms are nongroup rooms. Transient rooms differ from group rooms in that there is no guarantee of when the guests will arrive. Individual reservations are made at the guests' discretion, so predicting their level on any given night is difficult. Determining the most likely levels of transient demand entails looking at historical data. In the transient sales arena, the individual booking cycle dictates the historical transient demand levels. The **individual booking cycle** is the time between when an individual reservation is made and when that reservation is due to arrive. The booking cycle can be anywhere from a few days to a few months. The transient demand is low outside that traditional booking cycle and increases drastically within it. Whereas the group base can be reserved at a hotel far in advance, the individual booking cycle is more short term. Walk-in reservations, which are made by those arriving unannounced at a hotel in search of rooms, cannot be measured as part of the individual booking cycle because they are obviously difficult to predict. However, walk-ins can play a major role in the transient demand at certain hotels, which is why they are important to understand.

## YIELD MANAGEMENT

As was mentioned earlier, the combination of group and transient rooms makes up the hotel's occupancy, or overall room demand. It should now be noted, with the understanding of the group base and the individual booking cycle, how group and transient rooms come together. The group base is known before the individual booking cycle becomes a factor. Because a hotel has a group base before the booking cycle starts, transient room salespeople can charge room rates based on how many rooms are available. This pricing strategy is called **yield management**.

For example, Figure 1–2 shows a fictitious hotel's group base for a specific week. Imagine that the individual booking cycle is 1 week out. The hotel has 400 rooms for sale each night. In this example, the group base differs throughout the week as different groups come and go. While it comes close, the hotel never sells every room based solely on group demand. This is where transient rooms become a factor. Transient rooms fill the voids left by the group base on each night of the week (Figure 1–3). Using yield management, hotel salespeople try to come as close to full occupancy as is possible each night while maximizing the hotel's revenue potential. How exactly does yield management work?

Yield management incorporates two main factors: rate availability and length-of-stay restrictions.

**Rate Availability.** Yield management based on rate availability has the flexibility to tailor individual room rates based on the rooms already

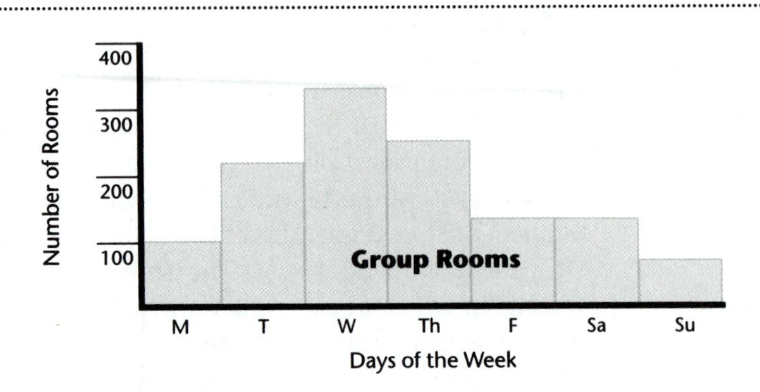


**FIGURE 1–2**
*Hotel group base for a specific week*

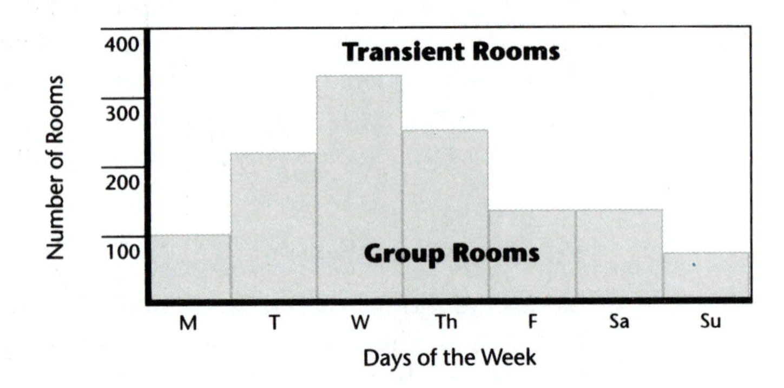


**FIGURE 1–3**
*Transient room sales*

on the books (the group base). In our example (see Figure 1–2), the group base is strongest on Tuesday, Wednesday, and Thursday. Under this yield-management strategy, the transient room salespeople should mirror the group-base pattern by charging more for a room on those three nights. Return to our example, this time knowing that the rack rate, or highest available published rate, is $150. The closer the room rate is to the rack rate, the closer the room comes to maximizing its revenue potential. Therefore, to maximize revenue potential, guests staying on Wednesday should be charged $135, while those staying on Monday should be charged $100 (Figure 1–4).

**Length-of-Stay Restrictions.** Like managing available rates, restricting the lengths of transient stays allows the hotel to manage its available rooms. The theory is that by restricting the number of nights a guest may stay at a certain rate, the hotel minimizes lower rates and maximizes revenue potential. In our ongoing example, if a guest made a reservation starting Monday for three nights at $100, he or she would be at the hotel on Wednesday night at a lower rate than that being offered to other guests. In this case, yield management would dictate that the $100 rate be available only for one or two nights. If the transient guest wanted to stay three nights, the available rate should mirror the rate on the busiest night, Wednesday.

Yield management of length of stay works in the other direction as well. A hotel may offer a lower rate for multiple nights if a portion of those nights are during lower occupancy periods. In our ongoing example, a guest making a 1-night reservation for Thursday may be offered a rate that corresponds to the available rate of $115. If that same guest wanted a 3-night stay extending into the weekend, however, the hotel might lower the available rate to more closely mirror the lower demand of Friday and Saturday. This application of yield management encourages the transient guest to stay when the hotel needs him or her most.

A hotel may decide which rate to offer by averaging the two rates in question (Figure 1–5). Averaging rates may be easier than applying the available rate restriction. For example, a guest wishing to stay at a hotel Wednesday, Thursday, and Friday nights may be quoted the average of the available transient rates:

$$\$135 + \$120 + \$110 \div 3 = \$122 \text{ (average rate)}$$

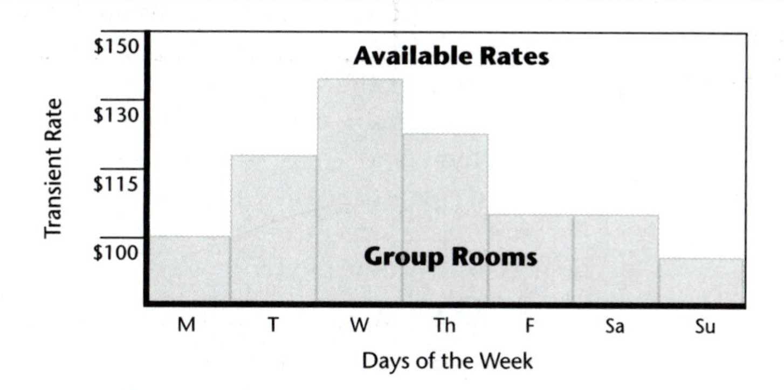


**FIGURE 1–4**
*Available daily room rates*

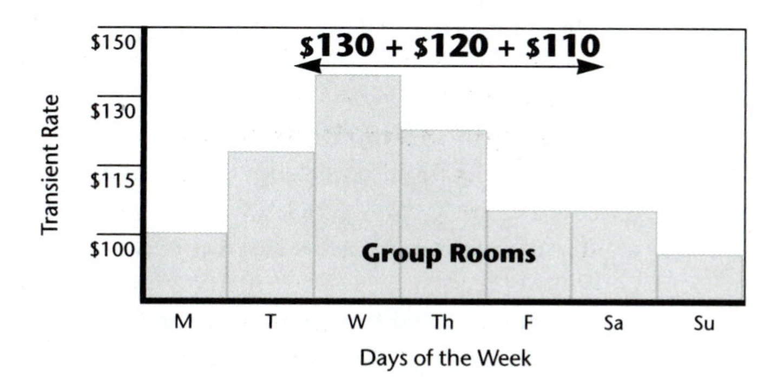


**FIGURE 1–5**
*Rate averaging*

## THE IMPACT OF ROOM SALES

The three sides of the hotel success triangle, room sales, catering sales, and outlet/ancillary sales (see Figure 1–1), direct the profitability and overall financial health of any hotel. Each plays an important role in that success. There is a reason room sales gain more attention, however. It can be said that the success triangle of any hotel would collapse without the strong base of room sales. Why? Because room sales are the foundation of hotel success.

In hospitality, financial health is measured by the strength of the three components of the hotel success triangle. The base of any triangle must be able to support the other two sides. Room sales, by definition, endeavor to fill the hotel. A full hotel dictates the hotel's financial health.

The sleeping room is the most profitable of all products and services sold in the hotel because of its profit margin and the captive audience quotient.

### PROFIT MARGIN

**Profit margin** is determined by comparing the sales revenue of a service or product with the costs incurred in providing the service or product. In hospitality, profit margins of each side of the success triangle can be derived from analyzing food cost and room cost.

**Food Cost.** The differences between the profit margins of food and room sales is at the heart of why room sales are so important. To determine profit margin, one must first determine the costs incurred in providing the item.

**Food cost** is the cost of a food item relative to its price. This cost is often measured as a percentage. The most simple way to understand this is to understand that the food cost percentage is the percentage of the profit that is taken by the cost of the item. To calculate this percentage, simply divide the purchase price of the item by the menu price and multiply by 100:

$$\text{Food Cost Percentage} = \text{Purchase Price} \div \text{Menu Price} \times 100$$

For example:

| Item | Purchase Price (Each)* | Menu Price* | Food Cost (Percent)* |
|---|---|---|---|
| Steak | $5.95 | $22.00 | 27 |
| Chicken | $3.95 | $17.95 | 22 |
| Caesar Salad | $1.99 | $ 9.95 | 20 |

*These prices and costs are strictly for demonstration. They include the total cost of the meal (starch, vegetable, and beverage, if applicable).

The preceding example shows the price for purchasing and reselling (menu price) each item. Each respective food cost reflects the hotel's cost relative to the menu price.

# *Industry Perspective*

## Sleeping Room Impact on Restaurant Sales

*Jim Craig*
*Assistant Food and Beverage Manager*
*Marriott Corporation*

What brings revenue to restaurant outlets within a hotel? The obvious answer is customers, but specifically what kind of customers make up the majority of the cover counts (customers per meal period)? This answer varies slightly, but not as much as might be expected. Whether the hotel is a resort or a downtown or an airport property, the basic answer is the same: in-house guests. While some hotel outlets may establish local, "regular" crowds, this type of business accounts for only a very small portion of the restaurant's total revenue. Typically, in-house guests make up approximately 70 to 80 percent of the total covers served in hotel restaurants.

It follows, then, that the higher the hotel's occupancy rate, the higher its potential for restaurant profits. Because sales and marketing team members are responsible for filling the hotel's rooms, they are valuable links to restaurant profits. Specific types of groups booked by the sales team can be the lifelines of a hotel restaurant. The customer with the highest "capture rate" (70 to 80 percent) is the group attendee who lacks scheduled meal functions. This capture rate is considerably higher than the 30 to 40 percent capture rate of the transient guest. This is simple to understand, because group functions are usually very structured and allow only short meal breaks. Adding to this, most group members do not have transportation to off-property dining, even if time permitted. Under these circumstances, the hotel restaurant is a welcome convenience.

The hotel itself has some opportunities to generate restaurant business, but overall the sales team provides the most consistent opportunity for restaurant business. The sales team brings guests into the hotel, both group and transient. It is up to the rest of the hotel to provide a favorable experience to ensure customer satisfaction and repeat business.

Hotel food and beverage options are often measured by how well they control food costs relative to profits. A high food cost could result if a hotel charges too little for menu items. A low food cost could result if the hotel overcharges for menu items. The measurement of "too low" or "too high" depends in large part on the management philosophy of the property and the market in which it is competing. For the sake of analysis, food cost percentages between 30 and 50 percent are common.

**Room Cost.** Relative to food cost, room cost is lower. Room cost has fewer relative fixed costs than does a food item. In room cost analysis, one must look at what it costs the hotel to prepare and maintain a room relative to what that room is sold for to the average guest.

The cost of providing a clean, comfortable room differs from market to market and from hotel to hotel. The basic components that make up room cost at most hotels are **heat/light/power (h/l/p)**, labor, and overhead. In combination, these may seem like imposing costs. In reality, however, they make up a small portion of the hotel room rate. Again, the actual numbers may vary, but in most markets the cost of preparing and maintaining rooms for sale to guests ranges from $20 to $50 per night.

**ROOM COST COMPONENTS**

| **H/L/P** | **Labor** | **Overhead** |
|---|---|---|
| Heat | Housekeeping | Debt Service of Owners |
| Light | Engineering (Internal | Marketing* |
| Power | Structure Maintenance) | Management Costs |
| | | Taxes and Related |
| | | Corporate Obligations* |

*See Chapter 2.

The following example relates this analysis to the fictional ABC Hotel, which sells rooms for an average of $150 a night. The costs incurred by the hotel in preparing each room for sale may be:

| **Component** | **Cost** |
|---|---|
| Heat | $ 3.00 |
| Light | $ 2.00 |
| Power | $ 2.00 |
| Housekeeping | $ 9.00 |
| Engineering (Internal Structure Maintenance) | $ 5.00 |
| Debt Service of Owners | $ 0.50 |
| Marketing | $ 2.25 |
| Management Costs | $ 2.75 |
| Corporate Obligations | $ 2.00 |
| Taxes and Related Obligations | $ 2.50 |
| | **Total: $31.00** |

Divide this actual cost by the price sold (room rate) and multiply by 100 to determine the room cost percentage:

$$\text{Room Cost Percentage} = \frac{\text{Actual Cost}}{\text{Room Rate}} \times 100$$

$$= \frac{\$\ 31}{\$150} \times 100$$

$$= 21\%$$

At first glance, one might assume that the cost percentages of food and rooms are fairly similar, and they are. Compare these percentages with average room rates across the country and you will see that the sleeping room has a much higher profit margin than does food.

Costs translate into profit margins, as was alluded to earlier in this section. In the analysis of cost percentages, the amount that is not consumed by the cost of the item equals the profit. If, as in our examples, the cost of a room or food is 20 to 40 percent, then the profit is the remainder, which is 80 to 60 percent. The following compares profit margins:

| **Item** | **Purchase Price (Each)** | **Menu Price** | **Profit Margin** |
|---|---|---|---|
| Steak | $5.95 | $22.00 | $16.05 |
| Chicken | $3.95 | $17.95 | $14.00 |
| Caesar Salad | $1.99 | $ 9.95 | $ 7.96 |
| | **Room Cost** | **Room Rate** | **Profit Margin** |
| Sleeping Room | $30.00 | $150.00 | $120.00 |

Extending this analysis further, assume that this hotel has 400 sleeping rooms. If each room generates a profit margin of $120, the total sleeping room profit on any given, sold-out night is $48,000 ($120 × 400). The food and beverage outlets would have to sell 2,991 steak dinners or 6,030 caesar salads to make the same profit!

This difference in profit margin is one part of the fundamental equation of room sales versus catering and outlet sales, because selling rooms is much more profitable for the average hotel than any other component. Another part of this equation is the captive audience quotient.

## CAPTIVE AUDIENCE QUOTIENT

A hotel cannot have significant outlet/ancillary traffic, or groups that contribute to the catering revenue portion of the success triangle, without occupied rooms. Beyond providing profit differences, occupied rooms provide a captive audience. A **captive audience** in hospitality is defined as customers who are staying at the hotel and will, for convenience and the lack of other options, partake in the outlets the hotel offers. A captive guest eats in the hotel's restaurant, uses the hotel's business center, and attends or hosts a meeting at the facility.

The captive audience quotient applies to outlet/ancillary sales as well as catering sales. Whether a transient guest or a group guest, the captive audience guest is at the hotel. Freestanding restaurants and conference centers must get their patrons into their facilities before making any sale. This is where the separation between relying on local traffic and a captive audience is most apparent. For convenience and other reasons, a transient hotel guest is more likely than a local-traffic patron to choose some outlet of the hotel (if the hotel offers outlets) at least once. The appeal of room service and specialty on-site restaurants drives many guests to full-service hotels. (See Chapter 2 for further information.) Hotel golf courses and other recreational facilities can be of such stature that transient guests choose hotels to use their facilities.

A hotel that has meeting space benefits from the same captive audience quotient. Group-related catering is measured by its contribution to the overall catering effort. The **group catering contribution** is defined as the catering business acquired by a hotel that has all, or a major portion of, attendees staying at the hotel. A local seminar may have only a few sleeping rooms, so it is not group related. In contrast, a major corporate convention may have all attendees staying at the hotel, so it is group related. All functions that result from this convention (e.g., all breakfasts, lunches, dinners, and receptions) become group-related catering functions and contribute to greater catering revenue.

The group catering contribution directly impacts the catering operation of the hotel. Periods of low group occupancy in a hotel invariably weaken catering performance and dictate low levels of the group catering contribution. In contrast, transient occupancy has no tangible effect on catering revenue.

An argument can be made that a hotel can derive a portion of its business from local traffic (see Chapter 2) to significantly impact both the outlet/ancillary and the catering parts of the success triangle. In this rare situation, a hotel may fill its meeting space with nongroup-related functions. In this case, the hotel precludes any group from booking, because most groups tie functions to their sleeping rooms. A hotel in this situation has to rely solely on transient demand to fill its rooms. With no group base, most hotels find it difficult to fill sleeping rooms, and empty sleeping rooms mean the profit margins of room sales go unrealized.

## REV-PAR

The previous analysis of room cost and profit margin illustrated how the room sales component of hotels can be measured. This analysis, while tailored to the hospitality industry, is not exclusive to the industry. Cost analysis, as well as profit and loss, applies to almost every industry today. However, the hospitality industry has developed tools for analyzing room sales that are unique to the industry.

Because hotels differed in size, they needed to compare performance on an even playing field. A tool for comparing room revenue from hotel to hotel is called rev-par. **Rev-par** is defined as revenue per available room. Rev-par divides the total sleeping room revenue for a predetermined time frame by the total number of hotel rooms. Rev-par goes beyond occupancy analysis because it factors in the **average daily rate (ADR)**. This tool allows hotels of different sizes to compare the revenue they generate by selling sleeping rooms.

Factoring in size allows any hotel to compare itself to another. Often, rev-par is analyzed when a hotel is considering changing its rate structure. The following example shows how rev-par is calculated.

From our previous example we know that the fictitious ABC Hotel sells a room for an average of $150 a night (the ADR). In this example, assume the hotel has 350 rooms and a 76 percent occupancy on a given night. Rev-par factors the ADR and the occupancy rate into one figure (Rev-par = ADR ×Occupancy). The rev-par calculation begins with these steps:

**Step 1** **Data collection**

a. The ABC Hotel has 350 rooms, an ADR of $150, and an occupancy rate of 76 percent.

**Step 2** **Revenue calculation**

a. At 76 percent occupancy, the hotel will sell 266 of its 350 rooms (0.76 × 350).

b. With 266 rooms and an ADR of $150, room revenue will total $39,900 (266 × $150).

**Step 3** **Rev-par calculation**

a. When the total room revenue ($39,900) is divided by the total number of available rooms (350), the rev-par equals $114.

The ABC Hotel had a rev-par of $114 on this night, but the rev-par can analyze the performance of a hotel over any time frame (nightly, weekly, monthly, or yearly). Rev-par analysis is useful because of its aforementioned flexibility in comparing differently sized hotels and their respective rates. Consider another example, the XYZ Hotel. The XYZ Hotel has 500 rooms, runs an ADR of $120, and has a 76 percent occupancy rate, which results in 380 rooms being sold (0.76 × 500). The total room revenue is therefore $45,600 ($120 × 380).

At first glance, a novice may look at the higher total room revenue of XYZ Hotel and incorrectly assume that it outperformed ABC Hotel. However, a rev-par comparison shows that the rev-par for ABC Hotel ($114) is higher than the rev-par for XYZ Hotel ($45,600 ÷ 500 = $91.2). This example shows that, when ADR and occupancy are factored in, the ABC Hotel outperforms the XYZ Hotel.

**Rev-Par as a Tool for Performance Analysis.** As was already discussed, the success of a hotel is measured by room sales and their effect on the rest of the hotel. The captive audience quotient contributes to outlet/ancillary sales and the catering operation. Occupancy measures the capacity at which rooms are being used, and rev-par measures the efficiency of occupancy.

Managers and owners use rev-par when looking at the rate structure of a hotel. The rate structure is the application of all rates at a hotel, both group and transient. The rate structure includes when certain rates are offered and how they are applied via yield management.

Hotel managers and owners have varying goals for hotel performance. Some want their hotels to be filled (high occupancy) year-round, while others opt for higher ADR. This comparison, while somewhat generalized, depicts the two major "camps" in hotel performance analysis:

Rate Driven = One Goal (Make Money)
Occupancy Driven = Two Goals (High Occupancy or High ADR)

These two camps are not mutually exclusive, but they do have different approaches. The rate-driven manager may forgo some low-rated group business in the hope of filling the hotel with higher-rated groups and/or transients. In contrast, the occupancy-driven owner may loosen the rate restrictions in his or her yield-management strategy in an effort to fill more rooms. The rate-driven manager hopes to maximize the room rates for revenue, while the occupancy-driven owner hopes to capitalize on the captive audience quotient for the total hotel.

It is logical to conclude, then, that the rate-driven camp measures its success by high rates and that the occupancy camp measures its success by high occupancy. A rate-driven hotel would therefore be difficult to compare to an occupancy-driven hotel in the same market. How can the performances of these two hotel management styles be compared? Rev-par analysis can bring these two camps together and compare them.

The previous example compared the ABC and XYZ Hotels. Initially, the hotels shared an occupancy figure (76 percent). Now compare the two, assuming that the ABC Hotel has an occupancy rate of 65 percent and is rate driven and that the XYZ Hotel has an occupancy rate of 80 percent and is occupancy driven.

**Step 1** **Data collection**

a. The ABC Hotel has 350 rooms, an ADR of $140, and an occupancy rate of 65 percent.

b. The XYZ Hotel has 500 rooms, an ADR of $110*, and an occupancy of 80 percent.

**Step 2** **Revenue calculation**

a. At 65 percent occupancy, the 350-room ABC Hotel will sell 228 rooms (0.65 × 350).

b. At 80 percent occupancy, the 500-room XYZ Hotel will sell 400 rooms (0.80 × 500).

c. With 228 rooms and an ADR of $140, total room revenue for the ABC Hotel will equal $31,920 (228 × $140).

d. With 400 rooms and an ADR of $110, total room revenue for the XYZ Hotel will equal $44,000 (400 × $110).

**Step 3** **Rev-par calculation**

a. When the total room revenue for the ABC Hotel ($31,920) is divided by the total number of available rooms (350), a rev-par of $91 results (or 0.65 × $140).

b. When the total room revenue for the XYZ Hotel ($44,000) is divided by the total number of available rooms (500), a rev-par of $88 results (or 0.80 × $110).

In this example, the rate-driven ABC Hotel had a higher rev-par than the occupancy-driven XYZ Hotel. The XYZ management might want to reexamine its booking decisions to boost rev-par performance. However, as was stated earlier, hotel performance is "in the eye of the beholder." Rate-driven managers may be satisfied with higher ADRs than their competitors. A comparison of two similar hotels could have easily resulted in a higher rev-par for the occupancy-driven hotel. If the XYZ Hotel booked higher rates and still achieved the same occupancy numbers, its rev-par would have been higher.

In later sections, which look at the selling of hotel rooms, rev-par serves as a tool for analyzing strategic decisions. Rev-par is an important basic concept in performance analysis as well as sales critique.

*Because the XYZ Hotel is occupancy driven in this example, its ADR was lowered to increase occupancy.

## THE HOTEL ORGANIZATIONAL CHART

For any group, an organizational chart outlines the positions and responsibilities of each member. Not unlike a team roster, which identifies the position each team member will take on the field, the organizational chart aids in identifying and directing the management team. Learning how a hotel organizational chart is laid out is important to understanding the different departments a hotel may have and how those departments work together.

It is crucial to have this understanding of differing hotel departments before analyzing hospitality sales theory further. The hotel sales team members work every day to commit all the hotel's resources to a group or an individual. Each department contributes in its own way to these efforts. A clear understanding of the functions and duties of different departments teaches salespeople both potential actions and limitations. That understanding will also aid the salespeople in better understanding their own roles within the hotel.

The makeup of a hotel's organizational chart is contingent on the hotel's size classification. The **hotel size classification**, which is a tool used by the industry to describe the relative size of a property, is based on the total number of sleeping rooms. Large hotels have the highest numbers of sleeping rooms and therefore the largest management teams. Figure 1–6 outlines one way of organizing a large hotel management team at the property level. As this figure shows, there are three distinct levels of top management in the hotel organizational chart: top level, executive committee, and department heads. These levels are the predominant method of deploying a hotel's leadership team.

“*An executive is a person who always decides, sometimes he decides correctly, but he always decides.*”

JOHN H. PATTERSON

**COMMON HOTEL SIZE CLASSIFICATIONS**

| **Classification** | **Number of Sleeping Rooms** |
|---|---|
| Small | 1 to 150 |
| Medium | 151 to 400 |
| Large | 401 to 1,500 |
| Mega | 1,501 and over |

### TOP-LEVEL MANAGEMENT

The top-level manager at any hotel is most commonly called the general manager. The **general manager** is ultimately responsible for the hotel. The general manager may report to a regional manager in a chain, or he or she may report directly to the hotel owner. Sometimes called the managing director or the general director, the general manager directly or indirectly (via other managers) coordinates the hotel's operational and sales efforts.

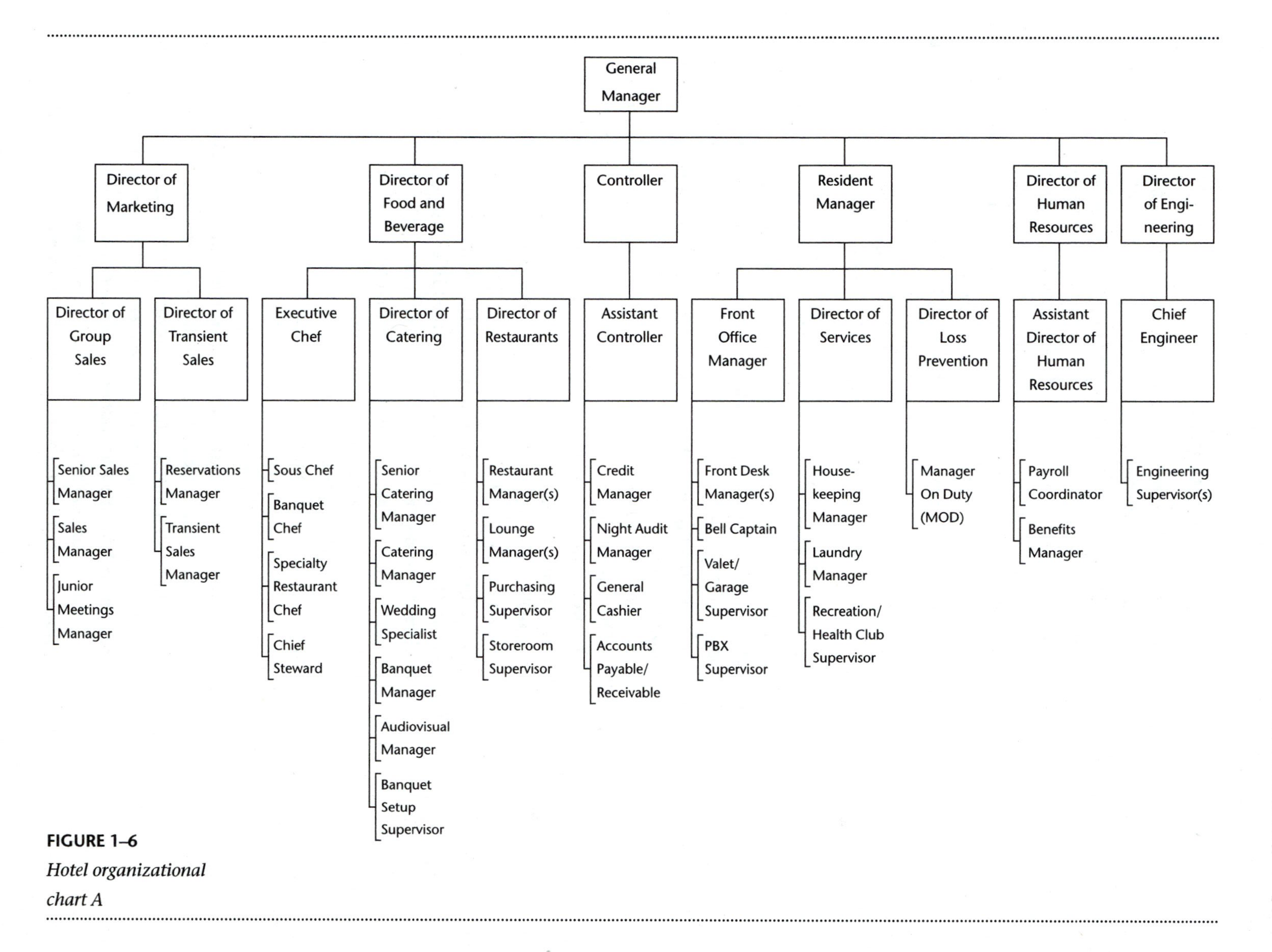


**FIGURE 1–6**
*Hotel organizational chart A*

## THE EXECUTIVE COMMITTEE

The **executive committee** is made up of senior-level managers who direct one or more facets of the hotel's operation. Reporting directly to the general manager, the executive committee sets specific revenue goals and operational targets. In some large hotel chains, regional managers are directly responsible for the strategic vision of each executive committee member. As Figure 1–6 shows, the executive committee may include the director of marketing, the director of food and beverage, the controller, the resident manager, the director of human resources, and the director of engineering. (Note: While these executive committee titles are the most common in the industry, they are not the only ones. Some hotels may place executive committee members in charge of public relations, casino operations, golf/tennis facilities, landscape/grounds, and information systems, to name a few.)

**Director of Marketing.** The **director of marketing (DOM)** oversees the hotel's sales and marketing operation, directing the group sales strategy in tandem with efforts to maximize transient revenue. He or she also implements long-range goals, mentors staff in career planning, directs all advertising, and helps determine the hotel's yearly budget and marketing plan.

**Director of Food and Beverage.** The **director of food and beverage (DOFB)** runs each department that sells, buys, or makes food and beverage products for guests. The catering, restaurant/outlet, and kitchen staff report to him or her.

**Controller** The **hotel controller** is in charge of the hotel's financial reporting and cash-flow management. The controller must monitor costs as well as help make cash-expenditure decisions. The controller typically has input in the operational decisions of most hotel departments.

**Resident Manager.** The title **"resident manager"** can be traced back many years. It started as the name for the manager who actually lived at the hotel (hence the term *resident*) and was available at all hours. Some time ago, it was determined that an individual should be in charge of the hotel when the general manager was unavailable. It soon became apparent that the after-hours responsibilities of this resident manager would center around sleeping rooms because of the 24-hour nature of hotels. Today, at large hotels it is rare to find the resident manager residing at the hotel but, because the age-old responsibilities of coordinating the operations of room-related hotel functions remain, the title remains. Some hotels use the title "rooms division manager" for this position instead.

**Director of Human Resources.** The director of human resources is in charge of all hotel personnel. His or her responsibilities include recruiting employment candidates and complying with all governmental regulations when hiring and terminating employees. Payroll and benefits are coordinated through this office.

**Director of Engineering.** The director of engineering is unique among executive committee members in that he or she is involved in the physical aspects of the hotel's operation. The conditions of the interior and exterior of the hotel fall under his or her purview. Controlling the costs of h/l/p as well as general maintenance are part of the engineering director's responsibilities. Long-term hotel improvement planning and renovations begin with this executive committee member.

## DEPARTMENT HEADS

The next level of management in the Figure 1–6 organizational chart includes the department managers, or department heads. Typically reporting to a member of the executive committee, **department heads** are the managers who are most directly involved in a department's day-to-day operations.

**Director of Group Sales.** The **director of group sales (DOGS)** is responsible specifically for the group room sales effort. On a day-to-day basis, the DOGS supervises and assists in the decision making of the senior and junior salespeople. Often, the DOGS is personally responsible for key/focus group accounts that have important and/or long-term impact on the hotel. Reporting to the DOM, the DOGS is accountable for achieving group revenue targets. He or she often works very closely with the director of transient sales and the director of catering.

**Director of Transient Sales.** Reporting to the DOM, the **director of transient sales (DOTS)** is responsible for the transient sales effort at a hotel. Working with his or her team of reservationists, the DOTS attempts to maximize the potential revenue of the transient market. In coordination with the DOGS and the members of the executive committee, the DOTS is the employee who is most responsible for the proper implementation of yield management. The DOTS is sometimes called the director of reservations.

**Executive Chef.** The **executive chef** is responsible for the hotel's overall food production. He or she must control food costs while ensuring that the hotel's level of food quality is maintained. More of a manager than a hands-on chef, the executive chef monitors the food production of the hotel's restaurants, lounges, catering/banquet functions, and in-house employee cafeteria. The executive chef reports directly to the DOFB.

**Director of Catering.** The **director of catering (DOC)** is responsible for the catering side of the sales effort. He or she must be able to direct all local and group catering efforts on hotel property. Typically, the DOC manages the catering sales staff as well as the operational catering staff directly. In very large hotels, the catering sales staff may report to the DOC while the operational staff may report to a director of convention services. (The convention service manager is discussed later in this chapter.) The DOC works closely with the executive chef to develop menus. The DOC can report to the DOFB or to the DOM.

**Director of Restaurants.** The **director of restaurants** is responsible for the staffing, quality, and cost control of all food and beverage outlets in a hotel. Reporting to the DOFB, the director of restaurants works closely with the executive chef's staff to ensure that all restaurants and lounges are up to standard.

**Assistant Controller.** The **assistant controller** (there may be more than one controller at large hotels) coordinates the day-to-day activities of the accounting office. The members of the accounts payable and receivable teams as well as the credit manager report to him or her. The general cashier and the night audit staff also report to the assistant controller. Financial reporting and compliance issues are large parts of the assistant controller's responsibilities.

**Front Office Manager.** The **front office manager** is responsible for a large portion of the most visible aspects of a hotel's operation. He or she directs the day-to-day activities of the front desk, the bell stand, and the concierge staff. Each of these departments is considered to be on the hotel's front line because it has a great deal of guest contact. The efficiency and service levels of each department under the purview of the front office manager are crucial to ensuring guest satisfaction. Some hotels include the PBX (internal switchboard or operator) staff in the front office manager's line of authority. Working closely with the director of services, the front office manager reports to the resident manager.

**Director of Services.** The **director of services** can be viewed as the "behind-the-scenes" version of the front office manager. The director of services is responsible for the hotel's housekeeping, laundry, and, often, recreational services. These departments are considered "back of the house" because they involve limited guest contact. The director of services must ensure that the quality of the guest rooms and the cleanliness of the hotel's interior are up to standard.

**Director of Loss Prevention.** The director of loss prevention can be a very important department head. His or her main priority is the safety and security of all hotel guests and employees. Members of the loss prevention staff patrol the hotel's halls and common areas. The director of loss prevention must ensure that all accidents and guest complaints are handled professionally and thoroughly. In many hotels, loss prevention also serves as a shipping and receiving department.

**Assistant Director of Human Resources.** The assistant director of human resources works closely with all other department heads to maintain employee satisfaction and to ensure that proper employment procedures are followed. He or she is often called upon to screen potential applicants in initial employment interviews.

**Chief Engineer.** The chief engineer coordinates the day-to-day maintenance of the hotel's physical structure. Often, his or her main priorities include assigning engineering staff preventive maintenance duties.

## SALES OFFICE ORGANIZATION

The preceding discussed a sample organizational chart and the management staff members composing it. As was mentioned earlier, understanding the duties of other departments complements any hotel salesperson's knowledge base. Because this book focuses on room sales, it is necessary to spend more time examining the organization of the hotel sales office.

The hierarchy of the sales office is not fixed throughout the hospitality industry. In fact, the hospitality industry views the sales office in different ways. The manner in which salespeople are deployed and to whom they report can differ from hotel to hotel. The specific titles and responsibilities of each salesperson also can differ. As a whole, the hospitality industry views sales office organization in two fundamentally different manners: traditional and revenue based.

### TRADITIONAL VERSUS REVENUE-BASED SALES DEPLOYMENT

The traditional organization scenario divides the sales efforts into two camps, employing the concept that room sales are unique and that catering sales are separate. As a result, those involved in group and transient sales report to one executive committee member while the catering salespeople report to another. All food and beverage departments, including catering sales and the outlets, report to the person in charge of the hotel's food and beverage arm. The person who directs the sleeping room effort manages the transient and group salespeople. The traditional organizational chart includes employees, namely the DOFB and the resident manager, whose respective responsibilities include the hotel's food and beverage side and its sleeping room operational side. Organizational chart A (see Figure 1–6) reflects the traditional sales organization at a sample large hotel.

The revenue-based organizational chart eliminates the resident manager position and adds an executive committee position, director of operations. (Figure 1–7 shows a sample revenue-based organizational chart.) As the latter title implies, the **director of operations** is in charge of the fundamental operational functions of the hotel. All operational departments that are not involved in the selling of a hotel product report to him

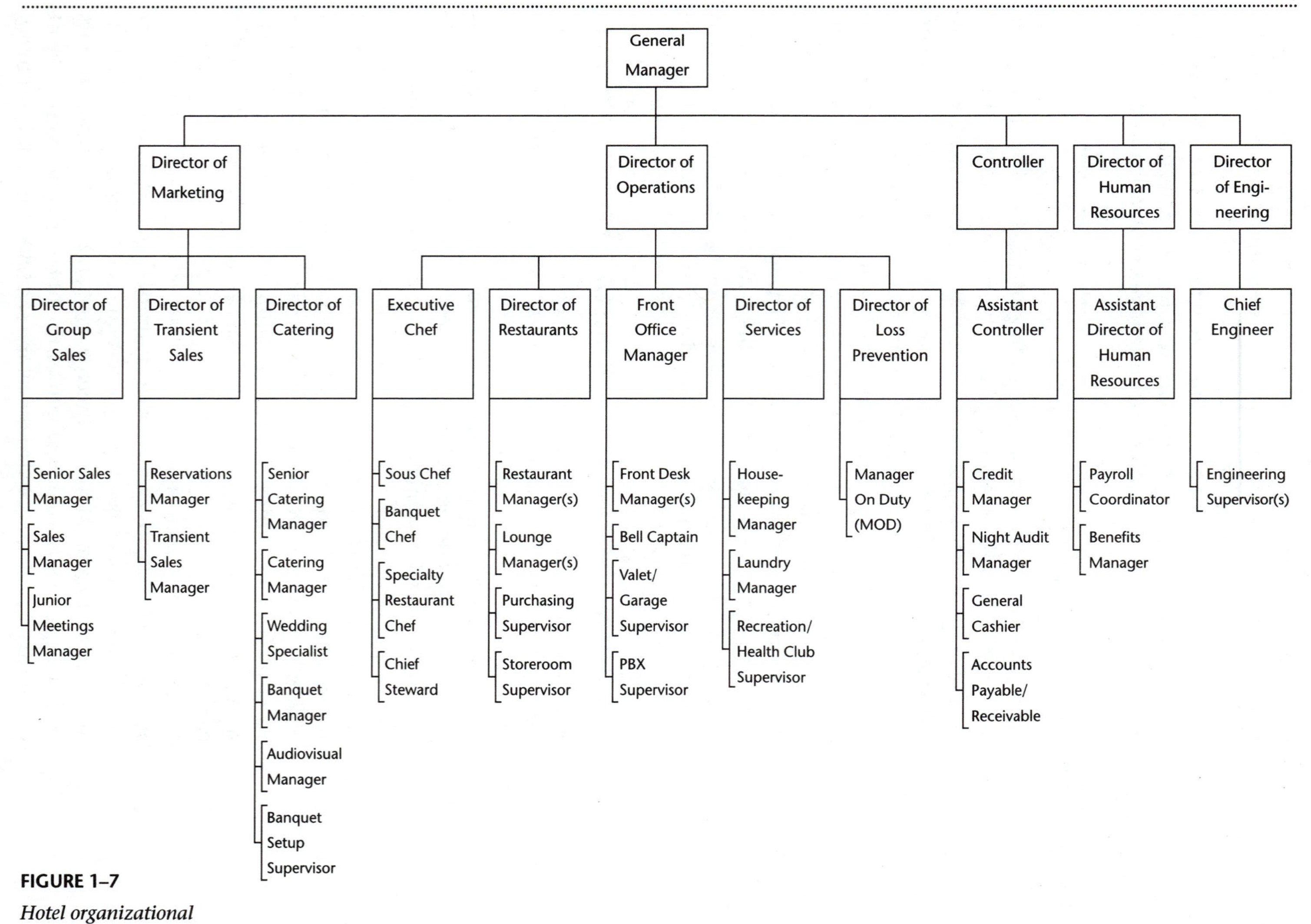


**FIGURE 1–7** *Hotel organizational chart B*

or her. In the revenue-based organizational chart, sales (proactive revenue) managers report to one executive committee member and the operational (reactive revenue) managers report to another.

The director of operations, in essence, combines the responsibilities of the DOFB and the resident manager. Rooms-related and food and beverage departments report to one executive committee member. The strategic vision that results when differing operational departments report to one individual can positively impact the hotel. This synergy is beneficial because the end result of total guest satisfaction can be coordinated easily by one individual. The director of operations deals more often with the guests in the hotel than the general manager because of this departmental synergy. Sometimes called an assistant general manager or a senior assistant manager, the director of operations position is often viewed as a stepping stone to the position of general manager.

The revenue-based organizational chart differs from the traditional in that it combines all sales-related departments under one heading. In this setup, the executive committee member in charge of the total hotel sales effort oversees the group and transient sales team as well as the catering sales team. Another way to view the differences between the revenue-based and the traditional organizational charts is to look at the way hotel revenue is generated in each. The sales team members (staff in group, transient, and catering) seek business for the hotel. They are proactive revenue generators. The outlets and other operational departments serve guests as needed. Therefore, the revenue they generate, if any, is more reactive.

## SALES OFFICE JOB DESCRIPTIONS

Whether traditional or revenue-based, the sales office organizational chart contains the same fundamental positions. The following identifies the most prevalent sales and catering job roles below department head on the organizational chart. All these positions report directly or indirectly to the DOM in the revenue-based organizational chart.

**Senior Sales Manager.** The **senior sales manager** handles major group accounts. Often, the senior sales manager is put in charge of grooming junior salespeople in the sales process. In the absence of a DOGS, the "senior" can assume group sales departmental responsibility. The groups a senior works with can be spread throughout the country, which translates into frequent travel duties. A senior sales manager may be tapped as a liaison in fostering better interdepartmental communication in the hotel. A senior is sometimes called a national account manager.

**Sales Manager.** Most hotels employ more than one **sales manager**. Most group-related business is booked by hotel sales managers. Hotels that employ more than one sales manager deploy them in different ways.

Whether deployed via market segment (see Chapter 2) or via geographic territory, sales managers work under the close supervision of the DOGS or the senior sales manager.

**Senior Catering Manager/Catering Manager/Convention Service Manager.** The **senior catering manager/catering manager/convention service manager** is primarily concerned with two things: booking local catering and servicing groups. **Local catering** is hotel business that has no associated group rooms. Specifically, local catering is business in which the function or the meal is the primary focus. Some local catering may have associated sleeping rooms, but it is considered local catering unless the client's main goal is to book rooms.

Group **servicing** is the on-property coordination of a group's specifics. Depending on the size of the hotel, these specifics can be food and beverage related or they can be rooms related. Again, depending on the size of the hotel, this servicing can be done by the catering or convention service departments. In some cases, three departments are involved in the booking and servicing of a group. The room salesperson books the group, the catering salesperson coordinates all menus, and the convention serviceperson manages the servicing once the group is on property. No matter how many departments are involved, however, the sales department books the group and another department takes over as the group's arrival date nears. (This is true except in the case of "meetings managers," which is addressed later.)

## CATERING/CONVENTION SERVICE DEPLOYMENT

Depending on the size of a hotel and its management philosophy, the relationship of group sales to the catering and convention service departments can differ slightly. Some hotels have no convention service department. In those hotels, the catering department assumes all servicing duties. The three most common ways to deploy the sales and service sides of a hotel are three-tiered, two-tiered, and modified two-tiered.

Three-tiered deployment (Figure 1–8) requires that the three branches of the hotel sales team work together. Each branch has a role in moving a group from booking to arrival.

Two-tiered deployment (Figure 1–9) exists in hotels with no convention service departments. The catering department assumes the servicing and menu-planning roles of all group business, as well as the booking of all local catering.

Modified two-tier deployment (Figure 1–10) employs both the catering and the convention service departments. However, the catering department does not play a role in servicing groups. The convention service department does all menu planning and group servicing, while the catering department works strictly on local catering.

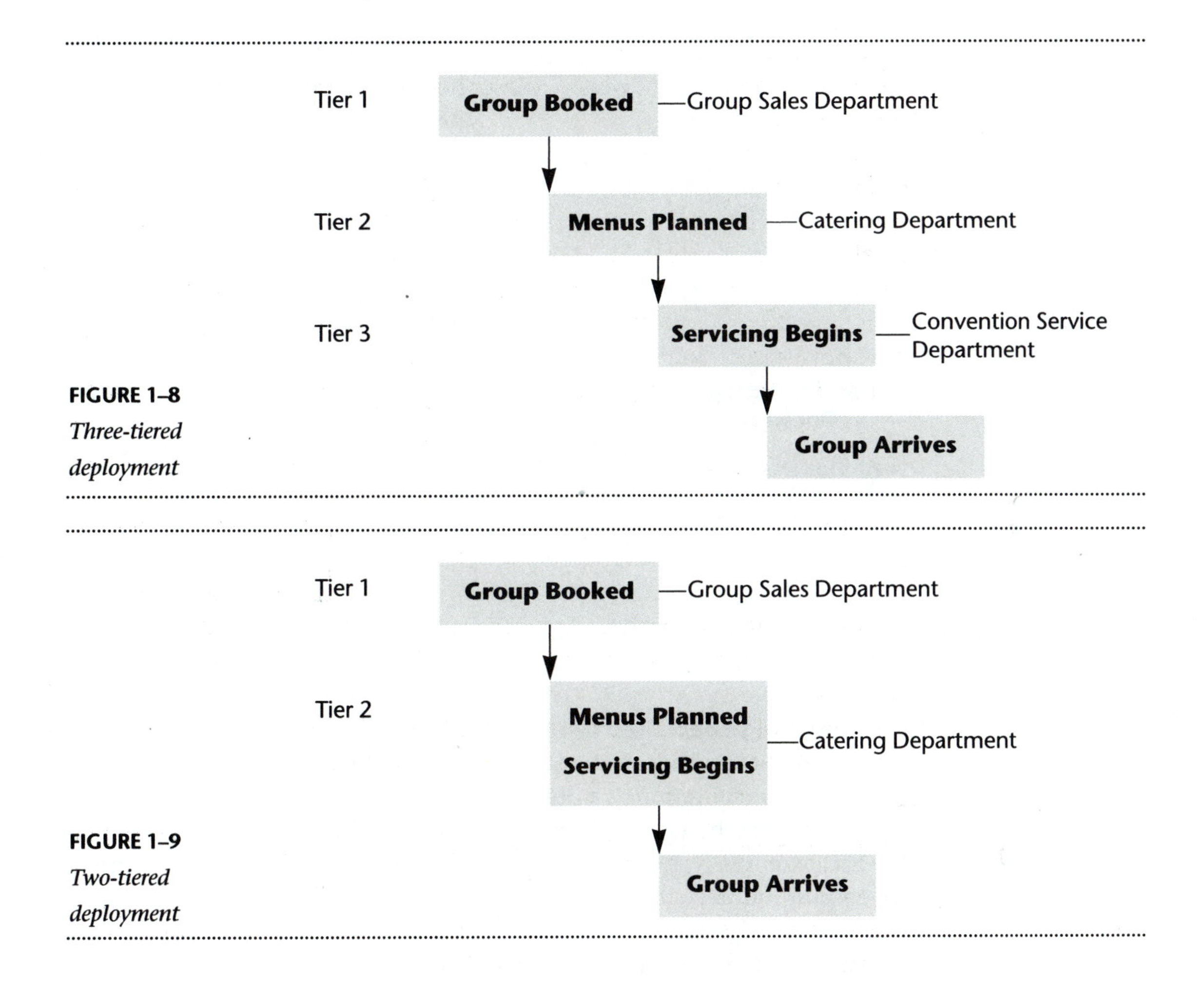


**FIGURE 1–8**
*Three-tiered deployment*

**FIGURE 1–9**
*Two-tiered deployment*

The management of group servicing at any hotel begins with communication between the room salespeople and the catering and/or convention service department about specific group details. This communication is called **group turnover**. Turnover is the process by which a group salesperson makes the catering and/or convention service department aware of the details of a group. Because the salesperson involved in selling rooms is most often the first to communicate with the group, and therefore knows more about the group than any employee at the hotel, the turnover process must be as complete and as detailed as possible.

The turnover process should be completed with ample time for the catering/convention service manager to prepare. A large convention should be turned over no later than 1 year out. The catering/convention service manager needs this time to coordinate the hotel's efforts on behalf of the group as well as to manage his or her slate of upcoming groups.

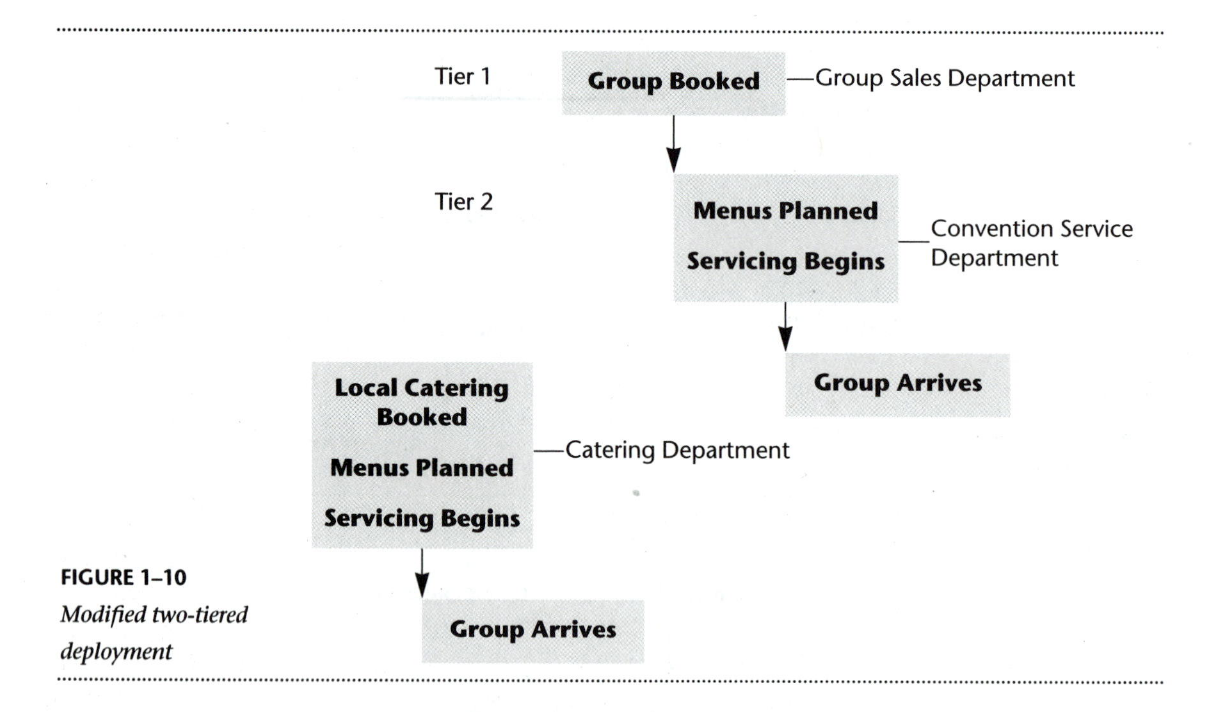


**FIGURE 1–10**
*Modified two-tiered deployment*

**Wedding Specialist.** Some hotels become very proficient at coordinating and executing weddings and wedding-related events. If a hotel establishes a reputation as a quality reception or rehearsal site, a **wedding specialist** may be employed by the catering department to develop this market exclusively. Developing the skills and knowledge required to effectively communicate in and coordinate this market can be time intensive, the wedding specialist frees the rest of the catering staff to concentrate on other local catering and group business.

**Junior Sales Manager/"Meetings Manager."** Many hotels employ one or more **junior sales managers/"meetings managers"** to coordinate small to medium meetings and conferences. The small meetings market is growing rapidly in many areas of the country. The idea is to employ a "one-stop shop" philosophy by empowering these salespeople to coordinate all the room and catering aspects of a group. In essence, junior sales managers can be considered both sales and catering managers. Combining these functions gives clients the ease of working with only one salesperson. The more senior salespeople can concentrate more of their time on large groups and conventions. This position is viewed as useful training ground on which entry-level hotel salespeople learn all aspects of the hospitality sales process.

**Reservations Manager.** The **reservations manager** is employed traditionally by large hotels as a day-to-day manager of the reservation agents in transient sales. Reporting directly to the DOTS, the reservations manager helps monitor the hotel's yield-management strategy and ensures that agents implement the strategy consistently.

**Transient Sales Manager.** The **transient sales manager** is primarily responsible for developing the nongroup room market at a hotel. Typically, the transient salesperson is the only proactive member of the transient sales team. He or she frequently approaches the local market to generate volume account agreements. A volume account is a contract between the hotel and an organization that trades lower rates for a guaranteed number of room nights. The goal of the transient sales manager is to create a first-choice hotel preference for any organization's transient room needs. The transient sales manager works closely with the DOTS and the reservations manager to fill the voids left by the group base.

## OTHER CATERING AND CONVENTION SERVICES JOBS

Other members of the catering and convention services team are listed in the organizational chart, but they are not considered parts of the sales team because their roles in any hotel are restricted to servicing. They are therefore reactive and not proactive in the sales equation. The group salesperson should be familiar in the duties of the following employees, however, because they play major roles in the success of any group program.

**Banquet Manager.** The **banquet manager** plays a very important role in servicing. He or she coordinates staff who are in charge of setting up function rooms, serving meals, and cleaning up. The banquet manager works with the catering and/or convention service departments to ensure all service sides of a program are completed correctly. The banquet manager is often the manager closest to the clients during a program, so his or her customer-service skills should be well-developed. Sometimes called a banquet maitre d', the banquet manager may report to the DOC or the DOFB.

**Audiovisual Manager.** The audiovisual (AV) manager is responsible for setting up and servicing all the AV needs of a function. Whether a group needs a simple slide projector and screen or a large multimedia satellite, the AV department ensures it is set up correctly. The role of technology in today's meeting and convention industry mandates that the AV department be aware of the latest trends and equipment in technology.

**Banquet Setup Supervisor.** The setup staff in a hotel are in charge of physically arranging meeting rooms. The tables, chairs, displays, and related items must be tailored for each function. The setup staff ensure that rooms are ready for the banquet manager to service.

The previous sections of this chapter addressed some of the basic concepts needed to understand why selling sleeping rooms is so important to

# Industry Perspective

## "Everyone at a Hotel Is a Salesperson"

*John Sweetland*
*Assistant General Manager*
*Hampton Inn*

Sales is not only the job of the dedicated hotel sales team, it is the responsibility of every member of the organization. Every employee in the hotel greatly influences the customer, which relates directly to the hotel's occupancy levels.

When a guest calls to inquire about a room or to ask specific questions, the PBX operator must have a great attitude and portray genuine enjoyment of what he or she is doing and where he or she is working. The operator must know the hotel thoroughly to answer basic questions before transferring the customer to the appropriate department. The operator should know things like shuttle service, the spa, restaurants, and gift shop.

The front desk must be friendly and courteous with all guests. The first 10 minutes of a guest's stay will, in large measure, determine how he or she perceives the hotel for the entire stay. These 10 minutes can make the difference between a repeat customer and a one-time visitor. The "10-foot rule" is an easy way to enhance the image of the front office. An employee who starts a conversation with a guest at least 10 feet before the guest reaches the desk makes a much better impression than an employee who allows the guest to reach the desk and wait to be acknowledged. At the very least, front desk associates must know where and how to get information for any guest need. Check-in speed must be quick, and check-in must be accurate. Check-in speed is one of the five key drivers (or critical success factors) to total guest satisfaction. The others are cleanliness, friendliness, value for price paid, and breakfast.

The lobby staff and courtesy van drivers are also key players in the guest's first 10 minutes. These staff members must be alert and friendly, welcoming guests as they step into the lobby or into courtesy vans. Anticipating a guest's needs (e.g., luggage storage or dinner ideas) also enhances guest satisfaction.

Recognizing guests by name makes them feel at home and has been shown to contribute to guest's loyalty to the hotel as well as to the hotel's chain. In my experience, repeat guests have been disappointed when no hotel employees remembered their names. Guests feel attached to their favorite hotels and expect the hotels' associates to be attached to them. This is a very important customer service tool.

Employees' knowledge and genuine enthusiasm for the hotel and its guests increases repeat business. In some cases, repeat business can result in 95 percent of a hotel's total sales. All front office employees must understand this notion of generating repeat sales through customer service. Any employee who can contribute to customer satisfaction must be considered a salesperson.

the hotel industry. The combination of group and transient sales strive to fill the hotel.

It should be noted that not only those involved in some aspect of the success triangle can sell a property. In fact, every employee at a property can be considered part of the sales team. The front desk can help sell a hotel by providing fast and friendly check-ins. A housekeeper can contribute to sales by giving sleeping rooms extra sparkle. The chef can help sell a hotel by ensuring that a special menu tastes as good as it sounded when it was sold.

The truly successful hotel is run by employees at every level who ensure that what the sales team promises a client is delivered. From the engineers who keep things running smoothly to the general manager guiding the entire operation, the total hotel sales approach translates into a hotel full of salespeople.

## CHAPTER REVIEW

### KEY CONCEPTS

Room sales
Catering sales
Outlet/ancillary sales
Success triangle
Group versus transient
Occupancy
Individual booking cycle
Yield management
Profit margin
Captive audience quotient
Group catering contribution
Rev-par
Size classification
Hotel organization
Traditional versus revenue-based deployment
Group turnover
Total hotel sales

## REVIEW QUESTIONS

1. What benefits does an occupancy-driven hotel have over a rate-driven hotel?
2. What costs are involved in selling a hotel, and what do those costs consist of?
3. Explain rev-par and its importance to hotel performance analysis.
4. Can the costs incurred in preparing a guest room for sale also affect food cost? Why?
5. Explain the different approaches to yield management.
6. What are the differences between group, transient, and catering sales?

# CHAPTER 2

# *Hotel Marketing Concepts*

> *"To guess is cheap . . . To guess wrongly is expensive."*
>
> CONFUCIUS

## INTRODUCTION

Marketing, as a term, is debated and argued about constantly. People disagree as to its definition. In hospitality, as in many other industries, marketing is commonly understood to be the process of bringing buyers and sellers together. **Effective marketing** consists of marketing a service, a product, or an idea in such a way as to invoke the perception of benefit to the consumer.

Benefit can be measured in monetary or emotional terms. Either way, knowing what the consumer wants enables the marketer to achieve the most success. In the hotel industry, as in other rapidly changing industries, most marketers agree that the goal of knowing the consumer absolutely is never achieved.

This is part of the reason the hospitality industry is so rewarding. The ever-changing consumer forces marketers to continually reevaluate and update their products and services. Working in hospitality exposes the professional to vastly different approaches to capturing consumers. Marketing in this evolving marketplace requires the professional to identify current products and understand the trends driving the industry.

## THE HOTEL BUSINESS MIX

The hospitality industry currently encompasses a wide variety of hotels. Each has unique characteristics that set it apart from the others. However, hotels also share many fundamentals. To study hotel similarities and differences, hotels must be classified on their most basic levels. The marketing analysis of a hotel begins with the hotel's location and product type.

Hotels are classified first by their physical positions relative to customers in the areas and to geographic landmarks. A **hotel location type** defines the hotel's position. The **hotel product type**, in contrast, determines the hotel's service and amenity levels as well as its target market. A product type, for all intents and purposes, defines how and for what the hotel is used.

Understanding a hotel's product and location type leads to general understanding of the hotel's traditional business mix. The **traditional business mix** is defined as the pool of potential customers who are, as a rule, tied to a location or product type. If the location type is known, the traditional mix can be determined for a hotel that has not yet been built. The traditional business mix should not be confused with the **actual business mix**, which is an analysis based on data accumulated over a period of time. The actual business mix is a running account of all types of customers who have stayed at an existing hotel. Market factors like economic slowdown/expansion, corporate relocation, national emergency, and weather play important roles in determining the actual business mix.

Before we can fully comprehend the business mix of a hotel, we must look briefly at the market segments that make up that mix. A **market segment** is simply a portion or segment of the actual or potential business pool at any given hotel. Market segment characteristics may differ from one hotel to another. Grouping this business pool into segments with similar characteristics is called market segmentation. Market segments can be grouped in many different ways. In various combinations, all hotel business can be classified in one or more market segments. The following analysis looks strictly at group market segments.

## MARKET SEGMENTATION

### CORPORATE SEGMENT

The corporate market segment consists of for-profit companies. The corporate market segment may have more money to spend than nonprofit or other business segments. As a result, corporate business is often more concerned with content than with cost. This market segment frequently pays higher rates than others to ensure quality programs.

### ASSOCIATION SEGMENT

Associations are, by their nature, groupings of individuals who or companies that share purposes or goals. In a way, associations are a market segment within a market segment. Individuals can band together in association to share ideas, hobbies, beliefs, or any number of things. Companies can band together in association for research, educational, political, or public relations reasons. This market segment may be more cost conscious than the corporate segment, because its members often pay for services out of their own pockets. Associations can have very large numbers and require large facilities.

### OTHER SEGMENTS

Most hotels group market segments that do not fall easily into the above two categories into an "other" category. Also called the primary market, this segment consists of groups that have characteristics that set them apart from the corporate or association category. This separation is not meant to diminish the quality or impact of this segment but rather to afford it the attention it deserves.

The "other" market segment has five primary components: **social, military, educational, religious, and fraternal (SMERF)**. These components meet for reunions, bonding, continuing education, or any number of reasons. The SMERF components, which can be large or small, tend to look for lower rates than the corporate or association segment. The lack of experienced meeting planners can make working in this segment challenging, but rewarding.

| Primary Component | Markets |
|---|---|
| **S**ocial | Weddings, Proms, Fund Raisers, Bar Mitzvahs |
| **M**ilitary | Reunions, Award Ceremonies |
| **E**ducational | Continuing Education and Certification Classes |
| **R**eligious | Revivals, Enlightenment Gatherings |
| **F**raternal | Fraternities, Sororities |

### MARKET SUBSEGMENTS

Markets can be analyzed more deeply to separate the potential business pool into even more defined and/or diverse subsegments, including:

| Corporate | Association | Other |
|---|---|---|
| Manufacturing | Local | SMERF |
| Construction | State | Tour/Travel |
| Distribution | Regional | Cultural |
| Retail | National | Sports |
| Printing | International | Government |
| Health | | Seminars |
| Insurance | | |
| Media | | |

Dividing the business pool can be important to hotel marketing, because the resulting subsegments can serve as markers. A **marker** allows the marketer to direct the hotel's marketing resources most efficiently and profitably. Understanding the market segments that make up the majority of a hotel's traditional and actual business mixes sharpens a marketer's focus.

## HOTEL LOCATION TYPES

In hospitality, the location type of the product you are marketing is very important. Being cognizant of a hotel's surroundings provides the means for effectively marketing the hotel to the immediate community. As was mentioned earlier, hotel location types are classified by their physical positions relative to customers in the area and to their tangible locales. The four main hotel location types are downtown, resort, airport, and suburban. The following looks at each location type and its corresponding traditional business mix.

## DOWNTOWN LOCATIONS

Downtown location types apply to hotels located in dense urban areas, which are not necessarily city centers, but often are. Hotels surrounded by large clusters of corporate structures or office parks can be considered downtown location types regardless of where exactly they are located in cities. Traditionally, however, downtown hotels are located in the centers of cities' business districts. These areas often include convention centers. A **convention center** is a locally funded or privately owned structure that caters to large groups and conventions of all kinds. It has its own salespeople who sell the center to various market segments. The size and capacity of a convention center may allow it to provide its own food and beverage service, or it may rely on outside providers.

Many times, the term *convention hotel* is used in classifying the location type of a hotel near a convention center. The difference between downtown or convention hotels, if both are near the city's convention center, is based on whether the hotels cater to business that is related to the convention center. Hotels located in dense urban areas or office parks without convention centers cannot be classified as convention hotels.

**Downtown Traditional Business Mix.** Because the downtown location type hotel is likely to be located near convention centers, its traditional business mix consists of convention center–related business. A convention hotel often works with other convention hotels to provide enough rooms to accommodate large groups using the convention center. These types of groups are called "city-wides," because the entire city often must participate to provide their accommodations.

Downtown hotels often court the corporate market due to their proximity to various office buildings and company locations, and they often offer substantial on-site meeting facilities and services that cater to the corporate market. During the week, the demand of a downtown hotel is often tied to what is happening in the city. Transient demand can be high on weekends if the local environment offers significant entertainment, shopping, or dining options. Cultural activities like museums and historical sites also drive transient demand.

## RESORT LOCATIONS

Hotels can be classified as resort location types only if they fulfill one of two main criteria:

1. A resort must be located near a special attraction that attracts guests for a reason other than the hotel. Attractions and the interest they generate vary from person to person. Special attractions can be as varied as the city or country in which the hotel is located. An ocean, a natural wonder, a mountain, an amusement park, or a

golf course can be a special attraction. Warm-weather areas with plenty of sun can also be special attractions.

2. The hotel must create its own special attraction. Health spas, private golf and/or tennis facilities, expansive pool areas, and other unique signature features allow the hotel to assume the resort location classification. A signature attraction is an event, an activity, or a facility that is identified with a hotel.

While resort hotels can be located anywhere, they often boast of signature attractions that provide perceived value to the receptive customer. A **receptive customer** is one who, due to personal interest or need, is more likely than the general population to be interested in a product or service. Receptive customers may feel they received special returns for their money if they perceive value in the products or services they purchased over and above what the general population may perceive. In the resort environment, this value can be derived from recreational skill enhancement. (Some hotels offer "schools" for golf, tennis, skiing, and other sports.) Customers can also perceive value from partaking in signature attractions like celebrity health/beauty salons and unique restaurants. Consumers will often be willing to spend more than they would normally when they perceive that the product or service is valuable.

The resort classification should apply only to hotels meeting the preceding criteria. A few hotels use the term "resort" to trick customers into believing that they offer special attractions. These hotels use deceptive location classification, which is most common in the resort location type. Some hotels add "downtown/convention" to their names because they wish to cater to the corporate market but lack the necessary meeting space.

**Resort Traditional Business Mix.** The resort relies heavily on transient demand for its traditional business mix. Resorts may cater to individuals, couples, or families, which often translates to high weekend demand and weaker weekday traffic. Family resorts may cater to their market by offering activities for children and more affordable rates. The term "family friendly" is often used in describing these resorts.

Resorts that are built near special attractions may be subject to the attractions' seasonality. **Seasonality** is a term used to define the time of year when a special attraction is open or at peak level. (Other terms for seasonality are *in season* and *off season*.) Most attractions, like amusement parks and ski slopes, are open during fixed times. Other attractions, like beaches, are open all year, but they peak during temperate weather months. Desert golf resorts are in higher demand during the more pleasant winters than during the hot summer months. The seasonality of resorts dictates their demand levels. Group business can be good off season at the more expensive resorts. Groups may also find perceived value in meeting during the week and avoiding the higher demand weekends.

## AIRPORT LOCATIONS

The airport hotel location type is perhaps the easiest to identify. Most major airports in the world are close to one or more hotels. It can be said that the special attraction of an airport hotel is the airport itself. The airport provides a steady stream of travelers going to and from the city at almost all hours.

Airport hotels commonly provide complimentary shuttle service to and from their nearby airports to make it convenient for the traveler. The airport hotel's restaurants, lounges, and other facilities may operate longer than those of hotels of other location types to accommodate travelers facing time zone changes and jet lag. In major, gateway cities, multilingual staff members are common at airport hotels to assist international travelers. **Gateway cities** are traditionally located in areas that make them practical first stops for international flights entering the United States. Seattle, San Francisco, and Los Angeles are gateway cities for Asia and the Far East. New York, Boston, and Washington, DC, are gateway cities to Europe and beyond. It should be noted that current improvements in airplane technology are allowing for longer direct flights from cities not commonly considered gateways.

**Airport Traditional Business Mix.** Airport hotels cater primarily to the business traveler, whose transient demand peaks during the week and falls drastically on weekends. Most corporate business travelers want to return home on weekends. The weaker weekend demand often pushes airport hotels to work with low-rated groups who may be more willing to forgo weekday stays for more attractive rates. Airport hotels look for SMERF groups to fill this void.

Major hotel chains (e.g., Marriott, Hyatt, Hilton, Sheraton) realized long ago that consistency was important to marketing their airport hotels. The traveler who knows what to expect from a hotel will likely look for his or her brand choice in an unfamiliar city. Therefore, many airports have many similar hotels. This similarity between hotels may also translate to similar rates. In this environment, the business traveler may be swayed by the chain that offers the most attractive frequent stay incentive program.

A **frequent stay incentive program**, or guest loyalty program, offers repeat guests earning points, which can be redeemed for some type of reward. Like the programs offered by airlines and car-rental companies, these rewards can be free room nights, vacation packages, and other perks. Most earning-points programs grade customers based on usage volume.

Those at top volume are often entitled to lower rates, upgraded rooms, and other amenities for each stay. Some business travelers become so loyal to a hotel chain's frequent stay program that they may pay higher rates or stay at subpar facilities to earn points. (This brand loyalty is addressed later in this chapter.)

### SUBURBAN LOCATIONS

The suburban location type is perhaps the most common. Suburban hotels are generally considered those that do not fit into the other three location types. Given that criterion, it can be said that most hotels in the world are actually suburban location types. These hotels are not located in downtown areas or near airports. They have no special attractions to qualify them as resorts. They are common on major roadways and near small office complexes. A large company headquarters or manufacturing site often warrants a small or medium suburban hotel.

Surburban hotels often thrive in environments in which the compression of demand in a city lessens the importance of a hotel's location type. **Compression of demand** is the theory that the need for hotel rooms in a city or a geographical region remains fairly constant despite occupancy level. In effect, if rooms in one part of an area are sold out, room demand will compress so as to drive those looking for rooms elsewhere. This compression often occurs first with downtown and convention hotels. A city-wide convention may consume all rooms in a downtown area, but the average demand for transient and other group rooms remains fixed. These guests must exit the downtown area to find rooms, which increases occupancy at hotels that are normally unaffected by downtown demand.

**Suburban Traditional Business Mix.** Suburban hotels vary greatly in their traditional business mixes. For most, transient demand plays a major role in occupancy. Suburban hotels near large corporate facilities may rely exclusively on one firm for most of their occupancies, but the social market typically provides the bulk of group business at suburban hotels. Weddings and proms can be lucrative events for suburban hotels. This location type is nearer the bedroom communities of many cities than other types, which is one reason the social market plays a major role in the suburban hotel's traditional business mix.

## HOTEL PRODUCT TYPES

Hotel location type is half the equation of marketing a hotel. Hotel product type is the other.

The hospitality industry is changing rapidly. New developmental and marketing ideas emerge almost daily. The hotel product type must grow and change to stay in step with this evolution. There are product types in the market now that were not even dreamed of 10 years ago. The first hotel product types can be traced back to the days of ancient Egypt. Mentions of inns can be found in various ancient religious texts. The evolution of modern hotel product types can be traced to the first roadside motels of J.W. Marriott and Howard Johnson almost 40 years ago.

Holiday Inn took its idea of clean, comfortable, and affordable accommodations to the nation. Since then, thousands of hotel developers, managers, and owners have put their marks on old, roadside motels. The roadside motel product type is still viable. Today, we can analyze how many more product types exist in the marketplace. New product types coexist with the oldest roadside motel. Looking at these new product types can be done in two ways: examining service levels and determining target markets. Hotel product types are defined by their service levels and their target markets.

## PRODUCT TYPE ANALYSIS BY SERVICE LEVEL

Analyzing product type by service level entails first understanding exactly what "service level" means. **Hotel service level** is measured by the amount of actual and perceived consideration a guest can reasonably expect to receive. This amount is based on a hotel's reputation as well as by comparison with other product types.

As a consumer, you experience different levels of service. A favorite restaurant or dry cleaner may make you feel special by reserving your favorite table or using your name in a greeting. The grocery store that special orders something for you provides a higher service level than one that does not. You may know by reputation where to go in your area for the best auto mechanic or barber. In many cases, you may pay more for the product you feel gives you more in return. However, service level is not necessarily tied to cost. A consumer perceives value in receiving quality service.

In the hotel industry, differences in service levels are often tied to incremental increases in cost. The following table shows the most common service level classifications and contemporary brand examples.

**ECONOMY, BUDGET, MID-MARKET, UPSCALE, AND LUXURY HOTELS**

| Limited Service | Full Service |
|---|---|
| Current Economy Market Examples* | Current Upscale Examples* |
| Budgetel Inn | Hyatt |
| Fairfield Inn | Marriott |
| Motel 6 | Hilton |
| Red Roof Inn | Omni |
| | Sheraton |
| Current Budget Market Examples* | Current Luxury Examples* |
| Best Western | Four Seasons |
| Econolodge | Intercontinental |
| Knights Inn | Ritz Carlton |
| Super 8 Motels | |

Current Mid-Market Examples*
- Courtyard
- Holiday Inn
- Howard Johnson
- Ramada Inn

*Note: These market examples are taken from *Hotel & Motel Magazine,* November 1996. The hotel companies may have other product types that are not listed here.

The table's two columns, full service and limited service, straddle the mid-market examples. The full- and limited-service definitions exemplify the differences in hotel service level. By definition, **full-service hotels** provide their guests with the services, amenities, and facilities they want or need to complete a total hotel experience. To varying degrees, these services can include:

On-site restaurant(s) serving breakfast, lunch, and dinner
Room service
Meeting space (on-site sales and catering staff)
Business center
Health club/recreation facilities
Gift shop
Complimentary services (e.g., bed turn-down and newspaper delivery)
Lounge(s)/entertainment
Suites, upgraded rooms
Concierge service
Express/video checkout ability
In-room amenities (e.g., minibars, voice mail, data ports with Internet access, work areas, oversized beds, sitting areas, toiletries, movies)
Security/loss prevention
Shuttle services

In contrast, **limited-service hotels** typically do not offer the preceding services, most notably food and beverage outlets and on-site meeting space. However, they do offer quality rooms for a fair price.

The preceding table lists mid-market service level as both limited and full service. This is because mid-market hotels can vary from one place to another. A mid-market hotel may be full-service in one location while another in the same chain may be of limited service.

As was stated earlier, the price versus service relationship is not universal. In most markets, increasing service level is tied to increasing price (room rate). Because differences occur from location to location, price and service must be compared within the same market. The prices of the same brand luxury hotel may differ from New York to Tulsa. Local market factors like competition, operating costs, and availability skew these numbers. Figure 2–1 illustrates the generic price versus service relationship as it relates to different product types.

## PRODUCT TYPE ANALYSIS BY TARGET MARKET

Service levels help in understanding half the product type. The other half is the target market. A **target market** is a market segment, or combination of market segments, the hotel wants to penetrate. The target market can be tied to a product type or designated by a marketer as a new focus.

The modern hotel market has available vastly different targeted markets. These markets contribute to each hotel's business mix. The target market includes consumers who want a different type of hotel room. The physical differences of a room (product and service level) reflect the differences in the intended target markets.

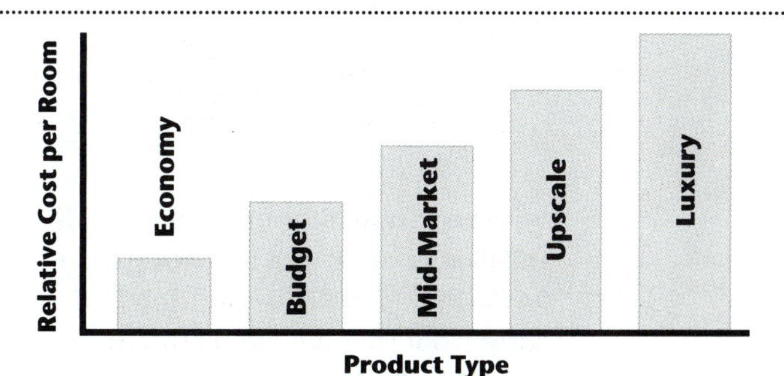


*Note: Price differences are not universal. Price relationships within markets could mirror this graph, but anomalies may occur.

**FIGURE 2–1**
*Relative cost versus product type*

**STANDARD/EXTENDED-STAY/ALL-SUITE TARGET MARKETS**

Current Standard Examples
- Economy
- Budget
- Mid-Market
- Upscale
- Luxury

Current All-Suite Examples
- Embassy Suites
- Marriott Suites
- Hilton Suites
- Doubletree Suites

Current Extended-Stay Examples
- Studio Plus
- Residence Inn
- Extended Stay America

*Note: These market examples are taken from *Hotel & Motel Magazine,* November 1996. These hotel companies may have other product types that are not listed here.

Notice that the standard market examples in the accompanying box do not list specific hotels. The standard target markets include the segments that made up the classification of service-level product types. The standard target market does not differentiate between service level and product types. Guests who are looking for traditional hotel rooms are the standard target market. Target markets that are looking for a different room product type differ from the standard. The physical differences in hotels set them apart. These differences become apparent when looking at the target markets that comprise those seeking different room types from the standard, namely extended stay and all-suite markets.

**Extended-Stay Market.** **Extended-stay hotels** provide their guests with the services, amenities, and facilities that they want or need to facilitate long-term stays in one location. To varying degrees, these services/facilities can include:

- Stove and/or microwave
- Refrigerator
- Dishes and kitchenware
- Limited housekeeping services
- Grocery shopping service
- Business services

The cost of a room in an extended-stay hotel is often less than that in an all-suite hotel (see following). Guests can rent rooms by the day, week, or month. Extended-stay hotels rarely have on-site food and beverage outlets, but they are often built in locations with restaurant options nearby.

**All-Suite Market.** Unlike the extended-stay hotel, the **all-suite hotel** is targeted to the consumer who is looking for a hotel experience that rivals those in upscale and luxury hotels. A hotel suite can appeal to consumers. All suites can have:

- Two or more rooms per suite
- Varying service level
- Limited on-site food and beverage facilities
- Complimentary receptions and breakfasts

Breakfast inclusive rates appeal to many. Staffing levels at all-suite hotels are generally leaner than those at upscale or luxury properties, but the reduced staff levels render the rates at all-suite hotels more affordable than those at upscale or luxury hotels.

**Target Market Variation.** In hotel marketing, there is a need to define precisely the many variations that can occur within the three main target markets (standard, extended-stay, and all-suite). The more specific the target market, the more easily a marketer can apply resources to reach the intended consumer. These variations are no more than combinations of service and product types. Combined target markets are called **hybrid markets**. Hybrid market classifications allow the marketer to determine the specific market segments within and among the three main market segments. The combinations among markets create numerous possible hybrid target markets. Hybrid markets are generally more defined and narrower than market segments because they focus on smaller, more specific business mixes.

The standard target market, which encompasses all service product levels, provides the starting point for analysis of hybrid markets.

## HYBRID MARKET ANALYSIS OF TARGET MARKETS

| STANDARD MARKET EXAMPLES | | |
|---|---|---|
| Economy<br>Budget | Mid-Market<br>Upscale | Luxury |

Combine the service levels with the product levels and the following hybrids appear:

- Economy long-term stay
- Budget long-term stay
- Mid-market long-term stay
- Upscale long-term stay
- Luxury long-term stay
- Economy all suite
- Budget all suite
- Mid-market all suite
- Upscale all suite
- Luxury all suite

The price relationships for hybrids mirror Figure 2–1. Economy and budget hybrids are on the lower end, and upscale and luxury hybrids are on the upper end.

# *Industry Perspective*

## "Extended-Stay Hotel Sales versus Full-Service Hotel Sales"

*Carolyn Porter*
*Preopening Sales Manager*

Extended-stay selling differs from full-service selling in a few ways. The full-service hotel can sell service and amenities (e.g., meeting space, restaurants, bell staff) as well as hotel rooms. Selling at extended-stay hotels focuses more on the room itself. Extended-stay hotels offer quality guest rooms with full kitchens and can keep rates low because they do not offer the services of full-service hotels.

When selling the extended-stay product, it is crucial initially to determine the correct target market. Because most hotels of this kind lack meeting space, group business is not a good market. The main focus should be customers who need interim housing. Guests who are seeking long-term housing solutions have unique needs, and extended-stay hotels offer services to match. For extended-stay hotels, people who are working on long-term projects, training, and development and people who are relocating are the biggest sources of business.

While extended-stay hotels do not have on-site restaurants, they are strategically positioned within walking distance of as many food and beverage options as possible. These hotels do not offer certain complimentary items, because those costs are always incurred by the customer in some way. Travelers in extended-stay hotels would prefer to fix coffee in their rooms rather than walk to the lobby early in the morning. Extended-stay guests also prefer not to have maid service every day. Guests tend to stay in extended-stay rooms longer than they do at full-service hotels, so they begin to feel at home and prefer to have maid service only a few times a week.

Selling the extended-stay product requires honesty. Customers who are picturing a full-service hotel experience cannot be persuaded to stay in an extended-stay hotel. Most hotels of this type have very limited staffing. Often, the front desk closes at night; there is no 24-hour service. It is important to communicate the benefits and limitations of extended-stay hotels.

# POSITIONING

**Positioning** is promoting a brand or product over the competition and how it is perceived by the consumer. In the hotel industry, positioning brings together the concepts of:

- Product type
- Location type
- Actual and traditional business mixes
- Service level
- Target market

The hotel marketer must apply these concepts to understand the *who, what,* and *where* of hospitality marketing. Positioning a hotel properly requires knowing whom to market to (actual/traditional business mixes), what to market (service levels/target markets), and where to market (product/location types).

## INITIAL HOTEL POSITIONING

Initial hotel positioning is the process of applying the who, what, and where concepts to a new hotel. The hotel will succeed if the marketer positions it correctly from the beginning. Service-level product types often can predict how a guest will feel at a hotel. The target market indicates who the marketer intends the guest to be. Product and location type knowledge direct the marketer to the proper hotel location. By combining these three concepts, the marketer should closely predetermine the traditional business mix.

The actual business mix can, in a way, gauge how well the marketer did with the initial hotel positioning. If the actual business mix is vastly different from the intended traditional mix, then the hotel's positioning could be improved. The difference in business mixes does not necessarily mean the hotel will fail, however. In many cases, a hotel can be profitable when the actual and traditional business mixes differ. Such differences can merely show a marketer where to look for improvement. The marketer who understands that changing a hotel's who, what, and where positioning could make the hotel more successful fully uses the hotel's assets and wastes none of its potential.

Successful positioning is ongoing. Long after a hotel is built and running, its positioning will need to be adjusted and refined. Market factors like competition, economic expansion/decline, and population changes can adversely affect a once thriving hotel. This refining of a hotel's positioning, or repositioning, is outlined in a hotel's yearly marketing plan.

## THE MARKETING PLAN

> *A good marketer has one ear to the ground and one eye focused toward the future at all times.*
>
> ANONYMOUS

A **marketing plan** is a document put together by a hotel's marketing leaders to chart a course for the next year. This plan dictates any repositioning actions that must be taken by surveying competitive and market factors. It also summarizes the hotel's next year's marketing budget, advertising plan, and fiscal goals.

From year to year, the hotel marketer must analyze the actual business mix and adjust the positioning as needed. The marketing plan is a useful tool because it forces the marketer to review the hotel's progress. A chronological marketing plan lays out the repositioning steps by date, which helps keep the marketer on schedule. Falling behind in the marketing effort of a hotel can sacrifice opportunities.

The marketing plan should not be unchanging. A good hotel marketing plan is flexible enough to allow the marketer to make adjustments as circumstances dictate.

### A MARKETING PLAN CASE STUDY

A major corporation located next to a hotel suddenly went out of business. This corporation provided the hotel with most of its group business. The hotel's marketing plan, which was written with the understanding that the corporation was going to continue to be a major business source, was now less effective. The hotel could lessen the impact of this loss by immediately redirecting marketing resources to other market segments. Good marketing plans consider the financial health of major business sources earlier.

# MARKET SHARE

Hotel marketing is challenging and rewarding. Successful marketing decisions can provide satisfaction in a job well done. Learning from mistakes only makes for better marketing decisions the next time.

How can one measure marketing successes and failures? In the hotel industry, measurements of success go beyond occupancy and rate levels. The best way to measure marketing success is to look at market share. **Market share** is a hotel's portion of the available market relative to the portions of the market taken by the competition. Market share analysis in the hotel industry has the added component of hotel size. A hotel's size dictates its potential market share. Therefore, hotel market share is further defined as the potential total market share relative to the actual market share.

It is important not to confuse hotel market share with traditional market share models in other industries. For example, if XYZ Company makes widgets in a market of three other widget makers, its market share is determined by how many widgets it sells relative to all four companies. If XYZ sells 10,000 widgets in a given year and the entire widget industry sells 100,000, then the market share for XYZ is 10 percent ([10,000 ÷ 100,000] × 100).

The XYZ Company can theoretically make as many widgets as it wants; widget supply has not limited XYZ to its 10 percent market share. Other factors (e.g., quality, marketing effort, price, distribution) must come into play.

This market share analysis does not apply to the hotel industry, however. Remember, hotels have a fixed number of rooms that can be sold in a given year. The hotel industry is limited in that a hotel cannot build more rooms when demand warrants and, conversely, it cannot remove empty rooms when demand lowers. Hotels have a fixed, limited amount of rooms they can sell in a given time frame. This concept is called available room potential. For example, imagine that ABC Hotel has 400 rooms.

The available room potential in a week is 2,800 rooms (7 × 400).
The available room potential in February is 11,200 rooms (28 × 400).
The available room potential in a year is 146,000 rooms (365 × 400).

The hotel industry uses the term *room night* to describe one hotel room that is occupied for one night. Room nights sold, therefore, can help measure a hotel's performance if they are divided by the available room potential. Room potential performance is the number of room nights sold relative to the potential available. This performance analysis is the first step in understanding market share. A marketer must know what the hotel can do before comparing it with others. Return to our example, in which the ABC Hotel has 400 rooms, and imagine that each night the hotel sells 300 rooms. The room potential performance in a week is 75 percent ([300 ÷ 400] × 100).

300 × 7 = 2,100 room nights
400 × 7 = 2,800 room nights

Of course, a hotel rarely sells the same number of rooms each night. However, the calculation remains the same regardless of how many rooms are sold each night.

One can argue that room potential performance is nothing more than another analysis of occupancy percentage. In fact, there are no real differences between the two except that occupancy is most often used to measure nightly performance while room potential is used to analyze longer time frames (e.g., weekly, monthly, yearly).

## SELECTING HOTELS FOR COMPARISON

The next step in market share analysis is to determine which hotels to compare and analyze. A crucial point is to ensure that the competitive hotels in this market share mix are similarly positioned. The market share mix is a pool of hotels that share product/location types, business mixes, service levels, and target markets. Determining this market share pool correctly enables the marketer to compare true competitors.

How valid is a market share analysis of a budget hotel to a luxury hotel? The adage "Do not compare apples to oranges" applies. Exceptions apply only in markets with few competitors of similar positioning. Markets with fewer than five competing hotels should include all competitors in the market share mix to generate statistically relevant data, even if the competitors have dissimilar positioning.

Next, the market share mix must be expanded so that available room potential for each hotel in the mix can be determined. This process entails determining the number of rooms for each hotel and multiplying that number by the chosen time frame. To obtain a total for the entire market, add the room potentials of each hotel in the mix. This step sets hotel market share analysis apart from the analyses of other industries. Again, there is a finite number of room nights available for sale in any market share mix.

## DETERMINING POTENTIAL MARKET SHARE

This leads to the next step, which is to determine the potential market share of each hotel. The potential share of a hotel is measured by comparing its total number of rooms to the total available in the market share mix. This number reflects the market share the hotel would receive if it sold every room every night. It is extremely rare for every hotel in a market to reach its potential market share. The essence of hotel market share is determining how a hotel performed by comparing its potential share of the market to its actual share.

The last step in preparing for market share analysis is to collect actual room potential performance data of the market mix for a specific time frame. Many cities, locations, and government tourism agencies prepare reports that list the occupancies and room night sales data for all hotels in their coverage areas. These reports, often called star reports, can cover any time frame, but the most common is a month. As a result, most market share analyses are conducted monthly. (In some markets, where star reports are difficult or impossible to obtain, hotels may exchange occupancy numbers monthly. Average rate figures cannot be exchanged due to antitrust concerns, but occupancy exchanges do not violate current laws.)

With a marketer's own hotel room potential performance, a valid market share mix, and the room potential performance of that mix (from a star report or shared data), a market share analysis can be conducted. Following is an example of this process.

**EXAMPLE**

Imagine that you are a marketer at the ABC Hotel from our previous example who wants to determine the hotel's market share for the last month. You know that the ABC has 400 rooms and that its available room potential in February was 11,200 rooms (28 × 400).

Now assume that you have already determined the competitive hotels in the market share mix and that they are similarly positioned. Those hotels are named A, B, C, D, and E. Their respective available room potentials are as follows:

| Hotel | Total Number of Rooms | Available Potential in February | |
|---|---|---|---|
| A | 800 | 22,400 | (28 × 800) |
| B | 650 | 18,200 | (28 × 650) |
| C | 500 | 14,000 | (28 × 500) |
| D | 250 | 7,000 | (28 × 250) |
| E | 200 | 5,600 | (28 × 200) |

The data from our ABC Hotel must now be added to reach a total available potential for the entire market share mix:

| Hotel | Total Number of Rooms | Available Room Potential |
|---|---|---|
| A | 800 | 22,400 |
| B | 650 | 18,200 |
| C | 500 | 14,000 |
| D | 250 | 7,000 |
| E | 200 | 5,600 |
| ABC | 400 | 11,200 |
| **Total Market** | **2,800** | **78,400** |

At this point you can determine the potential market share for each hotel. This potential is the measurement of a hotel's share of the total available market. It is determined by dividing the hotel's total number of rooms by the total available rooms in the market.

| Hotel | Total Number of Rooms | Potential Market Share (Percent) | |
|---|---|---|---|
| A | 800 | 28.6 | (800 ÷ 2,800 × 100) |
| B | 650 | 23.2 | (650 ÷ 2,800 × 100) |
| C | 500 | 17.9 | (500 ÷ 2,800 × 100) |
| D | 250 | 8.9 | (250 ÷ 2,800 × 100) |
| E | 200 | 7.1 | (200 ÷ 2,800 × 100) |
| ABC | 400 | 14.3 | (400 ÷ 2,800 × 100) |
| **Total Market** | **2,800** | **100.0*** | |

*The percentages must equal 100 when added.

You now know the available room potentials and the potential market share for all hotels in our mix. Now compare those figures with the actual room night performances from a fictional February star report:

| Hotel | Total Number of Rooms | Available Potential | Actual Room Night Performance |
|---|---|---|---|
| A | 800 | 22,400 | 15,680 |
| B | 650 | 18,200 | 13,104 |
| C | 500 | 14,000 | 9,100 |
| D | 250 | 7,000 | 5,530 |
| E | 200 | 5,600 | 4,760 |
| ABC | 400 | 11,200 | 8,960 |
| **Total Market** | **2,800** | **78,400** | **57,134** |

At this point, the actual market share can be determined by dividing the actual room potential performance by the total room nights sold in the market. This now illustrates how each hotel in the mix performed relative to the total market.

| Hotel | Market Share (Percent) | |
|---|---|---|
| A | 27.4 | (15,680 ÷ 57,134) |
| B | 22.9 | (13,104 ÷ 57,134) |
| C | 15.9 | (9,100 ÷ 57,134) |
| D | 9.7 | (5,530 ÷ 57,134) |
| E | 8.3 | (4,760 ÷ 57,134) |
| ABC | 15.7 | (8,960 ÷ 57,134) |
| | 100.0* | |

*The percentages must equal 100 when added.

The hotels ranged from an 8.3 to a 27.4 percent market share. Does this mean that Hotel A did 19.1 percentage points better than Hotel E (27.4 − 8.3)? Not at all. Hotel A is much larger than Hotel E, meaning its share of the market will almost always be greater than Hotel E's. Again, the comparison must be of similar objects. This is why a marketer determines market share performance by comparing a hotel's actual market share to its potential market share.

| Hotel | Actual Market Share (Percent) | Potential Market Share (Percent) | Difference (Percent) |
|---|---|---|---|
| A | 27.4 | 28.5 | <1.1> |
| B | 22.9 | 23.2 | <0.3> |
| C | 15.9 | 17.9 | <2.0> |
| D | 9.7 | 8.9 | +0.8 |
| E | 8.3 | 7.1 | +1.2 |
| ABC | 15.7 | 14.3 | +1.4 |

In this example, Hotel A actually lost market share, while Hotel E gained. ABC Hotel posted a very respectable 1.4 percent increase in market share.

It is now clear that selling more rooms than another hotel is not necessarily a sign that the hotel is doing a better job. Market share analysis provides the means to "level the playing field" by comparing what a hotel actually did to what it could have done. Over time, the marketers at each hotel can use this information as a valuable tool for evaluating their hotel's performance and determining future direction.

## OPERATIONAL HOTEL MARKETING

Being a skilled hotel marketer entails knowing sales and marketing theory. Most marketing directors in hotels have two main responsibilities. The first is supervising and motivating the sales staff. The second, which is covered here, is continuously observing and, if needed, repositioning the hotel as the first choice among consumers in the targeted market. The latter is accomplished by optimizing the resources and tools that make up operational hotel marketing.

**Operational hotel marketing** is defined as the methods, approaches, and collateral used to position and/or reposition a hotel property to meet the predetermined marketing goals of the hotel's marketing plan. Operational marketing is also the way a marketer redirects the marketing effort to compensate for unforeseen challenges and/or opportunities that can arise from changes in market factors.

Most industries have few entry-level marketing jobs. Those who enter their careers with marketing as goals often find themselves selling initially. Selling forces one to know the product. In the hospitality industry, a DOM is often a seasoned sales veteran who first and foremost understands the product being sold. The logic is simple. Understanding a product, and interacting over time with those who buy the product, teaches salespeople how to better position the product for the customer. That skill base, coupled with a mastery of hotel marketing concepts and operational marketing strategies, often predicts the profile of a successful hotel marketer.

> “*Sales knowledge leads to marketing knowledge.*”
>
> ANONYMOUS

The goal of the marketing effort in any hotel is like those of other industries: Get the end user to choose your product. The end user is the entity that will ultimately consume the product. In the hospitality industry, the end user is the hotel guest, and the product is the hotel. The following section covers the techniques needed to market to the end user. These techniques make up the basis of operational hotel marketing, which is divided into two categories: corporate and on property.

### CORPORATE MARKETING

The term **corporate marketing** suggests that the marketing effort originates from an executive boardroom at company headquarters, but this is not always the case. Corporate marketing is the effort of one or more hotels, working alone or in unison, to position as the consumer's first choice. This principle is exemplified in the national and regional marketing efforts of medium to large hotel chains that promote their products as one whole. However, small chain and independent hotels can also become parts of a corporate marketing effort. Local tourism organizations, convention bureaus, and destination areas (e.g., landmark commissions and cultural attractions) can pool their resources to create their own corporate marketing efforts within the hotel community. Large hotel entities that are in one or a few areas (e.g., Walt Disney or Opryland) can become a major presence in the target markets they pursue by using their substantial resources to support a corporate marketing effort. Corporate marketing's aim is to create awareness on a regional or national level, regardless of the size or type of hotel.

Corporate marketing is best understood by looking at its two most important components: broad-based marketing strategy and brand loyalty.

**Broad-Based Corporate Marketing Strategy.** The corporate marketing strategy of any hotel focuses on bringing guests into the hotel. The objective of creating the natural first choice for guests is the ultimate aim of corporate marketing.

Relying solely on the local community to fill a hotel's rooms is often unsuccessful. Group business often originates from outside the local area, which requires marketers to create awareness of their products on regional and/or national levels. A broad-based awareness among target marketers helps ensure that the end user stays at the hotel.

Broad-based awareness of a hotel is often necessary in markets with heavy competition, primarily resort and downtown/convention location types. Creating broad-based awareness of a hotel helps ensure that the guests in the hotel's target market remain. Broad-based awareness marketing aims to target the out-of-town hotel guest with no initial preference. Guests typically want to stay where they are most comfortable. Comfort often causes first-time guests to choose the hotel of which they are most aware.

The ultimate goal of broad-based awareness is achieved when the first-time guest walks into an unfamiliar hotel. The guest was comfortable enough in the hotel's name, image, or some other aspect to walk through the door or choose the property from a directory. If the service levels and quality meet the guest's expectations, the hotel becomes his or her preferred hotel. If, however, the hotel fails to live up to the image created by the broad-based awareness, the failure is difficult to overcome. In highly competitive markets, most potential guests have many choices, each of which participates in broad-based marketing efforts.

This broad-based awareness is usually created in two ways. First, hotels of any size can use pinpoint advertising to reach a specific guest or market. Second, medium to large chains have brand loyalty to help create broad-based awareness.

*Pinpoint Advertising.* **Pinpoint advertising** is the process of using advertising media and other resources to reach specific target markets on a regional or national level. Advertising that does not intend to reach non-target markets is considered pinpoint. Trade journal advertising reaches a specific target market, so it is considered pinpoint. A national television commercial running on major networks throughout the day is not pinpoint advertising.

It is fair to assume, therefore, that a properly completed marketing plan and predetermined target markets are crucial to effective broad-based marketing. Pinpoint advertising can be applied to specific target locations and/or market segments. This ability to pinpoint or direct advertising gives this marketing medium great impact.

A city or region from which a major portion of a hotel's actual business mix originates is called a feeder. In the winter, when many want to escape to warmer climates, New York may be a feeder city to south Florida. The south Florida hotels that want to capture these "snowbirds," as they are sometimes called, will want to pinpoint their advertising to New York.

Pinpoint advertising of market segments can increase demand for a specific type of guest. For example, a hotel in Aspen, CO, may advertise in a skiing magazine to create awareness in that segment. A convention hotel or convention bureau may advertise at a national trade show or in a meeting planner magazine to help create awareness in that segment.

**PINPOINT ADVERTISING TECHNIQUES**

| **Location*** | **Market Segment** |
|---|---|
| Local Television | Industry/Hobby/Trade Journal |
| Local Radio | Magazines |
| Local Newspapers | Trade Shows/Expositions |
| National Newspapers with Regional Editions (*USA Today, Wall Street Journal*) | Mass Mailings Targeted by Market Segment |
| Billboards | FAM Trips** |
| Mass Mailings Targeted by Zip Code | |
| FAM Trips** | |

*Note: These pinpoint techniques apply to the areas being targeted, not to the local market where the hotel is located.

**The acronym FAM, which stands for familiarization, describes trips that are conducted by one or more hotels or by a convention/tourism bureau to familiarize prospective meeting planners from a specific region or market segment with a product.

*Brand Loyalty.* Hotels of all sizes, as well as organizations that promote cities or regions, create broad-based awareness through pinpoint advertising. Medium to large hotel chains have an added advantage. Because of their size and marketing resources, large hotel chains can also use brand loyalty to create guest preference.

As was discussed earlier, guests make initial choices based on awareness. The ultimate goal of broad-based awareness is to bring the first-time guest into a hotel. After that, if the hotel's service and quality meet the guest's expectations, the hotel becomes the guest's preferred hotel. Brand loyalty, by its nature, creates predetermined guest preference.

**Brand loyalty** is defined as the institutionalized preferences of a consumer for a product or service based solely on a brand name or logo. Assuming he or she can choose among all similar brands and market factors are even (i.e., no significant price pressure), a consumer will choose a specific brand over all others due to brand loyalty. In hospitality, deviations from this rule occur when guests associate negative experiences with a specific hotel of that brand or when a hotel of that brand is significantly lower in quality than the rest of the chain.

Hotel chains rely on brand loyalty in highly competitive markets to create a preference among potential guests. In a competitive hotel market, marketers' biggest challenge is determining what drives the guest to choose a particular hotel (e.g., the one on the right versus the one on the left) if the hotels from which he or she is choosing are identical in price and quality. Broad-based awareness created through brand loyalty is one answer.

Unlike pinpoint advertising, brand awareness is created over time in the consumer's subconscious. The association of a brand or logo with real or implied feelings of satisfaction and consistency results in loyalty.

**EXAMPLE**

The McDonalds hamburger chain is perhaps one of the most successful examples of a corporation creating brand loyalty through consistency. A consumer knows that a cheeseburger purchased in Boston will taste the same as one purchased in Seattle. If the consumer enjoys that cheeseburger, brand loyalty will cause the consumer to choose McDonalds again when he or she wants a cheeseburger, especially when he or she has no other familiar choices.

Brand loyalty applies only when the consumer seeks the product or service the brand offers. The brand loyalty in the preceding example would not affect the consumer's decision of where to eat a steak dinner, for instance. In the hotel industry, brand loyalty applies only to the product types and hybrids the guest is seeking. If the guest desires an all-suite product in a specific situation, his or her loyalty to a budget hotel would not affect the decision.

Consistency in the hotel product type is the cornerstone of brand loyalty in the hospitality industry. Knowledge of, or the association of, a level of quality, service, and price fosters loyalty in the hotel guest. This guest will incorporate a predetermined preference for a specific chain when deciding where to stay in unfamiliar markets.

Beyond consistency, medium to large hotel chains use yet another tool to create brand loyalty: the frequent-stay program.

Frequent-stay programs create an incentive for the guest that can translate into brand loyalty. Cross-promotional tie-ins with frequent flier and car-rental programs can be further incentives for consumers. Linking travel-related products and services to hotel brands benefits hotels and consumers. These promotions will, for instance, give a guest who stays at a specific hotel bonus frequent flyer points. A hotel can also offer bonus points for flying a certain airline or using a certain car-rental agency. Certain credit card companies, American Express being the most visible example, reward their customers by giving them bonus points each time they check in and use their cards at a certain hotel brand.

However broad-based awareness is created, whether through pin-point advertising or brand loyalty, the goal is the same. Corporate hotel marketing seeks to instill in the end user a preference for a specific product on a regional or national level. The next section of this chapter discusses how to create that preference on a local level.

## ON-PROPERTY MARKETING

The luxury of relying on just the local market to fill rooms is afforded few hotels. The local market is generally defined as those guests residing within a comfortable driving distance from the hotel. This distance, which can differ throughout the country, is considered the hotel's sphere of influence. The **sphere of influence** (Figure 2–2) is the reach of the hotel's local marketing effort. How far from the hotel must one go before reaching a point at which no one has heard of a specific product?

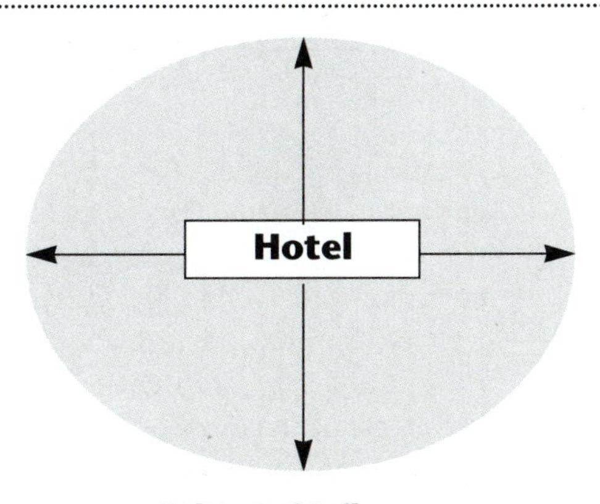


**FIGURE 2–2**
*Sphere of influence*

This sphere can be much larger with large hotel entities or destinations (e.g., Walt Disney or Opryland). Areas like south Florida have variable spheres of influence (Figure 2–3). In the wintertime, south Florida becomes attractive to many northern residents, primarily those from the East Coast and Midwest. In this case, the sphere of influence expands. In the summer, the sun and warmth are less appealing, for obvious reasons, which shrinks the sphere of influence. Seasonality can affect the sphere of influence.

The local market as is discussed here applies to properties regardless of the sizes and scopes of their spheres of influence. The local market should be considered static for the sake of this discussion. The business that comes from the local market can be generally counted upon year-round. That portion of the market, without the variable of seasonality, can be affected by the marketing effort of the hotel.

The local market can consist of members of that community or, many times, guests related to the community. Visiting relatives and friends compose a portion of local market demand. Local group business can also play a major role in a hotel's business mix because of the need for nearby meeting and convention facilities. This demand is nurtured primarily by on-property marketing.

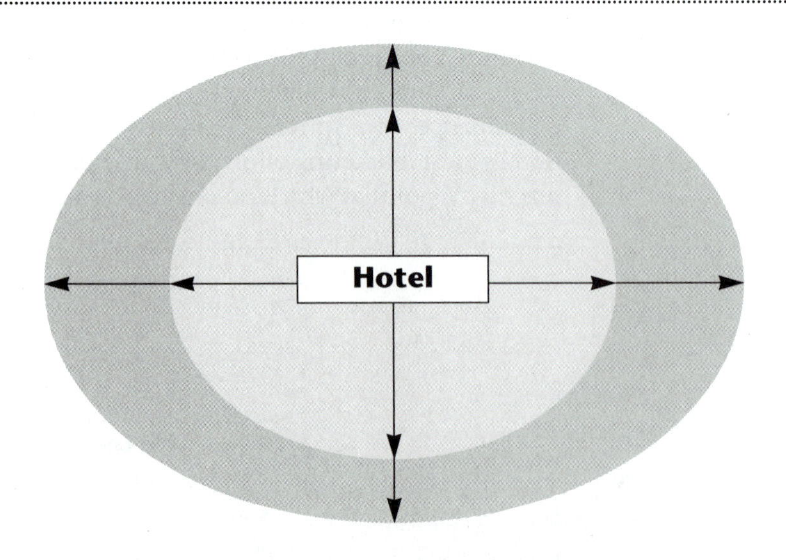


**FIGURE 2–3**
*Variable sphere of influence*

Unlike corporate marketing, which focuses on the hotel guest who is outside the sphere of influence, on-property marketing targets individuals and groups who are within the sphere of influence. The feeder cities of any hotel should lie within the hotel's sphere of influence. The tools and methods hotel marketing directors use to promote their hotels to their local communities share many similarities among differing hotel location and product types. On-property marketing gives marketers the freedom to adapt their efforts to the idiosyncrasies of differing markets.

The ability to tailor the marketing effort lies at the root of on-property marketing. This tailoring can boost the initial impact of corporate marketing because it brings the hotel home to the community. Identification with a specific property as part of the community in which it operates goes beyond pinpoint marketing or brand loyalty. For example, if a major hotel chain offered a "Fun in the Sun" package for guests nationwide in winter, it would have no effect on the hotel of that chain in Minnesota. Only the chain's warm-weather properties would benefit. This is why on-property, or hotel-specific, marketing is essential. A tailored marketing effort by members of that hotel chain who could genuinely boast of "sun" would be the most effective way to promote the package.

**On-Property Marketing Methods.** The following lists tools and techniques used by hotel marketers to promote specific properties to the local market. To different extents, these marketing avenues can prove very beneficial in promoting a hotel to its local community and sphere of influence.

*Collateral Materials/Brochures.* Collateral materials are preprinted advertising aids used to promote a specific hotel, a combination of hotels, or a region. A brochure typically highlights one hotel. Collateral materials and brochures both can be very useful visual aids when showcasing a product to an end user who cannot make an in-person visit. Creative use of colors and formatting heighten these materials' impact. A derivation of the hotel brochure is called a rack card. A rack card is a small, nonfolded, promotional piece that briefly but succinctly highlights a specific hotel or region. Rack cards, which are typically 3″ × 6″, are meant to fit easily into an envelope to send to prospective guests or clients.

*Tradeouts.* A tradeout is nothing more than an "in kind" exchange of goods or services. Hotels incorporate tradeouts into their on-property marketing efforts to maximize their return on investment. A hotel can, in essence, trade rooms or meeting services to an advertising agency or media outlet in exchange for goods or services. A radio station could, for example, exchange ten 15-second commercials for their equivalent in hotel products or services. Tradeouts are very popular in the industry because they entail no real exchange of money. One entity is trading something it can offer for something that it wants. Both participants benefit from the end result. Common tradeout opportunities for hotels exist in:

- Local radio
- Local television
- Local or regional magazines
- Outdoor advertising media (e.g., billboards and airport displays)
- Printed collateral producers and telephone directories
- Internet sites

*Co-ops.* As its name suggests, cooperative advertising and promotion entails "working together." A co-op would entail a hotel joining forces with another product or service provider for the benefit of both. A hotel that joined forces with a bus company, for example, could provide its guests with transportation, and the bus company could add the hotel's pool of guests to its potential customer pool. A local museum that promoted a specific hotel to its guests could get the benefit of that hotel promoting the museum to its guests. Co-ops commonly occur when hotels team with:

- Tour agencies, destination marketing firms, transportation providers
- Local attractions
- Entertainment venues

*Packages.* The hotel package is the most versatile means of local promotion at the marketer's disposal. A hotel package combines one or more hotel products or services to make the new entity more attractive. Often this entails pricing the package below the cost of purchasing the two separately. Most traditional hotel packages combine a room with a meal (e.g., breakfast), for one price. The perceived benefit to the guest can be monetary savings, convenience, or both. Variations on hotel packages can consist of:

- Meal packages, the most common of which are:
  **American plan**, which includes three meals a day with the room
  **Modified American Plan**, which includes two meals (typically breakfast and dinner) and the room
  **Continental plan**, which includes continental breakfast and a room
  (Note: The **European plan** is commonly mistaken for a package, but no meals are included. It is another way of asking for the room rate only.)
- Vacation packages, which bundle room rates and one or more of the following: airline tickets, transportation, tickets to local

attractions or shows, and "themed" amenities. A themed amenity could include sunglasses and suntan lotion for that "Fun in the Sun" package mentioned earlier. A honeymoon package could include champagne and strawberries with the room. A "Night on the Town" package might include a limousine ride and dinner. A concert package might include a ticket to a show and the musical group's latest compact disc (CD) in addition to the room.

- Meeting packages, which are values for the busy meeting planner. A typical meeting package that includes coffee breaks, lunches, or dinners in the cost of a meeting room can ease the planner's mind. Themed meeting packages can make the meeting experience more enjoyable for the jaded attendee. A "Day at the Ballpark" meeting break package might include hot dogs, peanuts, soft pretzels, and snow cones with baseball paraphernalia as decoration. Other packages group common AV needs (e.g., flipcharts, overhead projectors, 35-mm slide projectors, and screens) with the cost of a meeting room.

*Incentives.* When applied on property, an incentive differs from the corporate incentives many chains offer (e.g., frequent-stay programs, cross-promotional tie-ins). Incentives must be perceived as such to be of value to the end user. Offering free tickets to an unpopular attraction might not be an incentive. The flexibility of the hotel marketer to tailor incentives to match the hotel's specific needs are valuable. Lower room rates can be offered when the hotel traditionally underperforms. Certain room types (e.g., suites, upgrades) can be guaranteed available for a price. Room rental can be waived during certain times of the year if needed. The key to incentives is to create the perception in the guest that what the hotel is offering is something special.

The on-property marketing effort can result in short- and long-term success when applied correctly. With the analyses and techniques covered in this chapter, the hotel marketer can improve the overall performance of his or her hotel. As the first page of this chapter stated, taking the guesswork out of marketing inevitably leads to success.

## CHAPTER REVIEW

### KEY CONCEPTS

Product type
Location type
Actual business mix
Traditional business mix
Service level
Target market
Hybrid market
Positioning
Marketing plan
Market share
Operational marketing
Corporate marketing
On-property marketing
Broad-based marketing
Sphere of influence
Brand loyalty
Pinpoint advertising
Market segments
Perceived value
Deceptive location classification

### REVIEW QUESTIONS

1. How can marketing success be measured in a hotel?
2. What outside factors can influence or change the marketing direction of a hotel?
3. What differences can you think of between marketing a product and marketing a service?
4. How would the marketing plans for a luxury hotel differ from those for a budget hotel?
5. What forms of advertising could be incorporated into a hotel's marketing plan?
6. Describe the possible uses of the Internet in hotel marketing.
7. Provide examples of variable spheres of influence.
8. Explain the concept of compression of demand.

## CASE STUDY

This case study is an opportunity for a classroom or sales team to analyze the marketing situation of a fictional hotel. It has been organized to stimulate discussion. To get the most from this case, participants must thoroughly understand Chapter 2.

**BACKGROUND:**

**Hotel Name:** The Golden Bay Star Hotel
**Product Type:** Luxury
**Location Type:** Downtown San Francisco, CA
**Size:** Medium (400 rooms)
**Business Mix:** Corporate transient and group

**SITUATION:** The Golden Bay Star Hotel was developed by a group of investors in the late 1970s to be the premier luxury property of its type in the Bay Area. The downtown location was chosen for its proximity to the financial district and art-gallery community.

In its early years of operation, the Golden Bay Star enjoyed modest success, but the ownership felt better performance was possible. They decided they lacked name recognition. By 1982 the ownership had decided to affiliate the hotel with a national luxury management company. The hotel and management company signed an agreement that was renewable every five years.

For the next few years, the Star, as it is called, experienced record revenue performance. The boom in the financial markets was reflected in strong transient and group demand at high rates. The art market was experiencing strong interest from individual and institutional investors from across the world. Auctions and other meetings were traditionally held at the Star. All parties were satisfied with the arrangement.

By the late 1980s, hotel construction in the vicinity of the hotel accelerated. Properties of all product types and sizes began to appear around the Star. New hotel concepts (e.g., the extended-stay and all-suite) started to vie for the traditional business of the Star.

After several years of declining performance, Star owners began to get nervous. They needed to know why they were in this situation and how they could remedy it. The ownership sent a representative, Tom Anderson, to the hotel to monitor the situation. Tom met with the hotel's general manager, Shelly Burns. Shelly had been at the hotel for ten years. She had been on board for the hotel's period of exceptional performance and as the leader, she had been lauded. She was not used to having to explain poor performance.

Shelly Burns was a "hands-on" general manager. She involved herself in all aspects of operations and sales. She was so involved in sales and marketing, she saw no need for a director of marketing on her executive committee. The hotel had never needed to advertise, and the sales office seemed to run itself. After all, Shelly could make those decisions if needed, so why incur the extra salary costs?

The senior salesperson at the Star, Frank Nevins, had been on staff since the property opened. He had long enjoyed a healthy relationship with the local financial community. His contacts were renowned, and he spent a great deal of time cultivating those relationships.

Tom asked Shelly to take a good look at the current state of the hotel. He needed to report to the owners and wanted a solid plan from the hotel as to how it would improve performance. The owners were in the fifth year of their current management contract and needed to act quickly. Tom gave Shelly one week to develop a revised marketing plan.

**DISCUSSION:** If you were Shelly, what would you do? This case presented background on a fictional hotel, but these situations occur every day. As a group, or as assigned, develop a revised marketing plan for the Star. What factors should you consider?

**POINTS TO CONSIDER:**

- **The hotel's age** (A new hotel in the late 1970s is not new now. Does that matter?)
- **Location** (The Bay Area was in a downward business cycle. Is that cause for alarm? Should trends be anticipated?)
- **Management contract** (Could the management company be responsible?)
- **Target markets** (What are the pros and cons of relying exclusively on two market segments?)
- **Ownership** (Accountability to owners only when a hotel performs poorly is common. What can be done to improve the relationship?)
- **Competition** (How is supply and demand affected? What impact do the new hotel product types have on the Star?)
- **Management style** (Is it reasonable for a hotel general manager to be involved in sales and marketing? When is a director of marketing most needed, when the hotel performs well or poorly?)
- **Sales direction** (Frank Nevins spent a lot of time cultivating a slumping market. Was that the best use of his time? How might he better direct his sales efforts?)
- **Advertising** (What kinds of advertising, if any, could be incorporated into the new marketing plan?)

Use these points as a guide to developing your marketing plan. Share the results with others and see what ideas you devise.

(Note: This case study is a work of fiction. The names, locations, and situations are products of the author's imagination. Any resemblance to actual persons, events, or organizations is purely coincidental.)

# CHAPTER 3

# The Hospitality Sales Process

> *"Ninety-five percent of this game is half mental."*
>
> YOGI BERRA

## INTRODUCTION

Selling hotel rooms requires mastering basic concepts that are unique to hospitality. Both transient and group room sales require specific skills, but the student of hospitality sales should grasp group room sales initially. The ability to sell group rooms translates to an understanding of how to provide for a customer's any hotel room need. It also translates to transient sales. The salesperson successful in transient sales invariably has a strong background in group sales concepts.

This chapter outlines what is done inside the group sales office once a business opportunity is in place. A **business opportunity** occurs when an organization and a hotel communicate regarding sleeping rooms and/or meeting space. Sometimes referred to as a "piece of business," a business opportunity is not necessarily something a hotel may want; it is simply a possible booking. Analyzing what is done with a business opportunity is crucial in determining whether a hotel pursues the opportunity or not.

The hospitality sales process consists of applying specific analyses to a business opportunity. These analyses, which help determine whether to pursue or decline the opportunity, include:

- Qualification
- Room availability
- Arrival/departure patterns
- Need periods
- Slippage/history
- Rate quotes
- Function space considerations

The group salesperson must be able to apply each of these analyses when investigating the business opportunity. This chapter deals with these analyses under the assumption that the business opportunity already exists. The skills and techniques needed to create business opportunity are addressed in Chapter 4.

## QUALIFICATION

> *Knowing is half the battle.*
>
> ANONYMOUS

This quote tells the hotel salesperson to do his or her "homework." This is not homework in the academic sense, but homework in the sense that means "analyze a business opportunity." A salesperson's homework begins with qualification. **Qualification** is the process by which a salesperson learns the specific characteristics of a business opportunity. Qualification uncovers the who, what, where, when, and why (five *W*s) of a piece of business. Qualification of business is considered the first and one of the most important steps in hospitality sales.

The process of qualification begins and ends with questions. The salesperson must be able to ask the right questions at the right times. In fact, asking appropriate questions is a skill that applies to all aspects of hospitality sales. Asking is the only way to get answers. Whether via verbal or written communication, qualification endeavors to reveal as many of the 5 *W*s as possible. The qualification process should be considered a fact-finding mission. It is *not* the appropriate time for a salesperson to make or imply any commitments.

The following questions are good points from which to start the qualification of a business.

**THE 5 Ws OF QUALIFICATION**

Who . . .

- Is the client (name and title)?
- Is the organization (name, address, telephone number, fax number, E-mail address)?
- Is/are the decision makers (name[s])? (A decision maker is an individual or a group who makes the final decision on which hotel a business opportunity will choose. Identifying the decision makers helps the sales process later.)

What . . .

- Is the function (if applicable)?
- Are the function's characteristics (e.g., how many overnight rooms are needed)?
- Are the very important people (VIP) requirements, if any (are upgraded accommodations needed)?
- Are the general banquet requirements? What are the function space requirements (i.e., square footage needs)? How many meetings, meals, and/or displays are needed? How many will attend each event? The catering/convention service department will attend to the catering details, but qualifying space needs determines early if a hotel is large enough to accommodate a function.
- Is the organization's budget for this function?
- Is the purpose of the function? What do the planners wish to achieve?
- Message must be delivered, if any? The message may be one of celebration, enlightenment, training, promotion, or some other general theme.

Where . . .

- Is the function? Does the hotel of choice reflect the intended message? Is the hotel of choice the hotel of choice based on location? Is only one city under consideration? If so, is the client considering other hotels in the city? If the client is considering other cities, hotel chains could make one another aware of the business opportunity early in the qualification process.

When . . .

- Is the function to be held (dates)? Are the dates flexible?
- Has the function been held before? What succeeded in prior functions?
- Does the function recur (frequency)?

Why . . .

- Is the hotel under consideration?
- Is the city under consideration, if applicable?

### OPEN-ENDED QUESTIONS

Most of the questions in the qualification process require multiple-word replies, which means they are open ended. Words like *why, how,* and *what* encourage conversation. Open-ended questions bring out more information than their opposites, close-ended questions. Close-ended questions elicit yes-or-no responses. They begin with words like *is* or *if,* which often lead to one-word answers.

Answers to questions give the salesperson insight into the personality and character of the client or customer. Qualification, therefore, begins the process of establishing customer rapport. **Customer rapport** is positive interaction between a customer and a salesperson. Customer rapport means the customer and the salesperson are comfortable with each other and therefore exchange useful information.

Customer rapport enables the salesperson to uncover more than the 5 *W*s during the qualification process. It provides detailed revelations on why a customer called a specific hotel or what happened to cause the customer to call. Rapport aids the entire sales process. As the qualification process continues, new insights into the buying decisions of the customer reveal themselves (see Chapter 4).

## ROOM AVAILABILITY

To sell as many sleeping rooms as possible, the hotel salesperson must be able to track the rooms' availability. **Room availability** is the number of sleeping rooms that are available for sale on any given night. Armed with the room availability, a salesperson must be able to judge quickly the remaining group room capacity of his or her hotel to verify if a business opportunity is suited to the hotel or not.

Hotels of every size, product type, and service level have some type of internal tracking systems to monitor the availability of their sleeping rooms. These systems can be highly computerized or simple and manual. All such systems are intended to provide the salesperson an "at-a-glance" look at room availability.

Following is a sample availability report for a given week at the ABC Hotel, which has 500 rooms:

**SAMPLE ROOM AVAILABILITY CHART**

| Day | M | T | W | Th | F | Sa | Su |
|---|---|---|---|---|---|---|---|
| Date | 6/1 | 6/2 | 6/3 | 6/4 | 6/5 | 6/6 | 6/7 |
| Total Rooms | 500 | 500 | 500 | 500 | 500 | 500 | 500 |
| Group Ceiling | 200 | 200 | 200 | 200 | 200 | 400 | 125 |
| Groups on the Books | 100 | 125 | 100 | 75 | 100 | 300 | 25 |
| Group Availability | 100 | 75 | 100 | 125 | 100 | 100 | 100 |

A hotel salesperson can view the room availability data for a week to determine if a business opportunity fits the hotel or not. Fitting all possible business opportunities is important, because a hotel must come as close to filling all its rooms each night without overselling. **Overselling** occurs when a hotel sells more rooms than it has available on a given night. Many hotels oversell their rooms because of two factors that reduce the number of guests who arrive. These factors are no-show and slippage.

**No-show** is the term used in transient room analysis to describe the number of guests with reservations who do not arrive on a given night. Measured as a percentage, the no-show factor differs from hotel to hotel, but historical tracking gives hotel management a good idea of how many no-shows to anticipate on a given night.

**Slippage**, the term used when analyzing group room performance at a hotel, is the difference between what is contracted for and what actually arrives. Also measured as a percentage, slippage can be predicted, but it requires more than historical analysis alone. No-show and slippage are addressed in more detail later in this chapter.

Like the common practice of overbooking in the airline industry, overselling in the hospitality industry is a somewhat risky practice that managers engage in to sell exactly their total room allotments. A hotel that has sold all its rooms on a given night is considered sold out. Overselling can backfire when more guests arrive on a given night than there are rooms available.

If a hotel oversells too many rooms on a given night, it displaces guests with reservations. A common term for these displaced guests is "walked guests," because these guests must travel to other hotels for accommodations. Some hotels have policies to reimburse walked guests if those hotels oversell and cannot accommodate their guests' reservations. Most hotels pay for the guests' stays at other hotels and include meals, transportation, and a number of phone calls. Many chains offer free return stays at the hotels that walked the guests. Because these costs can add up, a hotel walks guests only as a last resort.

## GROUP CEILING

The **group ceiling** (see the preceding sample availability report) is the number of rooms the group sales department is expected to sell as part of the total rooms sold at the hotel. With the transient sales effort, the group rooms must bring the hotel as close to sold-out status as possible. This is where the group base is targeted. Based on historical group performance and anticipated increases/decreases in the current year (which correlate to goals set in the marketing plan), the group ceiling in the availability report dictates, day by day, where the group effort must be. The group ceiling may differ day by day as needed and in effect sets the limit for group rooms on a given night.

The on-the-books figure in the availability report represents what the group sales team has already accomplished. In this report, a salesperson can view what groups are booked and how many rooms each requires as part of the group ceiling. Many room availability reports list the booked groups and their respective group room allotments. An allotment of rooms for a group is called a **group block**. The term *block* is used because each allotment "blocks" or removes that number of rooms from overall hotel availability.

As the accompanying example shows, all group blocks make up the group rooms on the books:

**GROUPS ON THE BOOKS**

| Day | M | T | W | Th | F | Sa | Su |
|---|---|---|---|---|---|---|---|
| Date | 6/1 | 6/2 | 6/3 | 6/4 | 6/5 | 6/6 | 6/7 |
| "Appliance Store" | 50 | 25 | 10 | | | | |
| "Big Wig Car Dealer" | | | 55 | 75 | 75 | 100 | 25 |
| "Nice Restaurant" | 25 | 75 | 10 | | | | |
| "Retirement Party" | | | | | | 100 | |
| "National Beer Maker" | 25 | 25 | 25 | | | | |
| "Fraternity Group" | | | | | 25 | 100 | |
| Groups on the Books | 100 | 125 | 100 | 75 | 100 | 300 | 25 |

The difference between the group ceiling and what is on the books is what is available for the group salesperson to sell (group availability). Group availability is crucial to determining how a potential group business opportunity fits in the total hotel picture. Room availability drives the initial booking decisions of the salesperson.

**GROUP AVAILABILITY**

| Day | M | T | W | Th | F | Sa | Su |
|---|---|---|---|---|---|---|---|
| Date | 6/1 | 6/2 | 6/3 | 6/4 | 6/5 | 6/6 | 6/7 |
| Group Ceiling | 200 | 200 | 200 | 200 | 200 | 400 | 125 |
| Groups on the Books | 100 | 125 | 100 | 75 | 100 | 300 | 25 |
| Group Availability | 100 | 75 | 100 | 125 | 100 | 100 | 100 |

To determine the viability of a potential group, and to see how the group fits into the total hotel picture (group and transient), a salesperson must study the availability report closely. The availability report reveals which groups are booked and which groups are available to be booked. To be booked, a group must fit into the hotel's group availability. Assume the group "123 Ball Bearings" wants to host its national meeting at the ABC Hotel and that it needs 100 rooms on Friday, Saturday, and Sunday. In this example, the "123 Ball Bearings" group fulfills the hotel's group room needs on Friday, Saturday, and Sunday. Its block of rooms does not exceed the hotel's group ceiling.

**THE TOTAL PICTURE AT ABC HOTEL**

| Day | M | T | W | Th | F | Sa | Su |
|---|---|---|---|---|---|---|---|
| Date | 6/1 | 6/2 | 6/3 | 6/4 | 6/5 | 6/6 | 6/7 |
| Total Rooms | 500 | 500 | 500 | 500 | 500 | 500 | 500 |
| Group Ceiling | 200 | 200 | 200 | 200 | 200 | 400 | 125 |
| "Appliance Store" | 50 | 25 | 10 | | | | |
| "Big Wig Car Dealer" | | | 55 | 75 | 75 | 100 | 25 |
| "Nice Restaurant" | 25 | 75 | 10 | | | | |
| "Retirement Party" | | | | | | 100 | |
| "National Beer Maker" | 25 | 25 | 25 | | | | |
| "Fraternity Group" | | | | | 25 | 100 | |
| Groups on the Books | 100 | 125 | 100 | 75 | 100 | 300 | 25 |
| Group Availability | 100 | 75 | 100 | 125 | 100 | 100 | 100 |

**THE REVISED PICTURE AT ABC HOTEL**

| Day | M | T | W | Th | F | Sa | Su |
|---|---|---|---|---|---|---|---|
| Date | 6/1 | 6/2 | 6/3 | 6/4 | 6/5 | 6/6 | 6/7 |
| Total Rooms | 500 | 500 | 500 | 500 | 500 | 500 | 500 |
| Group Ceiling | 200 | 200 | 200 | 200 | 200 | 400 | 125 |
| "Appliance Store" | 50 | 25 | 10 | | | | |
| "Big Wig Car Dealer" | | | 55 | 75 | 75 | 100 | 25 |
| "Nice Restaurant" | 25 | 75 | 10 | | | | |
| "Retirement Party" | | | | | | 100 | |
| "National Beer Maker" | 25 | 25 | 25 | | | | |
| "Fraternity Group" | | | | | 25 | 100 | |
| "123 Ball Bearings" | | | | | 100 | 100 | 100 |
| Groups on the Books | 100 | 125 | 100 | 75 | 200 | 400 | 125 |
| Group Availability | 100 | 75 | 100 | 125 | 0 | 0 | 0 |

Room availability analysis in the group sales process is fairly straightforward when groups like "123 Ball Bearings" fit a hotel's room needs exactly as set out in the group ceiling. In today's hotel marketplace, however, a vast number of situations often complicate room availability. Variations in hotels, dates, groups on the books, and prospective business opportunities often make room availability analysis a more in-depth process. Questions among group salespeople arise most often when a group does not fit perfectly into the hotel's availability.

For example, assume the "123 Ball Bearings" group now needs 100 rooms on Friday, 150 rooms on Saturday, and 125 rooms on Sunday. The group now does not fit the hotel's availability as nicely as it did before. If

"123 Ball Bearings" were booked, the ABC Hotel would surpass its group ceiling on Saturday and Sunday. As was discussed, today's varied marketplace makes availability reports like this one much more common than that in the preceding example. When a group exceeds the group ceiling, the salesperson must consider other factors when deciding whether to pursue the business opportunity, including market conditions, displacement, and the nature of the group base.

**THE NEW PICTURE AT ABC HOTEL**

| Day | M | T | W | Th | F | Sa | Su |
|---|---|---|---|---|---|---|---|
| Date | 6/1 | 6/2 | 6/3 | 6/4 | 6/5 | 6/6 | 6/7 |
| Total Rooms | 500 | 500 | 500 | 500 | 500 | 500 | 500 |
| Group Ceiling | 200 | 200 | 200 | 200 | 200 | 400 | 125 |
| "Appliance Store" | 50 | 25 | 10 | | | | |
| "Big Wig Car Dealer" | | | 55 | 75 | 75 | 100 | 25 |
| "Nice Restaurant" | 25 | 75 | 10 | | | | |
| "Retirement Party" | | | | | | 100 | |
| "National Beer Maker" | 25 | 25 | 25 | | | | |
| "Fraternity Group" | | | | | 25 | 100 | |
| "123 Ball Bearings" | | | | | 100 | 150 | 125 |
| Groups on the Books | 100 | 125 | 100 | 75 | 200 | 450 | 150 |
| Group Availability | 100 | 75 | 100 | 125 | 0 | <50> | <25> |

## MARKET CONDITIONS

New hotel construction, economic expansion/decline, and population changes are some of the market conditions that determine room availability in hotels. Chapter 2 outlined the different hotel product/location types and their respective business mixes. These market factors can often dictate on which days a hotel will experience high and low demand. These factors reflect in the marketing plan, which in turn reflects in the room availability report via the group ceiling. Compression of demand also can affect the group ceiling. Hotels in sold-out status can press the room demand outward to other, surrounding hotels.

When analyzing whether to deviate from the group ceiling, the condition of the hotel marketplace at that point is important to consider. It is vital to remember that the group ceiling is set ahead of time with certain expectations. For example, a hotel community may set its group ceilings expecting a major, city-wide convention in a year. As the arrival date of the convention nears, however, the hotels may learn that the convention will be much smaller than expected. Hotels participating in the convention will need to recover their rooms, and surrounding hotels will be unable to count on compression of demand.

## DISPLACEMENT

When analyzing room availability, a hotel salesperson determines what impact a business opportunity will have on the group ceiling for the dates under consideration. Exceeding the group ceiling on certain occasions can be a good decision if potential displacement is determined first. **Displacement** is most commonly defined as the impact created when the rooms taken by a group piece of business exceed the group ceiling. Displacing rooms that are available for sale is called room displacement. For example, a block of rooms may displace the transient rooms that are available for sale. Displacement also occurs with revenue. This is called rate displacement. In this case, a group of low-rated rooms may displace the revenue that a higher-rated group of rooms or transient rooms might bring in.

The ongoing example of the ABC Hotel and "123 Ball Bearings" can show how to analyze displacement when deciding whether to exceed the group ceiling. The rate factor must be included in the analysis. Assume the group rate is $150 and the hotel's rack rate is $175. In this example, the "123 Ball Bearings" group adds to the hotel's total rooms without surpassing the ceiling on Friday. On Saturday and Sunday, however, the group puts the number of group rooms on the books beyond allocation. Displacement analysis looks at how the "123" group affects rate revenue and the gain/loss in rooms.

**DISPLACEMENT ANALYSIS**

| Day | M | T | W | Th | F | Sa | Su |
|---|---|---|---|---|---|---|---|
| Date | 6/1 | 6/2 | 6/3 | 6/4 | 6/5 | 6/6 | 6/7 |
| Total Rooms | 500 | 500 | 500 | 500 | 500 | 500 | 500 |
| Group Ceiling | 200 | 200 | 200 | 200 | 200 | 400 | 125 |
| "Appliance Store" | 50 | 25 | 10 | | | | |
| "Big Wig Car Dealer" | | | 55 | 75 | 75 | 100 | 25 |
| "Nice Restaurant" | 25 | 75 | 10 | | | | |
| "Retirement Party" | | | | | | 100 | |
| "National Beer Maker" | 25 | 25 | 25 | | | | |
| "Fraternity Group" | | | | | 25 | 100 | |
| "123 Ball Bearings" | | | | | 100 | 150 | 125 |
| Groups on the Books | 100 | 125 | 100 | 75 | 200 | 450 | 150 |
| Group Availability | 100 | 75 | 100 | 125 | 0 | <50> | <25> |

The first step in this analysis is to calculate the room revenue impact the group has, day by day. To do this, multiply each day's room number by the group rate ($150):

Friday 100 × $150 = $15,000
Saturday 150 × $150 = = $22,500
Sunday 125 × $150 = $18,750

To calculate the total room revenue impact of the group, add the subtotals from the 3 days:

$$\$15{,}000 + \$22{,}500 + \$18{,}750 = \$56{,}250$$

Note that the preceding analysis of rate displacement only considers the room revenue portion of a hotel's success triangle. A group may add significant revenue via its group catering contribution or its planned outlet/ancillary activities (e.g., golf tournaments at the hotel's course). These considerations are addressed in more detail later in the discussion of profitability. In this example, assume the "123" group offers only room revenue. A group that offers only room revenue is called a "rooms-only" group.

Rate displacement of the "123" group looks at the revenue generated by the group versus the revenue displaced by the loss of transient sales. Remember that the "123" group creates displacement on Saturday and Sunday. The total number of rooms displaced is 75 (50 + 25). These rooms are precluded from sale by the transient sales team. If the transient team sold rooms on Saturday and Sunday for $175 or more (as was determined via yield management), the rate displacement would be:

| | |
|---|---|
| 75 rooms × $175 (transient rate) | $13,125.00 |
| minus | |
| 75 rooms × $150 (group rate) | − $11,250.00 |
| displaced revenue | $1,875.00 |

It would not be in the best interests of the hotel to book the "123" group on Saturday and Sunday alone, because it would lose revenue. However, when the total revenue of the group is factored in, the picture changes. Friday has no transient displacement. Recall that its room revenue impact is $15,000 (100 [rooms] × $150 [group rate]). Subtract from that the revenue lost on Saturday and Sunday to calculate the total revenue impact:

| | | |
|---|---|---|
| Friday | | $15,000 |
| Saturday | ([50 rooms × $175] −<br>[50 rooms × $150])<br>($8,750 − $7,500) = | − $1,250 |
| Sunday | ([25 rooms × $175]) −<br>([25 rooms × $150])<br>($4,375 − $3,750) = | − $625 |
| | total revenue impact | $13,125 |

Therefore, the total revenue impact of booking the "123" group is $13,125. This indicates that, based on room revenue, the correct decision is to book the group.

### NATURE OF THE GROUP BASE

Like market conditions and displacement, the groups on the books can affect the availability of a hotel's group rooms. Most availability reports in the industry reflect the number of rooms a group is allocated at the time of booking. Over time, some groups change their room needs. Analyzing the rooms on the books is a useful addition to the tools of availability analysis already covered.

The term *slippage* was defined as the difference between the number of rooms contracted by a group and the rooms the group used. This term applies to groups that have come and gone at a hotel. The term used before the group arrives to define how well the group is doing relative to the rooms it contracted for is called **pickup performance**. The pace of reservations over time can indicate how well a group may do. Pickup can be stronger or weaker than what is reflected in the availability report.

The sales office must have strong lines of communication between its members to know the pickup performances of all groups on the books. A potential business opportunity may appear on the availability report to fit within the group ceiling on a particular day. If a booked group is picking up very strongly, however, it may require more rooms than what were allocated. This knowledge might alter the hotel's decisions for a new business opportunity.

Some hotels allow groups to go beyond their contracted blocks if the groups' pickup rates are favorable. Others hold firm to all blocks regardless of pickup performance. Poor-performing groups may be contractually liable for all unused rooms, in which case they pay for the rooms whether they fill them or not. Most states prohibit the "double sale" of hotel rooms.

Decisions based on the group base are only to be made with the other analyses of availability. All availability analyses combine to provide useful starting steps for the salesperson considering business opportunities.

## ARRIVAL/DEPARTURE PATTERNS

The availability reports in the previous sections showed differing numbers of group rooms on the books on consecutive days. As some groups arrive at the hotel, others remain and still others depart. The pattern of groups' arrivals and departures dictates how many rooms are on the books and therefore what rooms are available on a given day. A group salesperson must be aware of arrival and departure patterns and how those patterns can affect the total hotel sales effort.

Arrival and departure patterns are referred to in two distinct ways. Both arrivals and departures can be classified as major or soft. A **major arrival** is the day when most group rooms are needed. Most groups, however, need some rooms before most attendees arrive. For example, convention coordinators, meeting facilitators, corporate executives, and meeting planners may arrive early to plan and prepare for an upcoming meeting. These early arrivals are considered soft because they do not significantly impact the hotel. All soft arrivals should be blocked ahead of time, if known, because rooms may not be available in a sold-out situation.

A **major departure** occurs when most attendees check out of the hotel. Soft arrivals may remain after the event concludes to attend to all remaining details. For example, planners and facilitators may stay to review the bill or to ensure that all departing attendees find appropriate transportation. The rooms that make up soft departures are sometimes called "stayovers."

In the process of qualifying a business opportunity, one of the questions was, "Are program dates flexible?" This flexibility applies directly to arrival/departure patterns. A group with a flexible major arrival date allows the salesperson to book the group on dates that are more attractive to the hotel. Not unlike a puzzle in which pieces of different shapes and sizes create a bigger picture (Figure 3–1), groups with differing arrival/departure patterns create the big picture for the hotel's group effort (i.e., group base).

Before analyzing arrival/departure patterns in depth, one must understand the way in which the hotel industry categorizes the days of the week. Hotel classification shifts the days of the week 1 day earlier than the traditional classification. **Weekdays** in the hotel industry are therefore Sunday through Thursday and **weekends** are Friday and Saturday. Hotel classification differs from the traditional because guests spending the night at a hotel stay at the hotel the next day. For example, guests looking for a "weekend getaway" spend the nights of Friday and Saturday and the days of Saturday and Sunday. A guest staying Sunday night is preparing for an activity at or near the hotel on Monday.

**FIGURE 3–1**
*Puzzle pieces*

The following example illustrates the concept of arrival/departure patterns. The accompanying availability report shows the ABC Hotel's group availability and its groups on the books. Assume that "Sunny Real Estate" wants to host a program at the hotel. To host the program, "Sunny Real Estate" needs 75 rooms on Thursday, 100 rooms on Friday, and 125 rooms on Saturday. The first step for the salesperson is to see how the availability report changes with the "Sunny Real Estate" rooms.

**ROOM AVAILABILITY AT THE ABC HOTEL**

| Day | M | T | W | Th | F | Sa | Su |
|---|---|---|---|---|---|---|---|
| Date | 6/1 | 6/2 | 6/3 | 6/4 | 6/5 | 6/6 | 6/7 |
| Total Rooms | 500 | 500 | 500 | 500 | 500 | 500 | 500 |
| Group Ceiling | 200 | 200 | 200 | 200 | 200 | 400 | 125 |
| "Appliance Store" | 50 | 25 | 10 | | | | |
| "Big Wig Car Dealer" | | | 55 | 75 | 75 | 100 | 25 |
| "Nice Restaurant" | 25 | 75 | 10 | | | | |
| "Retirement Party" | | | | | | 100 | |
| "National Beer Maker" | 25 | 25 | 25 | | | | |
| "Fraternity Group" | | | | | 25 | 100 | |
| Groups on the Books | 100 | 125 | 100 | 75 | 100 | 300 | 25 |
| Group Availability | 100 | 75 | 100 | 125 | 100 | 100 | 100 |

**ROOM AVAILABILITY WITH "SUNNY REAL ESTATE"**

| Day | M | T | W | Th | F | Sa | Su |
|---|---|---|---|---|---|---|---|
| Date | 6/1 | 6/2 | 6/3 | 6/4 | 6/5 | 6/6 | 6/7 |
| Total Rooms | 500 | 500 | 500 | 500 | 500 | 500 | 500 |
| Group Ceiling | 200 | 200 | 200 | 200 | 200 | 400 | 125 |
| "Appliance Store" | 50 | 25 | 10 | | | | |
| "Big Wig Car Dealer" | | | 55 | 75 | 75 | 100 | 25 |
| "Nice Restaurant" | 25 | 75 | 10 | | | | |
| "Retirement Party" | | | | | | 100 | |
| "National Beer Maker" | 25 | 25 | 25 | | | | |
| "Fraternity Group" | | | | | 25 | 100 | |
| "Sunny Real Estate" | | | | 75 | 100 | 125 | |
| Groups on the Books | 100 | 125 | 100 | 150 | 200 | 425 | 25 |
| Group Availability | 100 | 75 | 100 | 50 | 0 | <25> | 100 |

As the accompanying box shows, "Sunny Real Estate" fits into the hotel's overall group base fairly well except for Saturday, when it displaces 25 rooms. A displacement analysis on the total revenue impact may reveal that the group is profitable with these arrival/departure patterns. However, if during qualification it was determined that the group was flexible with its arrival/departure pattern, the salesperson could move the group (like a piece in a puzzle) into dates that would work better for the hotel. The availability report looks quite different when the group's arrival/departure pattern is changed to Tuesday through Friday.

**ROOM AVAILABILITY WITH FLEXIBLE ARRIVAL/DEPARTURE**

| Day | M | T | W | Th | F | Sa | Su |
|---|---|---|---|---|---|---|---|
| Date | 6/1 | 6/2 | 6/3 | 6/4 | 6/5 | 6/6 | 6/7 |
| Total Rooms | 500 | 500 | 500 | 500 | 500 | 500 | 500 |
| Group Ceiling | 200 | 200 | 200 | 200 | 200 | 400 | 125 |
| "Appliance Store" | 50 | 25 | 10 | | | | |
| "Big Wig Car Dealer" | | | 55 | 75 | 75 | 100 | 25 |
| "Nice Restaurant" | 25 | 75 | 10 | | | | |
| "Retirement Party" | | | | | | 100 | |
| "National Beer Maker" | 25 | 25 | 25 | | | | |
| "Fraternity Group" | | | | | 25 | 100 | |
| "Sunny Real Estate" | | 75 | 100 | 125 | | | |
| Groups on the Books | 100 | 200 | 200 | 200 | 100 | 300 | 25 |
| Group Availability | 100 | 0 | 0 | 0 | 100 | 100 | 100 |

As a rule, arrival/departure patterns differ from hotel to hotel based on product and location type. Market factors and the business mix play major roles in determining which days are better for arriving at and departing from certain hotels. Maneuvering a business opportunity into a preferred arrival/departure pattern enhances the attractiveness of the group. In most hotels, a Sunday arrival is valued because guests often do not like to travel on traditional weekend days.

## NEED PERIODS

The analysis of a business opportunity continues beyond arrival/departure patterns. Broader than the day of the week, the time of year at which a piece of business arrives at the hotel can be very important. If a group can book at a hotel when the group base is low for many days, it would fill the hotel's needs. Consecutive days of underperforming room revenue constitute a period of need for a hotel. Need periods are the times of year during which a hotel traditionally performs at lower levels than others (Figure 3–2).

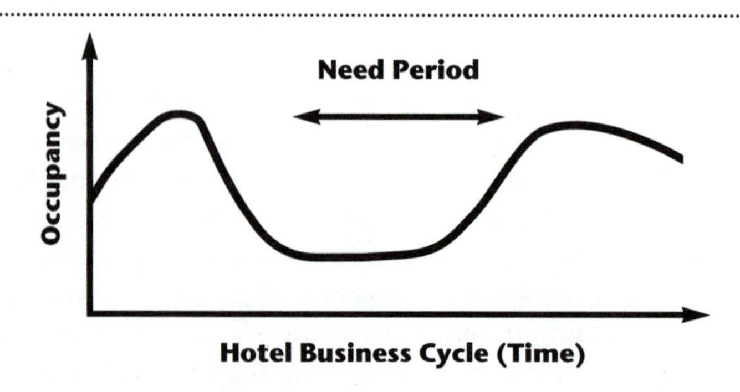


**FIGURE 3–2**
*Need period*

The nature of modern business is cyclical. Most businesses experience highs and lows based on the markets in which they operate. In the hotel industry, the need period is the time of year at which that cycle is on a down slope. Ideally, a hotel has no need periods. A consistently high performance is the goal of any hotel manager and owner. In reality, however, even high-performing hotels have time frames in which their success levels are lower than others. Knowing when and how severe need periods will be can allow a hotel to change its approach and therefore compensate. Reevaluating yield management and group sales decisions are the best ways to counter need periods. (Specific actions are addressed later in this section.) Need periods can be defined more narrowly as traditional or situational.

## TRADITIONAL NEED PERIODS

**Traditional need periods** occur at a hotel with predictable regularity year after year. A hotel's business cycle traditionally drops during these need periods. Traditional need periods most often result from a hotel's seasonality and/or its special attractions.

Chapter 2 addressed the concept of seasonality. The seasonality of a property primarily drives its need periods. For example, an Arizona resort will traditionally experience increased demand during winter, when Arizona's climate is most appealing. The state's sweltering summertime temperatures make that season an off season. Therefore, the summer can be generally categorized as a need period for much of Arizona. The rainy winters in Seattle are need periods for many hotels in that city.

A hotel's special attractions can also play a role in need periods. If a local amusement park that creates demand for the hotel when operating closes for part of the year, it could adversely affect guest demand and lead to a need period. A resort with a championship golf course that closes for maintenance a certain time each year could experience a need period during that time.

## SITUATIONAL NEED PERIODS

The fundamental difference between traditional and situational need periods is predictability. Traditional need periods recur regularly at the same times each year. In contrast, **situational need periods** are not necessarily predictable. For example, a situational need period could occur when a major, 2-week convention holding most of a hotel's rooms for a long time suddenly cancels. In this situation, the host hotel would face a gaping hole in its group base, and the hole would create a need period where one did not exist before.

Situational need periods do not have to be tied to the actions of specific groups or conventions. For example, a hotel that is located by a major highway may rely heavily on motor travelers for transient demand. If that stretch of highway were to close for repair and a detour were to be erected, the hotel would lose access to a significant portion of its demand. This situation also creates a need period where one did not exist before.

**Addressing Need Periods.** Whether the need period is situational or predictable, its impact on a hotel can be significant. As previously mentioned, the tools for counteracting a need period (changes in yield management and sales strategy) should be implemented far in advance for traditional need periods, and as soon as possible for situational ones.

Traditional need periods should be addressed in the hotel's marketing plan with detailed actions for the group and transient teams to implement. The group sales team may loosen restrictions on size and room rate for group business that fills a need period. Situational need periods are more difficult to address in that they do not have much lead time and are unpredictable. Group and transient sales may take advantage of promotions and specials to fill these need periods. The group sales team may have time to contact groups that did not fit into the sales strategy before the situational need periods. A group with a lower rate may be more attractive to a hotel given these new need periods.

It is important to note that need periods can evolve as results of the actions taken to address them. If the group and transient sides of a hotel work diligently to fill need periods, those need periods will eventually cease to exist. This is the goal of addressing need periods as soon as possible. Therefore, both transient and group salespeople should make it a habit to review the statuses of need periods. A need period can evolve to a sold-out period with the booking of just a few groups.

## SLIPPAGE/HISTORY

As was discussed earlier in this chapter, slippage is the difference between the number of rooms a group contracted for and the number of rooms the group occupied. The transient equivalent is the no-show factor. Both come into play when overselling a hotel.

Both the group and transient sales teams endeavor to minimize the effect of slippage and no-shows respectively. The reason for this is that, taken together, excessive slippage and no-shows can turn a sold-out night into one of much lower occupancy. Overselling transient rooms usually cannot overcome excessive group slippage. There are methods to address each factor.

## METHODS TO MINIMIZE TRANSIENT NO-SHOWS

The transient sales effort in the hotel industry has developed ways of addressing and limiting the impact of no-shows. The guaranteed reservation and the advance purchase reservation are the two most prevalent ways of combating no-shows.

**Guaranteed Reservations.** **Guaranteed reservations** are made by transient guests who wish to ensure that rooms await them when they arrive. A reservation is guaranteed by cash deposit or credit card. A guest must cancel a guaranteed reservation by a specific time on the day of arrival (usually 4–6 P.M.) to avoid being charged for the room. Guests with guaranteed reservations are much more likely to arrive at the hotel because of the potential penalty. A hotel can offer guests nonguaranteed reservations that are not held by cash or credit. These guests are not obligated to occupy the rooms. However, if it chooses the hotel can release nonguaranteed reservations by a certain time on the day of arrival (again usually between 4 and 6 P.M.). The no-show factor dramatically decreases with guaranteed reservations because the reservations oblige the guest to show. The mix of guaranteed and nonguaranteed reservations is a primary component of how far to oversell a hotel.

**Advance Purchase Reservations.** **Advance purchase reservations** are becoming more and more common in the hotel industry. Not unlike the advance purchase fares offered by many airlines, hotels may offer reduced rates for reservations that are booked far in advance. The tendency of transient demand is to be short term, which does not allow for significant yield management far into the future. An advance purchase reservation induces transient guests to make their reservations ahead. No-shows are dramatically reduced with these reservations because they are nonrefundable. Penalties are imposed on changes or cancellations.

## METHODS TO MINIMIZE GROUP SLIPPAGE

Managing slippage on the group side is as involved as it is on the transient side. The group sales effort uses other tools to minimize the impact of slippage. Analyses of the group's market segment, reservation method, and history give good indications as to the group's propensity for slippage.

**Analysis of Market Segment.** Market segments differ in their tendencies to "slip" upon arrival. While exceptions do occur, predicting the tendencies of groups to slip based on market segments can be valuable. Corporate groups tend to place experienced meeting planners in charge of establishing group blocks of rooms. Planners' knowledge of the groups they are working with enables them to make very good estimates of the group's final room occupancies. Final room usages for social groups (e.g., weddings) can fluctuate wildly from initial room blocks. The group salesperson must be able to work with each market segment to adjust room blocks to realistic numbers. That ability positively impacts slippage.

**Analysis of Reservation Method.** **Group reservation methods** are the ways in which group reservations enter the hotel. Most hotels offer group attendees three ways to make reservations for an event:

1. individual call-in,
2. rooming list, and
3. registration cards.

The individual call-in method is the most common way for groups to fill room blocks. In this method, a hotel holds a contracted number of rooms and attendees simply call to make their reservations. The second method, the rooming list, is supplied by the meeting planner. This list includes a list of predetermined attendees. Individual group members do not have to make their own reservations; the rooming list makes them. The list can indicate room preferences like smoking/nonsmoking and single/double. The third method for making reservations, registration cards, are supplied by the hotel so group attendees can make their reservations by mail. These preprinted cards indicate the group meeting dates and rates. Although used less frequently than in the past, some associations prefer this reservation method.

In terms of slippage, the three reservation methods differ. The rooming list is a very good indicator of how many rooms a group will bring in. Because the attendees are "prescreened" (committed to the planner) before being placed on the rooming list, they are more likely to arrive. The individual call-in method tends to slip more than the rooming list because control is taken out of the planner's hands. In this method, individuals must be counted on to make their own reservations. No prescreening is involved, because attendees do not have to commit to anyone. The registration card method tends to have slippage factors even greater than the individual call-in method. Filling out a card and mailing it takes more time than calling in, and lost mail and incomplete addresses compound the potential problems with this reservation method. A hotel incorporates the slippage potentials of the three reservation methods into its overselling and availability projections.

**ESTIMATED SLIPPAGE**

| Reservation Method | Slippage Percentage |
|---|---|
| Individual Call-In | 10 to 15 |
| Rooming List | 5 to 10 |
| Registration Cards | 15 to 20 |

**Analysis of History.** History in the hotel industry is defined as the documented historical room performance of a group relative to the rooms the group contracted. Beyond market segment and reservation method, history can show how an organization, a company, or an association has done over time. For example, a company that has held its annual meeting for the last 10 years will have 10 years of history of how many rooms were booked and what the slippage percentage was each year. Hotels in the hospitality industry have a good record of providing historical information to other hotels when requested. As a courtesy, hotels exchange historical information willingly on the assumption that their gestures will be reciprocated.

History can reveal the trends of a particular group. Slippage factors are the most important trend, but other factors can be revealed in the analysis of history. Early arrivals and stayovers (soft arrivals/departures), group block excesses, last-minute suite requests, and outlet/ancillary usage can all be useful historical information.

Adjusting a group block according to history is a good idea in most cases, but not all cases. For example, if a hotel near a corporation's headquarters is tapped to host the corporation's annual board meeting for the first time but the last few years of the corporation's history comes from a remote, inaccessible property, the hotel should adjust the interpretation of history. The organization's slippage might be dramatically reduced at the more convenient hotel. The reverse could also apply.

## RATE QUOTES

Chapter 1 introduced the success triangle (Figure 3–3). Its three components of room sales, catering sales, and outlet/ancillary sales combine to create success for a hotel. The revenue generated by the sale of sleeping rooms makes up the foundation of the success triangle. The sales team (group and transient) is responsible for selling these rooms. It is logical to conclude then that the pricing of these rooms is the most important function of the sales team. Transient sleeping room rates are determined, in large part, by yield management strategy. On the group side, determining room rates is more involved. The group side is responsible for creating the base of rooms over which transient sales must fill. Determining the rates quoted to groups requires integrating many factors, including availability, arrival/departure patterns, need periods, and slippage. All these factors are revealed through efficient qualification.

The question most frequently posed to a hotel salesperson is, "What is the room rate?" Every client wants to know the costs incurred by staying at a hotel. Rate quoting requires significant analysis and consideration. To accurately quote group rates, the salesperson must be able to

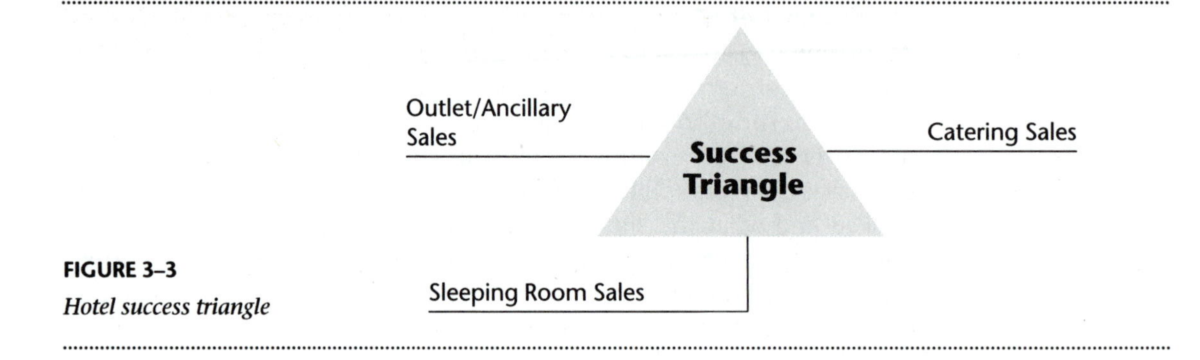


**FIGURE 3–3**
*Hotel success triangle*

evaluate target rates, peaks and valleys, profitability, and the group sales equation.

## TARGET RATES

Group room sales is considered separate from the transient sales effort because selling multiple rooms at once is both desired and time-intensive for the salesperson. If this was not the case, all rooms at a hotel could be sold by the transient team and the meeting space could be sold separately by the catering team. The objective of group room sales is to effectively trade a lower room rate for multiple reservations on a given day. To differing degrees, this trade-off creates the base of rooms for transient sales. On a given day, the rate to offer a group in exchange for its higher occupancy is outlined by target rates.

**Target rates** are the minimum rates the group sales team must reach to achieve the hotel's predetermined revenue target. Target rates may also be called pickup rates, because if all booked groups meet or exceed the determined rate the group budgeted goals will be met or picked up. Target rates are established initially by the hotel's marketing plan, which sets out the group revenue goals. In most hotels, availability reports outline the target rates, day by day. Target rates are flexible in that they may change (higher or lower) to reflect the groups on the books and the final revenue goals as different groups are booked. Target rates may be lower during need periods to enable the sales team to book differing groups. Periods with high group bases or predetermined seasonalities may have higher target rates.

Target rates consider, in an evolving process, all groups that are booked. The target must be high enough to meet the group revenue goal but not so high as to lessen the benefit the client derives from trading multiple reservations for the lower rate. The client must perceive that buying sleeping rooms in bulk is valuable.

**ROOM AVAILABILITY REPORT WITH TARGET RATES**

| Day | M | T | W | Th | F | Sa | Su |
|---|---|---|---|---|---|---|---|
| Date | 6/1 | 6/2 | 6/3 | 6/4 | 6/5 | 6/6 | 6/7 |
| Total Rooms | 500 | 500 | 500 | 500 | 500 | 500 | 500 |
| Group Ceiling | 200 | 200 | 200 | 200 | 200 | 400 | 125 |
| "Appliance Store" | 50 | 25 | 10 | | | | |
| "Big Wig Car Dealer" | | | 55 | 75 | 75 | 100 | 25 |
| "Nice Restaurant" | 25 | 75 | 10 | | | | |
| "Retirement Party" | | | | | | 100 | |
| "National Beer Maker" | 25 | 25 | 25 | | | | |
| "Fraternity Group" | | | | | 25 | 100 | |
| "123 Ball Bearings" | | | | | 100 | 150 | 125 |
| Groups on the Books | 100 | 125 | 100 | 75 | 200 | 450 | 150 |
| Group Availability | 100 | 75 | 100 | 125 | 0 | <50> | <25> |
| Target Rate | $125 | $150 | $125 | $125 | $175 | n/a | n/a |

As an example, assume that the rack rate at the ABC Hotel is $175. As the accompanying table shows, the days with the most rooms available for the group team to sell (Monday, Wednesday, and Thursday) have lower target rates in an effort to attract more groups. The day with a higher group base (Tuesday) must have a higher target rate because the remaining group rooms are at a premium. On Friday, the target rate matches the rack rate because the group team met its predetermined room goal (group base). Any more group rates on that night would not make sense. Exceeding the group ceiling would take from transient rooms which, by their nature, sell at higher rates. The same theory applies to Saturday and Sunday. These days have no target rates in the table because the group team exceeded the group ceiling on each. It must be assumed that the hotel conducted a displacement analysis to show that the group that put the sales team over the limit was profitable. No more group rooms should be booked on those days.

Target rates must be viewed as a goal, not as a beginning. Rate negotiations with a client should therefore not begin with the target rate. Because most bargaining situations bring the seller's price lower and the buyer's price higher, a group salesperson should make the initial room rate quote higher than the target when possible and fall back to the target rate when needed. Target rates ensure that salespeople know where their quotes must be and that the sales team is not quoting haphazardly.

## PEAKS AND VALLEYS

Situations arise in which the target rate may be too high. Availability reports may have "holes" or "valleys" between dates of strong group performance. While need periods consist of multiple days (weeks or months) of low demand, peaks and valleys occur when 1 or 2 days of low demand occur between days of higher demand (see Figure 3–4). Peaks and valleys most often result directly from arrival/departure patterns of groups that were not placed together well (remember the puzzle).

**AVAILABILITY REPORT RESULTING FROM INFLEXIBLE GROUPS**

| Day | M | T | W | Th | F | Sa | Su |
|---|---|---|---|---|---|---|---|
| Date | 8/1 | 8/2 | 8/3 | 8/4 | 8/5 | 8/6 | 8/7 |
| Total Rooms | 600 | 600 | 600 | 600 | 600 | 600 | 600 |
| Group Ceiling | 400 | 400 | 400 | 400 | 300 | 300 | 400 |
| Groups on the Books | 400 | 325 | 175 | 75 | 250 | 250 | 150 |
| Group Availability | 0 | 75 | 225 | 325 | 50 | 50 | 250 |
| Target Rate | **$150** | **$125** | **$110** | **$110** | **$135** | **$135** | **$110** |

Consider as an example a 600-room hotel with a rack rate of $150. As the accompanying table shows, Wednesday and Thursday have fewer "Groups on the Books" than the rest of the week. There is a gap between the departure of a large group on Wednesday and the arrival of the next major group on Saturday. Large groups cannot arrive on Tuesday and depart on Friday because of the hotel's group availability. Peaks and valleys in the hotel's group availability block certain arrival/departure patterns.

The target rates for Wednesday and Thursday are lower than those for the rest of the week, but they may not be low enough for this example. In this example, the hotel has no option but to fill these two days exactly. A lower target rate for these two days may induce a group to book on these days, which is when the hotel needs the business. (Note: This example assumes that the transient demand is no stronger than what was allocated when the group ceiling was determined. A strong transient-demand hotel, which could fill these nights without a group room contribution, would

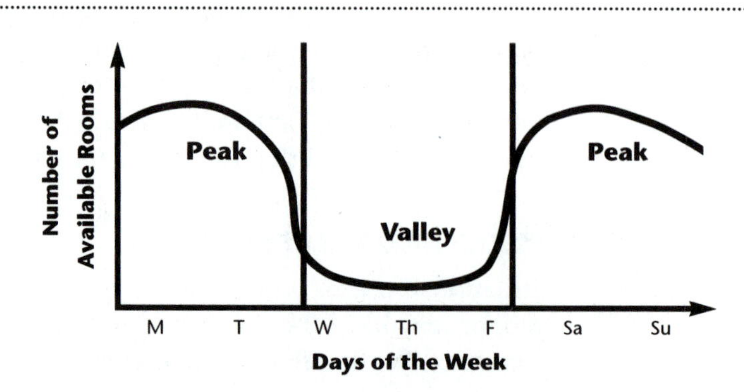


**FIGURE 3–4**
*Peaks and valleys*

not need to take groups rated lower than what was determined by the target rates. The airport hotel product type [see Chapter 2] may fit this profile.)

## PROFITABILITY

The quoting of group rates should consider more than just the rooms themselves. As was reviewed in Chapter 1, the low cost of a sleeping room provides a hotel the greatest profit margin. The three sides of the success triangle (see Figure 3–3) depend on the triangle's foundation of room sales to impact the rest of the hotel's revenue sources. In the ideal scenario, strong room sales benefit the catering and outlet/ancillary revenue centers of a hotel. However, situations arise in which salespeople focus less on the room rate portion of groups and incorporate the impact the groups may have on the other side of the success triangle. Room rate quotes can be affected by the total hotel impact of a business opportunity.

**Total hotel impact** is a group's revenue contribution to all three sides of the success triangle. Sleeping room revenue, the group catering contribution, and outlet/ancillary usage combine to give a big picture of the revenue impact on the hotel.

A salesperson may deviate from the target rate when the total hotel impact surpasses any loss in room revenue. Groups that schedule catered breakfasts, lunches, and dinners provide the catering department substantial revenue. Groups that do not schedule catered functions and limit attendees' free time force attendees to use the hotel's food and beverage outlets. A group that plans a major golf tournament off season may be viewed favorably even if the room rates are lower because the hotel needs the golf revenue at that time.

Need periods are not strictly a group room phenomenon. Because room sales drive the rest of the hotel, a period of low room sales may lower catering and outlet/ancillary sales for the same time frame. Need periods are another instance in which a salesperson may reevaluate target rates to contribute to the total hotel impact of a business opportunity. Profitability must be viewed with all sides of the success triangle in mind.

# Industry Perspective

## "Transient Business Travel"

*Carolyn Morton*
*Business Transient Sales Manager*
*Omni Hotels*

The definition of business transient travel, or volume account, is simple. Any organization that trades a guaranteed volume of room nights to a hotel in exchange for a discounted rate is considered a business travel account. The room rate discount is based on the volume and pattern of the room nights provided by the organization and the revenue goals of the hotel.

This segment of transient demand can be vital to hotels because of its consistent volume throughout the year. Unlike group business, the business travel segment should need a hotel's services 12 months a year, 7 days a week. Business travel can be viewed as a supplement in times when the group sales effort experiences lower demand due to need periods or market conditions.

A business travel account can be viewed as needed by one hotel while unneeded by another. The definition of "good" depends largely on the hotel's product type. A small to medium luxury hotel may not need to commit itself to discounted transient business. In contrast, a large, upscale hotel may be willing to make that trade-off.

The salesperson who is interested in pursuing this market segment must ask the following qualifying questions:

- What is the nature of the company's business? Does the company fit the image of the hotel?
- Who is the hotel's competition? Is the company looking at other hotels of similar product type? Are the hotels' service levels the same? What about their locations?
- What is the company's budget? Can it afford your hotel? Is your hotel a good value for the company? Do you offer more/less than the company needs?
- What hotels has the company used in the past? What is the company's volume history? Why is the company looking to change hotels?
- How will the company's travel patterns impact your hotel's average rate and occupancy?

- Does the company have a mandated travel policy? In other words, must all members of the company stay at your hotel when in town, or can they choose from several options?

The answers to these questions will help a salesperson evaluate new business travel opportunities. The salesperson should carefully decide whether to pursue those opportunities or not. Unqualified accounts should not be considered. A poor decision will adversely affect a hotel's business mix, occupancy, average rate, and rev-par.

## THE GROUP SALES EQUATION

Rates = Dates + Space

Dates = Rates + Space

Space = Rates + Dates

Rates—Group sleeping room rates
Dates—Dates of the group's function
Space—Function space needed in the hotel

The accompanying equations encompass a fundamental rule in group sales. This rule, called the **group sales equation**, sets a standard for group negotiations. The group sales equation states that three basic components make up a group negotiation. The three components, rates, dates, and space, are equally important. In group negotiations, the hotel must have one of the three components in its favor. The client can, in effect, take any two of the components and the hotel will claim the third. How does this work?

The group sales equation provides a guideline for the salesperson who is qualifying a group program. As the client reveals the details of the program, the salesperson should begin to think about which components of the group sales equation must be given to the client and which component the hotel must retain. For example, if a client cannot pay targeted rates for a program and the arrival/departure pattern is not flexible, then the hotel should insist on some leeway in the reserving of function space. A group who must meet on certain dates and cannot alter the function space of its program should be booked at a room rate the hotel wants or needs. A hotel should be able to move a program into need periods or valley dates if that program cannot pay target rates or alter its meeting space requirements to better suit the hotel.

The group sales equation is introduced here, in the rate quoting section, because rate is often the most delicate item in group negotiations. A salesperson knows what rate he or she must book on any given day via the target rates. In initial negotiations, the client often puts equal value on each of the three components in the group sales equation. As the qualifying process continues, however, it may become apparent that rate is the least flexible component for the client. A skilled salesperson addresses the rate issue by altering dates or space requirements and thereby makes the client aware how valuable the other two components of the equation are to him or her.

The group sales equation dictates a trade-off between the client and the hotel. This does not mean that rate quoting must take a backseat to space and dates, however. On the contrary, the group sales equation gives a salesperson the tools to address all issues a client may raise. The ability to lower a rate quote to benefit the hotel (with space or date adjustments) gives the client a "win" while the hotel also gets a "win." This "one for two" trade-off in equation components is viewed as a benefit to both the hotel and the client.

> “
>
> *Give the clients the sense that they have won and it creates a win-win situation for both them and your hotel.*
>
> 
>
> JAMIE DOYLE, DIRECTOR OF SALES

## TIPS AND HINTS FOR RATE QUOTING

Beyond the aforementioned concepts of target rates, peaks and valleys, profitability, and the group sales equation, the skill of rate quoting involves many nuances. The experienced salesperson can hone his or her rate quoting ability over time so that all these concepts become second nature. The following lists some time-honored rate-quoting tips:

- Do not quote a rate too quickly. Always take the time to fully qualify and determine the specifics of a business opportunity. Some clients do not understand that a salesperson must get the "big picture" of a program before quoting a rate. Clients who are shopping (calling many hotels to get a range of rough quotes) may not be serious. They will not give the salesperson enough time to fully qualify. As a last resort, the salesperson should quote the rack rate and hope the client will call back to allow for further negotiation and qualification.
- A salesperson should take the time before quoting a rate to see what rates are on the books for a certain date. Other groups will indicate the market tolerance level. The market tolerance level may reveal that a hotel's target rates are too high or too low. A series of group rates that far exceed the targeted group rates may indicate that group rooms are at a premium for those dates. If compression of demand is taking place in the group market, certain parts of the surrounding hotel community may be sold out or have exceeded their group availabilities in their group ceilings. In these instances, a rate quote that strictly

adheres to the target rate loses potential room revenue. The converse is also true. A period of rates that are below the target rate may indicate that the hotel market has become a "buyer's market." If the supply far outweighs the demand, and all else remains equal, the supply-and-demand curve mandates a reduction in prices.

- When a salesperson qualifies a business opportunity, the group's rate history is helpful. A group's rate history (the rates it paid in the past) is only available to a salesperson if the group met at the salesperson's hotel. Documents exist for all groups that have used a hotel. These documents, called group files or account profiles, which are addressed in more detail later, can give the salesperson an idea of the rates a group is accustomed to paying. The idea is not to jolt the group with a room rate quote that is vastly different from the quote it received the last time it met at the hotel. A drastically reduced rate may hamper the hotel's chance for a rate increase next time. Consistency in rate quoting is called "rate integrity." Rate integrity mandates that any change in a rate quote be accompanied by a reason. Changes in the hotel's status (e.g., occupancy level or city-wide compression) may necessitate a different rate quote. Changes in the group (e.g., size, arrival/departure patterns [need periods], total hotel impact) can also necessitate a change in the rate quote.
- If a piece of business returns to a hotel at the same size and scope and on the same date, a slight rate increase is warranted. A 5 percent increase in room rate is considered industry standard because it mirrors the rate of inflation. All organizations, including hotels, face increases in price for goods and services. If the client resists a slight increase in room rate, the salesperson can use the client's business as an example. For example, if a car dealership wants to return to a hotel with a similar program and market conditions remain the same, but the dealership resists a slight rate increase, the salesperson should ask the dealership if the prices of car makes and models remain the same year after year. The client gains new perspective when the salesperson relates price considerations in terms the client understands.
- If a new business opportunity with no rate history approaches a salesperson, the qualification process should uncover where the group met in the past. Knowing other hotel property types and service levels can help the salesperson understand the rates the group may have been quoted. If the group's past hotel is

unknown, the salesperson can get an idea of the group's rate structure by uncovering its AAA or Mobile rating. Both Mobile and AAA rate hotels on a scale of 1 to 5, with 5 being the top level. AAA uses stars as measurement; Mobile uses diamonds. In either case, a client frequenting 5-star hotels probably is less averse to high rates than one frequenting 2-diamond properties.

- It is important to note that just because a group has paid significantly more than current target rates in the past, the salesperson should not artificially inflate rates. A hotel should not over- or undercharge for its services. Groups who trade up a level of hotel product or service should be quoted the same rates as consistent customers. The converse is also true. Assuming it chooses a hotel in the same market, a group choosing a hotel of lower quality or service level should not expect rates to remain the same. Integrity in rate quoting applies as much to the hotel as it does to the client.
- Always be cognizant of how rate quotes relate to rev-par. A hotel filled with higher rates achieves a better rev-par than one filled with lower rates. Room rate drives the most important revenue source of the hotel.

In summary, every group or transient business opportunity demands that the salesperson thoroughly complete his or her homework. Completing homework simply entails thoroughly qualifying and researching. It is important that questions are asked (qualifying) and documented data (history) is gathered so that an intelligent and equitable decision is reached. Experienced salespeople often ask sales teammates for opinions and review each other's work so that different perspectives are considered.

## FUNCTION SPACE CONSIDERATIONS

The previous section introduced the group room equation:

$$\text{Rates} = \text{Dates} + \text{Space}$$

Function space plays a major role in this equation. Determining how much function space a business opportunity requires entails in-depth analysis.

Stand-alone conference centers and hotels with meeting space must make the best use of their function space to maximize their catering revenue potential. A conference center is a facility that provides meeting and food and beverage services but not sleeping rooms. Some conference centers work with hotels, but they are fundamentally different entities. Both hotels and conference centers rely on their salespeople to reserve meeting space for groups effectively. Reserving space, also called blocking space, and ensuring that the space derives sufficient revenue helps the hotel to determine whether to pursue or decline business opportunities.

This section looks at the rationale behind determining function space usage in a hotel facility with meeting space. Nonsleeping room entities like conference centers can apply some of these concepts, but the role space plays in the group sales equation does not apply to them. The hotel salesperson must understand the types of functions a client may request, namely the event and food function, before attempting to secure function space.

When qualifying, the salesperson should initially determine a group's function space requirements because, outside of sleeping rooms, function space is usually the main reason a group chooses a hotel. If a group does not need sleeping rooms, it may choose a conference center. If a group does not need sleeping rooms and is focused on a food or an event function type, the sleeping room salesperson should not be involved because:

1. The catering-only group does not need sleeping rooms. When a meal or a meeting is emphasized, most attendees are from the local area. The distinction between local catering and group business centers is the need for sleeping rooms.
2. Meeting and food functions are the areas of expertise of the catering salesperson and therefore best lay exclusively within the catering arena.

## EVENT FUNCTION TYPES

The vast majority of groups a salesperson books at a hotel require function space for meetings or conventions. These are classified as **event functions** because the focus is on the events themselves. This is not to say that these groups do not require food function space in addition to the event spaces, but the need for food function space would not exist if not for the events. Following are the most common event types:

Meeting—This "catchall" term refers to the most frequent need for event space. Sometimes also called a general session, the **meeting** is the most important event a group plans. The business conducted and the topics addressed in meetings generally bring groups to the hotel.

Breakout Room—The **breakout room** is designed to allow attendees of a general session to "break" into smaller groups for more intensive discussion. A breakout room is generally much smaller than the main meeting room. The need for breakout rooms is common among large groups.

Exhibit/Display Space—Large groups, namely associations and trade groups, may provide **exhibit/display space** near their general sessions for displays and exhibits from various providers. For example, academic groups may provide display space for attendees to share new ideas with each other. Often called trade shows, these events are designed to allow attendees of large groups to mingle and network with vendors. A vendor is a small group or an individual who is interested in selling an item to a group's attendees.

Office Room—An area set aside as a central point of operations for the meeting planner and his or her staff is called an **office room**. Large groups may require small meeting rooms to house all their equipment and materials (e.g., copiers and fax machines). The office room is often held on a 24-hour basis.

Registration Space—Set up in front of the general session room, **registration space** is made up of one or more 6-foot tables and serves as a meeting check-in point. The meeting planner may staff this area to hand out conference materials, identification credentials, and other items needed by attendees.

## FOOD FUNCTION TYPES

Groups that are meeting at a hotel with meetings as their main goal still must eat and relax. Because food functions may need to accompany events, salespeople must be aware of the differing types of food functions and their typical requirements. The definition of **food function types** focuses on the meals in question.

Breakfast—A **breakfast** is typically a sit-down meal in the morning that serves traditional breakfast fare. The breakfast, as a food function, is usually held in a room separate from the meeting.

Continental Breakfast—The **continental breakfast**, which is a lighter version of the sit-down breakfast, serves cold food items and hot and cold beverages. The continental breakfast can be served in a separate room, but most often it is served in or around the central meeting room of a group. It is a common starting event at which attendees congregate and get to know each other before the program begins.

Coffee Break—The **coffee break** food function is designed to break up meetings. The coffee break can be set up inside or outside the main meeting room. It allows attendees to stretch their legs and network between sessions. Coffee does not have to be served during this food function, but it often is during early and mid-morning breaks. Afternoon breaks can include any type of beverage and snack. These breaks can be themed to match the mood and feeling of the planner and attendees.

Lunch—**Lunch**, which is a midday food function, serves a full meal in the meeting room or in a separate room. Lunch menus can be similar to those for dinner, but they have slightly smaller portions. A roll-in lunch allows the meal to be served while attendees continue to conduct business in the same room. A sit-down lunch is more structured in that attendees must adjourn to another room to dine. Lunches can be plated and served as complete meals or they can be buffets from which attendees serve themselves.

Reception—Often a precursor to dinner, a **reception** is designed to promote mingling and communication among attendees. Hard and/or soft beverages may be served with light snacks. A formal reception may include a full bar and an assortment of hors d'oeuvres. Hors d'oeuvres can consist of many selections, but they are commonly thought of as heavier "finger foods" like shrimp, canapés, and fruit and cheeses. Receptions can occur at any time of day in today's market.

Dinner—**Dinner** is the last formal food function type in a given day. It can encompass several courses and menu items. The dinner can lead to formal business presentations or less structured events. Dances and celebrations that are scheduled after dinner are not classified as food functions because the focus of the events are activities, not food. These events are classified as function events.

Each food function type has distinct characteristics. Some are obvious: One would not serve scrambled eggs for a hotel dinner or set up a hotel breakfast in the lobby. Some are not so obvious: Receptions do not have to be evening functions. Morning receptions can serve cakes and fruit without alcohol. In qualifying, the salesperson must not assume that common terms for food functions mean the same to the client as they do to him or her.

One way to differentiate between food and event function types is to view the potential catering revenue contribution of each relative to the number of attendees. A meal (e.g., dinner or breakfast) generates more catering revenue per person than does a meeting.

Because of the division of responsibility in the sales office, the group salesperson should not be too concerned with the specific menus tied to food functions. These details are best left to those in catering, who better understand menu planning, or meeting managers, who are engaged in planning all aspects of small group functions.

## COMMON ROOM SETS

After the salesperson determines the nature of the event and its food function types, the function space in the hotel must be secured. The term *blocking space* is used to describe the act of reserving function space for a group. Blocking both sleeping rooms and function space correctly is vital to the success of the hotel as well as the group.

The availability report/display of function space in hotels is not unlike the availability report for sleeping rooms. Some hotels have fully computerized their internal sales and catering functions. Currently, a few of the large chains have computer programs that allow salespeople to view availability displays of any given day and function room. Some hotels use some of the sales and catering programs that are currently on the market, namely Delphi and Miracle. Other hotels use the more traditional slash books, which are nothing more than large books that display a hotel's inventory of function space, day by day, on each page. With slash books, the salesperson simply turns to the day in question and slashes with a pencil all the space needed for the appropriate time frame.

Whatever system a hotel has in place, salespeople must have very good understandings of what groups can fit in the hotel and where. This entails knowing in-depth common function room sets and the capacities of different styles of seating. Figure 3–5 outlines some of the basic and most common seating styles in today's meeting industry. These setups are the most frequently used, but this is not to say that new and unique setups are not being created every day. Various setups combine to create new setups. The experienced salesperson can visualize each function room in varying setups.

Each setup requires a differing square footage. For example, a 40-person meeting in theater style requires fewer square feet than a 40-person meeting in schoolroom seating. Because hotels have different room configurations, it is difficult to provide rules by which to determine the number of square feet for every room set. All hotels have, as part of their printed marketing collateral, room-capacity charts that outline each function room and its capacity in different seating configurations.

When evaluating what function space to allocate a group, the salesperson must keep in mind the extra items that will occupy square footage. A function room capacity chart outlines the number of people a room can accommodate without other items. Some of the most common items requiring space at a food or an event function are AV, buffet tables, and miscellaneous.

**Audiovisual Needs.** When blocking function space, the salesperson must understand that many types of AV equipment can require some square footage in a function room. In the ideal qualification process, the client details the group's AV needs. The salesperson must understand basic AV terminology to carry on basic yet intelligent AV conversations with clients. The following terms constitute what is considered to be the *minimum* level of familiarity for anyone working in the hospitality field.

**Banquet Style or "Rounds"**

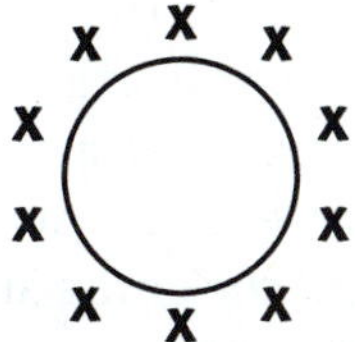

Usually seats 8 to 10 people per round table, depending on table size. Works well for all meal functions and breakout rooms in which team building or brainstorming is needed.

**Schoolroom Style or "Classroom"**

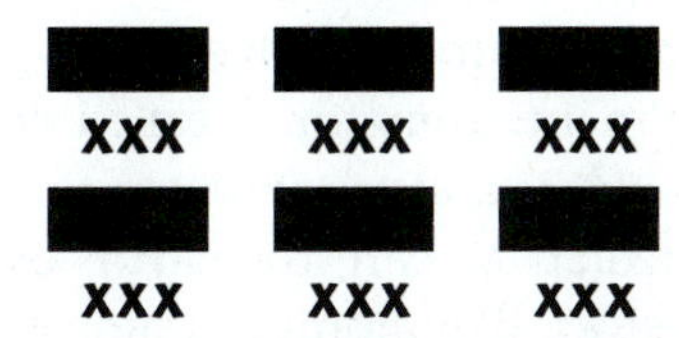

Typically seats 2 to 3 people per 6-foot table or 3 to 4 people per 8-foot table. Works well for presentations in which participants must work with information at the front of the room. Provides a surface for note taking and/or handouts.

**Herringbone or "Chevron"**

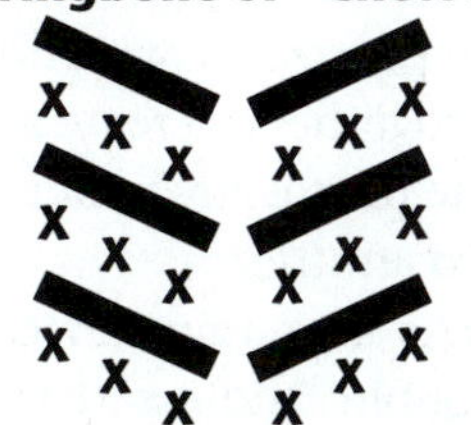

Variation on schoolroom or theater style that angles tables to the front of the room. Can help seat more attendees in a smaller room.

**U-Shape or "Open End"**

Good for intimate or intense meetings that require interaction. Natural location of the presentation source is at the open end of the *U*.

**Conference Style or "Boardroom"**

Seats people around a solid, rectangular table. Very flexible style that can be built with schoolroom-style tables to accommodate any size group. Tends to work better for smaller numbers. Large, conference-style tables can keep attendees too far apart for effective interaction.

**Theater Style or "Auditorium"**

XXX XXX XXX XXX
XXX XXX XXX XXX
XXX XXX XXX XXX
XXX XXX XXX XXX

Simply rows of chairs facing the front of the room. Easiest setup from a labor point of view. Works best for attendees who only need to listen to what is being presented in the front of the room, because there is no work area for writing or note taking. Best setup in terms of space use in that the maximum number of people can be seated in the least amount of space.

**Star**

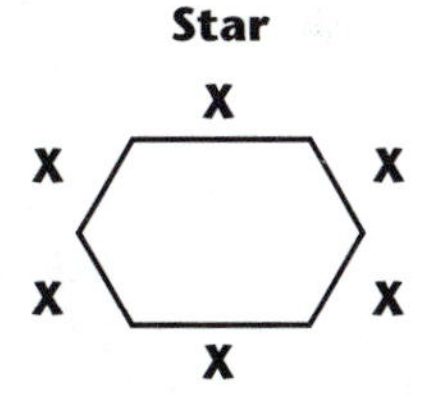

Good for diplomatic or sensitive discussions in which the aim is to avoid seating anyone at the head of the table.

**Hollow Square or "Open Conference"**

Not as conductive to presentations or other styles, but often used for board meetings.

**FIGURE 3–5**
*Seating styles*

Amplifier—The **amplifier**, which is used with some type of audio source, allows sound to be enhanced or, more often, intensified before presentation.

Audio Monitor—The **audio monitor** is useful in any setup with a live music source. It is usually a small speaker in a stand-alone configuration near the mixer. It serves as a "listening ear" as to how something is being heard throughout the entire audio system.

Audio Source—The **audio source** is any device or entity that creates a sound to be fed into an audio presentation system. It can be a presenter, a speaker, a live band, and so on.

Boom Microphone—A **boom microphone** is attached to some type of extension. It is used when the operator wants to capture the audio source but cannot get very close to the audio source.

Cable—**Cable** is a generic term that covers all types of connecting cables used in AV equipment. Sometimes called coaxial or "coax," cables come in various lengths and gauges to perform various tasks.

Cart—Sometimes called an AV cart, the **cart** is used as a mount to transport other AV devices, like monitors, slide projectors, and overhead projectors.

Dimmer Switch—A **dimmer switch** is a light-control device that is often mounted on function room walls to control the intensity of the house lights. Dimmer switches can be connected to remote switches to control the lights from the podium or somewhere away from the function room wall, or they can be stand-alone controls for portable lights.

Dissolve—**Dissolve** is the process by which two or more projection units are faded in and out together to create a seamless presentation.

Dubbing—**Dubbing** is the process by which recorded audio is transferred from one recording to another.

Equalizer—An **equalizer** is an audio device that is often used with an amplifier and/or a public address (PA) system and that allows for adjustments in bass, treble, and mid-range frequencies. It can be employed when the audio source lacks sound quality or the room acoustics are less than ideal.

Feedback—**Feedback** is a high-pitched squeak or squeal that results when audio from the speaker system recirculates through a microphone.

Flipchart—A **flipchart**, a large pad of paper mounted on a tripod or another type of easel, is used to illustrate a point. It is useful in team building, brainstorming, and other types of meetings.

Freeze-Frame—A **freeze-frame** is one frame of video or motion picture that is stopped for display.

Front Projection—**Front projection** is a style of light projection that uses a standard front reflective screen of any size. The light source (often a projector of some kind) must come from the front side only.

Hot—**Hot** is the descriptive term for the state when a coaxial cable carries a live feed or some type of AV device is on or in use.

House Lights—**House lights** are the permanent lighting system in a function room.

House Sound—**House sound** is the permanent audio system in a function room.

Lavaliere Microphone—The **lavaliere microphone** is a small microphone that can be attached to a speaker to allow freedom of hand movement. It can be wireless or corded.

Level—**Level** is the measurement of volume or intensity.

Liquid Crystal Display (LCD) Computer Panel—The **liquid crystal display (LCD) computer panel**, a unique computer monitor that allows light to pass through it, is used with an overhead to display its contents on a screen to a large audience.

LCD Computer Projector—The **LCD computer projector** is similar to the LCD panel, except it uses its own light source to project a computer's image on a screen. There is no need for an overhead.

Mixer—A **mixer** is an audio device that combines audio sources. It is often used to create a seamless recording level. A mixer must be used whenever sound is being amplified or multiple microphones are being used.

Monitor—A **monitor**, a common term for television monitor, is used most often as a video playback viewer but it can be used in many other ways. It is about the size of a television. Monitor is sometimes used as jargon for audio monitor.

Multimedia—The term **multimedia**, which refers to the use of two or more AV devices in a presentation, is most often used to describe high-end and extravagant programs.

Overhead Projector—An **overhead projector** is a device by which light is sent through a directional lens and is displayed in a forward direction. Overhead projectors most often use transparencies or LCD computer monitors as their presentation sources.

Pan—**Pan** is the rotation of a camera around the viewing area. The goal often is to simulate a panoramic view.

Pipe and Drape—**Pipe and drape** is a common term for portable dark draping that can be set up as a divider (useful in exhibits) or as a barrier to conceal something (rear screen).

Podium Microphone—A **podium microphone** is attached to a podium or lectern.

Public Address (PA) System—A **public address (PA) system** is a portable audio speaker setup that is generally used in large areas or auditoriums. It is useful in situations when house sound does not suffice.

Rear Screen—**Rear screen** is a style of light projection that uses a rear-generated light source. The nonreflective screen can then be viewed from the front of the room. The rear screen is useful in that the audience cannot view any AV device, but it tends to take a lot of function space. Often, pipe and drape is used to hide everything behind the rear screen.

Remote—A **remote** device activates an AV device from some distance. A remote, which can be attached via wire or wireless, is used often in slide projector and video presentations.

Satellite Downlink—A **satellite downlink** is the connection made to an orbiting communications satellite to link audio and video from other locations.

Skirting—**Skirting** is using fabric or linen to wrap an AV cart or a table to make it look more professional.

Slide Projector—A **slide projector** is a video device that is used to project one slide at a time. It is sometimes called a carousel projector because it usually uses the carousel tray to hold and advance the slides.

Speaker Phone—A **speaker phone** is a "hands free" telephone that allows more than one person to communicate at the same time.

Spotlight—The **spotlight**, which targets light on a person or an object, can be part of the house lights (permanent in a function room) or it can be portable. The spotlight is useful when a stage is in use.

Standing Microphone—A **standing microphone** is attached to a freestanding device that can be adjusted for height and angle.

Strobe—A **strobe** is a rapidly blinking, high-intensity light. It is often used in multimedia presentations to add visual impact.

Surge Protector—A **surge protector** is an electrical device that acts as a buffer between sensitive equipment and an electrical outlet.

Table Microphone—A **table microphone** is attached to a small, flexible stand that is mounted on a tabletop for seated speakers. It is used in panel discussions.

Throw—**Throw** is the projection distance.

VHS—**VHS** is standard videotape format. The VHS system uses ½-inch wide videotape.

Video Cassette Recorder (VCR)—A **Video cassette recorder (VCR)** is a device used to record and play back video.

Video Projection—**Video projection** is the display device that is used to project VCR playback onto a screen. It is often used when a standard monitor is not big enough to be seen by all attendees.

Zoom—**Zoom** is the action of magnifying a subject without changing the camera or video source location.

Rear screen, video projection, large front-display screen, and other AV setups can reduce by up to a third the total capacity figures in a hotel's meeting space capacity chart. A salesperson should not discount the tendency of clients to add to their AV requirements after blocking space. If possible, all client needs should be fully uncovered during qualifying. Last-minute space changes can only be accommodated by what the hotel has available.

**Buffet Tables.** When blocking space for a buffet meal function, the salesperson must consider the size of the group and any requisite buffet tables. Buffet tables take up square footage that cannot be allocated for seating. Menu selection plays a part in the size of the buffet (extensive menus require more space), but the room salesperson blocking the space may not know the menu.

Buffet tables can be single-sided or double-sided, meaning that people can get their food from one or two sides of the buffet. On a double-sided buffet, each side of the table has the same salad, entree, and so on as the other side. A simple rule of thumb is to plan one double-sided or two single-sided buffet tables for every 100 attendees. The tables can be set up inside or outside the function room depending on the space available. Setting up the buffet outside the function room gives the group more seating space inside, but the salesperson must ensure that attendees can access the room easily and that the buffet does not interfere with activities outside the meeting space.

**Miscellaneous.** Miscellaneous items are not part of the main setup but are revealed during the qualification process. These items can include:

Display Tables—**Display tables** are tables that are used inside a function room to display materials and other items. Six-foot tables are most common. Display tables can impact the usable square footage. Several display tables drastically reduce the seating capacity.

Exhibits—If a group uses the general session room or some other event room to meet as well as to display **exhibits**, it reduces seating. Exhibits can vary in dimension. Large exhibits should be set up in separate areas whenever possible.

Decorations/Props—When, during the qualification process, a client suggests that he or she needs extensive **decorations/props**, the salesperson should take notice. Without addressing specifics, the salesperson should explain to the client that these items may take usable square footage and that a larger room may better suit him or her.

Additional Work Space—Clients may require additional space if they need expanded work areas for their attendees. For example, groups using large binders or computer workstations need more space than others.

## SPACE EFFICIENCY

When blocking space for meetings, it is imperative to keep in mind how efficiently the hotel's resources are being used. Blocking space efficiently means a hotel can book more groups, which equates to increased sales.

**Space efficiency** is the method by which a hotel's available space is allocated relative to other events in the hotel and upcoming functions. Optimizing the revenue potential of function space, while minimizing labor and other costs, is considered efficient space use.

When salespeople block space for groups, they commit other hotel departments to expend labor and inventory. Careful examination of the hotel's function space book or computer display reveals what else is booked on the day in question. A salesperson should endeavor to minimize the changing or turning of room sets. For example, if a hotel has a breakfast scheduled on a particular morning for one group and another group needs lunch space, it would save time and labor to put the lunch in the same room. This is called a "stay set." When the breakfast concludes, the banquet staff could prepare the room for lunch using the same round tables. If there are no other alternatives but to block event or meal functions into rooms with different setups, the hotel must do so, because it is necessary to generate revenue. Minimizing the turning of function rooms helps the hotel's bottom line, however.

Typically, the time available between functions to change sets, what is called **turn time**, is the measure of how long the staff has to prepare for an upcoming function. A good rule of thumb is to allow at least 1 hour turn time from the previous function to clean up and prepare for the next. This rule may differ from hotel to hotel, however. Hotels with function space spread over wide areas may require longer turn times for staff and equipment to arrive. A hotel with all its function space in a central area may be able to turn a room in a shorter amount of time. The availability of staff members to turn the room may also come into play.

Turning a room from event function to food function takes more time than changing it from food function to food function. Setting up for meals typically takes longer than setting up for meetings because of the extra labor required to lay down linen and napkins, pour water, set the table with silverware, set salads, and so on.

## ROOM RENTAL

As a part of the products and services a hotel offers, the function space itself can generate revenue. Not unlike the rates charged for a sleeping room, room rental from function space generates revenue for usage of the space for a specific time frame. **Room rental** is the cost of function space. The cost of this space is not considered a part of the cost of a meal or a

# *Industry Perspective*

## "Creativity in Blocking Function Space"

*Lisa Darlington*
*Catering Manager*

Creativity comes into play when maximizing space. If function space is limited or a group cannot afford the cost of separate meeting and meal space, the salesperson has several options.

A meeting set in classroom style could incorporate a roll-in lunch. Sometimes referred to as a "working lunch," the roll-in lunch allows the hotel to use the meeting room for lunch as well as to conserve space for other bookings. Buffets can be rolled in to the back of a meeting room. Box lunches can be provided at the lunch break, which allows attendees to take their meals and eat anywhere. A meeting room can be set in round tables and, with a short break to allow the banquet staff to set up, the room can serve as the lunch or dinner room as well as the meeting room.

What the salesperson should consider when exercising such options is setting aside space at the back of the meeting room or in the foyer for buffet tables or roll-in carts.

meeting. Often called a "setup fee," room rental can add significantly to the overall revenue generation of a group, because most room rental is pure profit.

**Quoting Room Rental.** In the qualifying process, the salesperson must evaluate many aspects of a program to determine pricing. The decision to pursue or decline a business opportunity hinges on many items already covered, namely profitability, need periods, the success triangle, and so on. While the qualifying process is being conducted, the function space needs of the group must be determined. It is important that an honest price for this space (room rental) is quoted to the client right away.

Many salespeople fear that charging for the use of meeting space will discourage potential customers. What must be understood is that charging room rental is the same as charging a sleeping room rate. A hotel should no more give away a function room than it should give away a sleeping room. Room rental is a bargaining tool that can be incorporated into the selling tools available to a salesperson, and it should not be discounted.

Room rental is considered part of the revenue the catering department receives from a group. Therefore, it plays a role in the profitability of the catering sales portion of the hotel success triangle. Any revenue generated from the use of function space is viewed as having the same profit margin as sleeping rooms.

This section looks at the many aspects of room rental and how room rentals should be quoted. Market factors like market tolerance and client education level are addressed first. The starting point for quoting rental is the concept of predetermined room rental. Room rental as viewed in the group sales equation and rental as it applies to space use, specifically space intensity and room-to-space ratios, must be understood by the group salesperson.

**Market Tolerance.** A hotel that is in the enviable, and rare, situation of being the "only game in town" does not have to concern itself with competition. In reality, today's hotel marketplace is made up primarily of hotels of similar sizes and product positions that are competing with each other in close proximity. These competing hotels often seek the same client pool.

Depending on the city in which a hotel and its competitors find themselves, the market dictates a level of cost for similar hotels. Competing hotels quote room rental rates differently based on different criteria, but rates that are drastically different from what the market will tolerate translate into little business (too expensive) or lost potential profit (too inexpensive). This rationale applies to room rentals as well as to sleeping room rates.

In general, hotels quote room rental rates based on the market tolerance they use to quote sleeping room rates. Some hotel managers view room rental differently. Some managers view their hotels' function spaces as superior to those of their competition. Others discount the value of their function spaces because the spaces are in poor condition. Managers who drastically reduce function space fees to guarantee group bookings may not place as much value on room rental. A hotel with unique function space characteristics may have a product no competitor has, which translates into premium room rental rates. These function space characteristics can include:

- High ceilings
- A large, continuous ballroom (no pillars, posts, or other obstructions)
- New carpeting, lighting, equipment, and so on
- Advanced in-house sound systems or multimedia control centers

- Theater auditoriums
- Windows with unique views
- Centrally located meeting space
- Soundproof walls and room dividers

**Client Education Level.** Like market tolerance, the level of client education can impact the rental rates quoted by a hotel and its competition. In certain location types (e.g., downtown), potential clients may find that meeting space cannot satisfy the demand. In these situations, in which meeting space is at a premium, most hotels charge higher room rental rates. The market in turn assumes that value on function room rates. In other words, clients expect high charges for room rentals in the downtown market. The clients in this market have been educated to expect these charges as standard.

The opposite also applies. If hotels in certain locations find that they are losing business to other locations due to high room rental costs, those hotels will likely discount their rental prices quickly. A historical record of hotels giving away discounted or free meeting space teaches clients that they can avoid room rental cost.

**Predetermined Room Rental.** The room rental rates of any hotel should be broken down by specific times of day and meeting room. A room rental tariff sheet, which breaks down what management has predetermined are the values of each meeting room and all function space for specific time frames, should be available at any hotel. These figures can be divided by length of time and time of day.

*Length of Time.* The length of time a group holds function space dictates how many groups can use function space at the hotel. The 24-hour hold reserves space for an entire day and night and precludes the hotel from reselling that space to any other group that might have a multiple-day program. The weekend hold on function space is common for groups that require large amounts of setup or teardown time. For example, conventions may have intricate displays and ancillary material. The time needed to put all facets of a meeting room together (set up) or to clean up and pack for removal (tear down) often falls over weekends. Social events like weddings may require partial weekend holds for decoration.

*Time of Day.* The standard breakdown of when groups meet encompasses the average length of time room rental tariffs are applied. The most common breakdowns are half-day, full day, and evening.

Half-day groups meet between 8:00 A.M. and 11 A.M. or 2 P.M. and 5:00 P.M. The half-day time frames most often occur between major food functions (e.g., after breakfast, before lunch, after lunch, before dinner). Groups meeting for full days usually request the hours of 8:00 A.M. to

5:00 P.M. Evening functions most often occur after 5:00 P.M. Receptions and dinners may be precluded from booking at a hotel that has an evening function booked in the corresponding meeting space.

With these standard time frames, a general room rental quote can be determined. The hotel management should preset a value for its function space without considering other factors, like sleeping room usage or food functions. These predetermined room rental rates are similar to target rates in sleeping room quotes.

Predetermined room rental tariffs can be established in different ways. The most common way is to determine a dollar value for each square foot of function space based on the room rental revenue budget set in the marketing plan. If, for example, a hotel has 10,000 square feet of function space and the daily room rental target is $5,000, the predetermined room rental for each square foot of function space is $0.50 (5,000 ÷ 10,000). Applying the square footage guideline for rental to the specific time frames discussed earlier indicates the predetermined room rental charge for any event function type. Again, it should be noted that the predetermined room rental tariff for any hotel does not consider other revenue factors, like sleeping room usage and food functions, which are addressed later. This tariff is simply the cost of the function space.

**SAMPLE ROOM RENTAL TARIFF SHEET**

| **Function Room/ Square Footage* (in Dollars)** | **Room 1/ 1,500** | **Room 2/ 1,500** | **Salon A/ 1,500** | **Salon B/ 2,500** | **Salon C/ 3,000** | **Total Rental (Dollars)** |
|---|---|---|---|---|---|---|
| **Time Frame** | | | | | | |
| Full Day | 750 | 750 | 750 | 1,250 | 1,500 | 5,000 |
| Half-Day | 375 | 375 | 375 | 625 | 750 | 2,500 |
| Evening | 375 | 375 | 375 | 625 | 750 | 2,500 |
| 24-Hour Hold* | 1,125 | 1,125 | 1,125 | 1,875 | 2,250 | 7,500** |

*At $0.50 per square foot.

**The 24-hour hold rental tariff is greater than the predetermined square foot allotment because holding a room beyond a full day involves holding the additional evening time frame. Because a 24-hour hold on a room precludes the room from availability for evening functions, the room rental loss should include both tariffs. Weekend holds, because they can vary in length, can use the same guideline. Any setup or teardown time that is needed should be included in the rental quote based on the time frames that are precluded from sale.

A salesperson can use the tariff sheet as a starting point to negotiate the space charge. Because the salesperson is not generally involved in room rental negotiations without a sleeping room component, predetermined room rental rates may not always apply. The following section reveals how and when a salesperson can deviate from the predetermined rental tariffs.

## ROOM RENTAL AND THE GROUP SALES EQUATION

In the qualifying process, a salesperson uncovers a group's function space requirements. Space requirements must be known before rates are quoted because the hotel's size and space availability must be considered first. A hotel must want to and be able to accommodate the business opportunity.

The group sales equation, Rates = Dates + Space, mandates that the three components have equal value. The equation dictates that the client receives two components in his or her favor and the hotel receives one. Room rental plays a role in how each of the three components is allocated. Room rental provides revenue for the hotel to offset the impact of space in the group sales equation.

It makes sense for the hotel to give the client two components and itself one if all three components impact the hotel in exactly the same way. That is, if the client dictates the parameters of his or her two components and the hotel dictates the parameters of its one, the hotel must be prepared to disregard the revenue impact of the client's two components. Room rental, because it generates revenue, can skew the equation. The space component positively impacts the hotel even if it is not the one component of the equation initially in the hotel's favor. For example, if a group wants to meet at a certain time of the year (dates) and its function space requirements (space) are not flexible, the hotel should hold firm on room revenue (rates).

If, in this example, the hotel was able to generate room rental revenue from the sale of the function space, the need for high sleeping room rate quotes would be slightly diminished because the sale would offset the hotel's revenue impact. The three components of the equation are no longer equal. A room rental quote at or near the predetermined rental tariff may not seem like a loss to the client, and it is a gain for the hotel. The salesperson must be able to view all incoming revenue as benefiting the hotel. This is the total hotel perspective.

**Space Intensity.** Function space use in a hotel must be optimized at all times. Blocking space effectively makes the best use of function space. When looking at how well space is being used, one must understand the concept of space intensity. **Space intensity** analyzes the amount of function space being used for an event or a group versus the amount that is considered typical for that hotel. A hotel with limited function space cannot allow a group to use all its available space. In contrast, a large convention hotel with tens of thousands of square feet of meeting space may be more generous in space allocation.

The "typical" amount of function space differs from hotel to hotel. The fundamental question a salesperson must ask him- or herself is, "Is this the best use of the function space?" If a 30-person group wants to book at a hotel but insists that its meeting be held in the large ballroom instead of a smaller salon, the meeting could be considered space intensive. A small lunch for a 10-person group might fit into a hotel's breakout rooms instead of its rooftop dining hall.

Using a function space capacity chart as a guide, the salesperson must be able to direct clients to function space that can accommodate their functions while optimizing space usage by the hotel. Figure 3–6 illustrates the concept of space intensity. In this example, the XYZ Company wants to book a meeting for 12 people in conference style setup. The hotel has two options for blocking the meeting. Option A uses a permanent conference room that can accommodate up to 15 people. Option B uses one section of a 10,000-square-foot ballroom. Which option is the least space intensive?

Option A, the conference room, is set up to host conference-style meetings exclusively. No business would be displaced or lost if the XYZ meeting was blocked there. Realistically, no larger groups or meal functions could better use the space. Option B requires the hotel to use Section D of the ballroom, which precludes the hotel from using the entire ballroom for a much larger meeting or meal function. The risk is high with this option, because the hotel no longer has the opportunity to book other business. Remember that functions on 24-hour hold and setup and teardown times can complicate space intensity. A hotel's meeting space capacities chart shows where functions best fit.

As the salesperson evaluates all the specifics of a function, he or she should consider the total hotel revenue impact. Remembering the hotel success triangle, a salesperson should ask him- or herself if the group is:

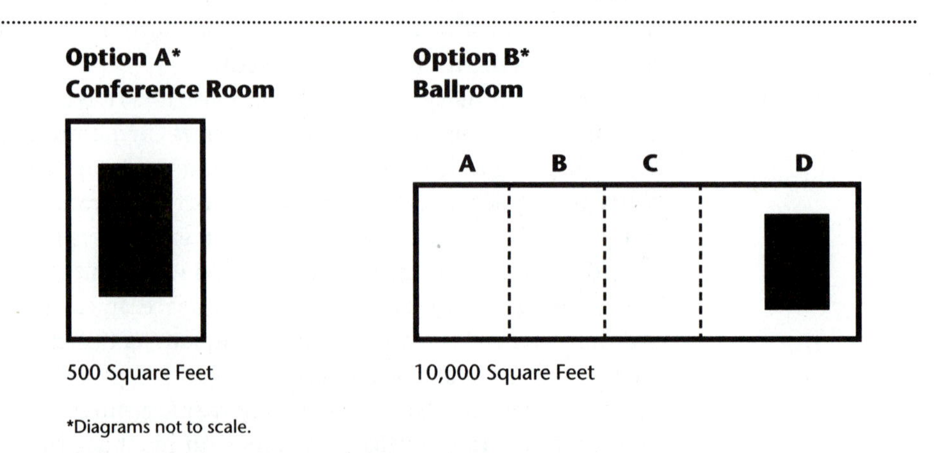


**FIGURE 3–6** *Function space intensity*

1. Using many overnight guest rooms;
2. Generating more revenue from above-average meal prices or high room rentals; or
3. Providing above-average outlet/ancillary revenue.

If the salesperson answers "yes" to any of the preceding questions, he or she should consider booking a space-intensive group. A space-intensive group that offsets the potential loss of catering dollars may appeal to a hotel.

**Sleeping Room-to-Space Ratio.** The concept of optimal space use does not end with space intensity. A similar analysis, called room-to-space ratio, applies more to the group room salesperson in that it looks at the usage of function space and the usage of overnight guest rooms.

**Room-to-space ratio** is the number of overnight rooms needed by a group relative to the total amount of square feet the group needs for function space. The actual ratio differs from hotel to hotel, but in general the total number of rooms within the group ceiling on a given night dictates the number of sleeping rooms that should be occupied each night by the group effort. This number, when divided by the available function square footage, results in the number of square feet allotted each sleeping room. The lower the number of rooms left to book within the group ceiling, the greater the amount of function square feet for sale.

As has been discussed previously, group rooms are almost always tied to functions that require meeting space at a hotel. Therefore, if a hotel filled only half its group ceiling but all its function space, it would not be able to book additional group rooms. Remember, the group ceiling is calibrated to supplement the number of rooms the transient sales team must sell. This scenario will not occur if the sales team analyzes the room-to-space ratios of groups before booking those groups. Maximizing the group room commitment of each new group, while keeping in mind the function space availability, ensures that space is optimized.

Consider an example of room-to-space ratios as they might relate to a new business opportunity. Figure 3–7 looks at a day in the availability of the XYZ Hotel, which has booked the ABC Group. Assume that the group ceiling for the night in question is 250 rooms and that the ABC Group has taken 175. The hotel has committed half its ballroom, one-third its breakout space, and all its specialized food function space to the ABC Group. Specialized space is simply function space that cannot be used for any other function. Specialized function rooms are permanently set up to host specific food or event functions.

If a new group, the 123 Company, approached the hotel salesperson and asked for 25 overnight rooms and all remaining space, should the salesperson book it? The revised availability display would look like Figure 3–8. All remaining function space at the XYZ Hotel is now taken by the 123 Company. At first glance, this may seem like the correct booking decision. On closer examination, however, the rooms portion of the 123 Company is not as appealing. An additional 25 sleeping rooms brings the hotel's total number of group rooms on that night to 200. The XYZ Hotel set a goal of 250 rooms in its group ceiling. Booking the 123 Company

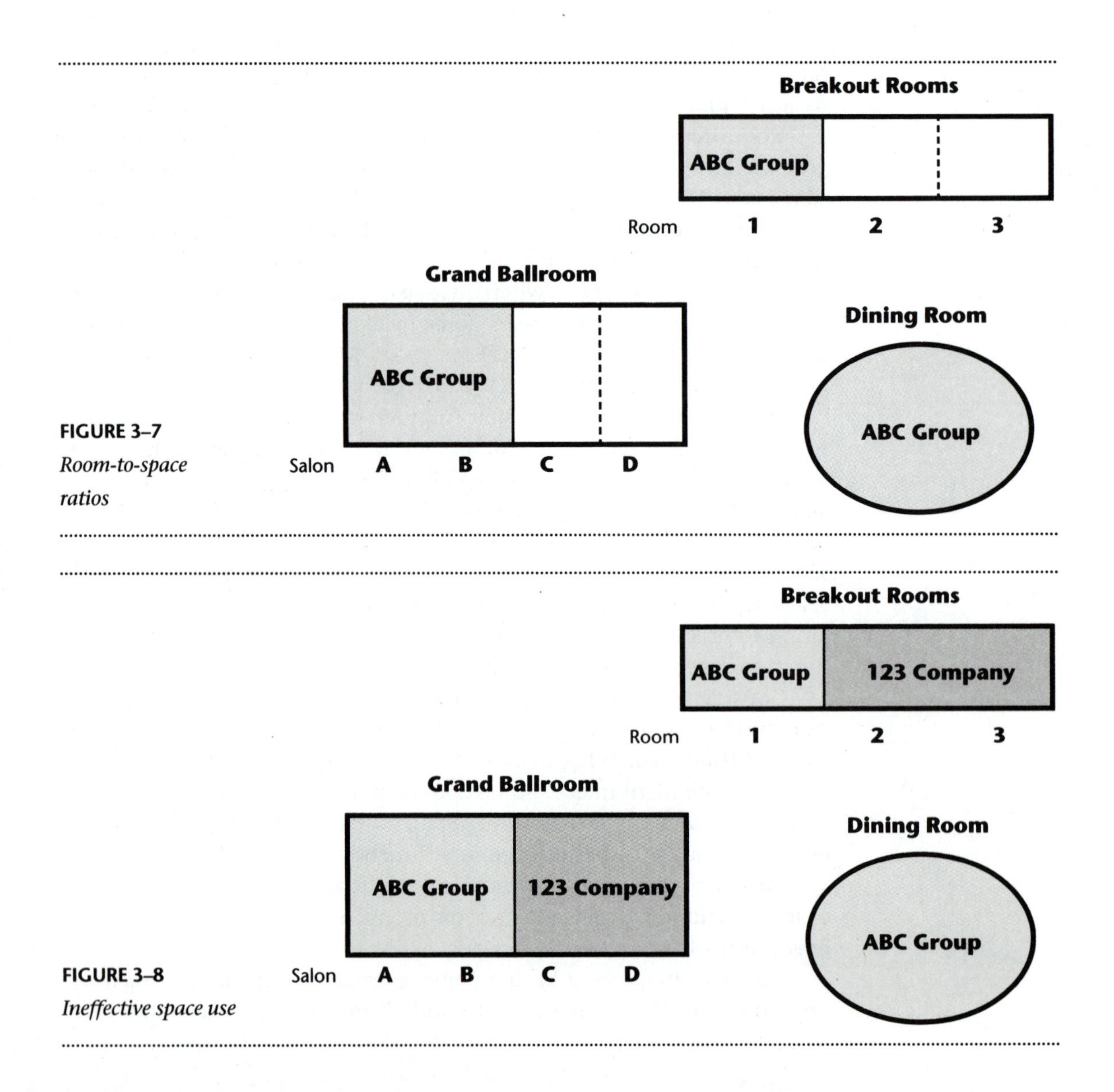


**FIGURE 3–7**
*Room-to-space ratios*

**FIGURE 3–8**
*Ineffective space use*

precludes any additional group rooms from being booked, because no space remains. If the hotel booked the 123 Company, it would probably not attain the group ceiling and would have empty rooms. Room-to-space ratio analysis indicates that booking this group is not a good decision.

## FUNCTION SPACE EXCEPTIONS

There are unique exceptions to the analyses of room-to-space ratios and space intensity. While these exceptions may not always apply to group salespeople, they are beneficial to understand because they can benefit the hotel in certain circumstances. These exceptions are national holiday time frames and winter holiday parties.

**National Holiday Time Frames.** Holiday time frames are unique when it comes to analyzing the space intensity of a potential function. National holidays like Memorial Day, Labor Day, Fourth of July, and Thanksgiving are often quite slow for group business. Therefore, these dates should be left open to group booking without consideration of space use. Any group that is booked on these days will likely not displace any potential group revenue. Religious holidays can have a similar impact, depending, in large part on the hotel's location in the country.

National holidays are not limited to American holidays. An American group may avoid booking a function on the Fourth of July, but a Canadian group may not. The international market can provide plenty of opportunities to fill holiday time frames.

**Winter Holiday Parties.** Sometimes called Christmas parties, winter holiday parties occur during the late fall and winter. Many organizations host parties during this time of year to thank their employees and members. These functions are not listed among functions in holiday time frames, because winter holiday parties are a unique type of food function and have different characteristics. Most notably, these parties produce very high food and beverage revenue. Also, they are seldom held on the winter holiday itself. Most holiday parties are held on the Fridays and Saturdays in the first 2 or 3 weeks in December, and possibly in the last week of November. They are even held in January to accommodate holiday schedules.

The job of a salesperson to analyze these groups differs from that in previous situations. These parties are, by nature, off-peak time functions (traditional need periods). Very few instances preclude the salesperson from booking them. Space intensity should not be a concern. Any revenue during this time of year positively impacts the hotel. The salesperson should remember, however, that holiday parties may require additional setup times. Blocking group space past 6 P.M. on a Friday or Saturday in

December could negatively impact the ability of the catering department to maximize revenue over these time frames.

## QUALIFYING WORKSHEET

Figure 3–9 is a sample qualifying worksheet, also called a "lead" or an "inquiry" sheet, that is used by most hotels in one form or another. This chapter introduced the main points that must be uncovered by a salesperson to best understand, or qualify, if a business opportunity is right for the hotel.

A worksheet that takes the salesperson through the initial qualifying questions step-by-step ensures that vital information is uncovered. Names and addresses can be forgotten in the excitement of a new business opportunity. These questions help the salesperson to think while communicating with a contact, because their answers may lead them to further questions. A "next step checklist" is helpful because it ensures action is being taken at each point in the sales process. Over time, these worksheets become familiar and can be scanned in a file quickly, which helps the salesperson better qualify future business opportunities.

Qualifying worksheets should be completed for all business opportunities, whether they come to fruition or not. A business opportunity that is turned down initially might become more attractive as market conditions change. Often, qualifying worksheets are the only records of refused business.

## CHAPTER REVIEW

### KEY CONCEPTS

- Qualifying
- Open-/close-ended questions
- Room availability
- Slippage
- Group ceiling
- Displacement
- Arrival/departure patterns
- Need periods
- Target rates
- Profitability
- The group sales equation
- Food/event function types
- Common room sets
- AV requirements
- Room rental
- Space intensity/room-to-space ratio

### REVIEW QUESTIONS

1. What are the differences between peaks and valleys and need periods?
2. How might a hotel's group ceiling be determined?

## Deluxe Suites Hotel
### Inquiry/Lead Worksheet

Contact Name: ______________________ Lead Taken by: ______

Organization Name: ______________________ Date/Time: ________

Phone and/or Fax Number: ______________________ Salesperson: ________

Mailing Address: ______________________ E-Mail: ______________

**Overnight Rooms (Pattern and Number)** **Year**

| Day: | M | T | W | Th | F | Sa | Su | M | T | W | Th |
|---|---|---|---|---|---|---|---|---|---|---|---|
| Date: | / | / | / | / | / | / | / | / | / | / | |

Number of Rooms:

Suites: Yes/No

Status: Tentative/Definitive/Actual

**Market Segment:**

Corporate Association Other

**Meeting Frequency:**

First Time Weekly Monthly Biannual Annual

**Subsegment**

**Catering/Function Space Requirements**

**Date** **Meeting Space/Number of Attendees/Setup Requirements**

Coffee Breaks

Exhibit Space/Square Feet

**Meal Functions/Number of Attendees**

Breakfasts

Lunches

Receptions

Dinners

**Qualifying Checklist**

- Ask open-ended questions (the 5 *W*s). ____
- Check sleeping room availability (group ceiling, market conditions, displacement, group base). ____
- Is the arrival/departure pattern attractive to the hotel? ____
- Is this a need period? ____
- Check history for slippage and other information. ____
- Is the hotel's target rate within the group's budget? ____
- Can the group sales equation be implemented to mutual advantage (rates/dates/space)? ____
- Are there other function space considerations? ____
- What is the room rental? ____

**Next Step Checklist**

| | | |
|---|---|---|
| Hold Sleeping Rooms ____ | Send Brochure ____ | Send Menus ____ |
| Hold Meeting Space ____ | Send Proposal ____ | Send Contract ____ |
| Turndown ____ | Trace Date ____ | Send Thank You ____ |

**FIGURE 3–9**
*Qualifying worksheet*

3. What are the differences between situational need periods and traditional need periods?
4. How are target rates determined? How might they change during a year?
5. Why are quick rate quotes not advisable?
6. Explain the concept of displacement.

CHAPTER 4

# *The Hotel Sales Triangle and Action Triangles*

*"Garlic is to food, as sales is to the bottom line."*

UNKNOWN

## INTRODUCTION

The skill of selling a service differs greatly from that of selling of product. Much of the value a customer receives from a service is implied, perceived, or felt. While the main drivers of product sales are arguably price and quality, service sales requires a greater level of customer understanding. In hotels, this understanding begins with the creation of a business opportunity.

The hotel sales triangle (Figure 4–1) creates that business opportunity and enables the salesperson to begin the analyses and comparisons reviewed in earlier chapters. Knowing what is done to a business opportunity after it is created is crucial to understanding the business opportunity while it is being created. A salesperson who knows the end point of his or her journey makes better decisions along the way. These are the reasons that foundation of hotels sales and the sales process were introduced before this chapter.

The sale is created by implementing the points of the hotel sales triangle. After it is created the sale must be completed, or closed. Closing a sale is accomplished by the win triangle (Figure 4–2). Together, these two triangles ensure that a sale is made. This chapter analyzes the two triangles and how they work together.

The hotel sales triangle concept is based on the equilateral triangle (Figure 4–3). This geometric shape has three equal-length lines. These three lines join at points equidistant from each other. Conceptually, these three points are as different as they can be from each other. Together they create something entirely different. This idea forms the basis for action triangles. Like the hotel success triangle, which was covered earlier, the hotel sales triangle encompasses the notion of three different sides contributing to a new, different whole.

In hospitality, rarely do situations arise that the salesperson can address with single solutions. In fact, most sales situations force the salesperson to decide between three equally important options. The hotel sales triangle illustrates this notion with its three equidistant points.

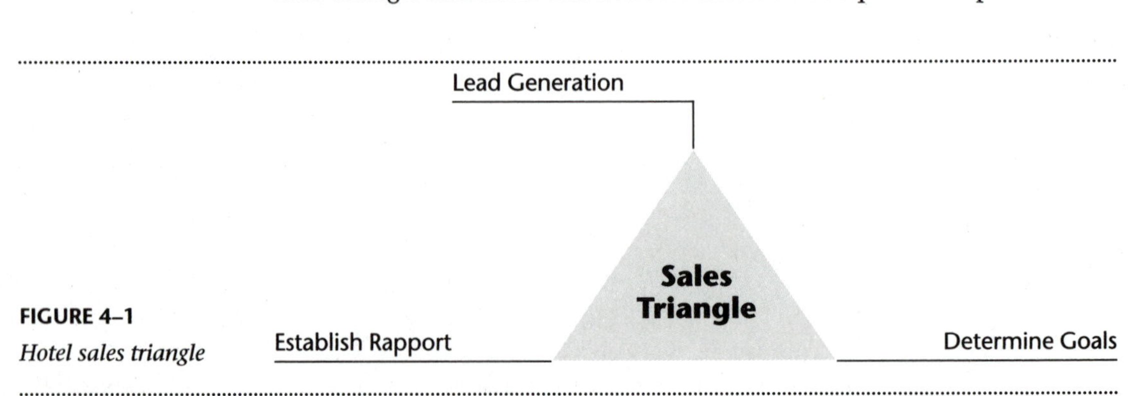


**FIGURE 4–1**
*Hotel sales triangle*

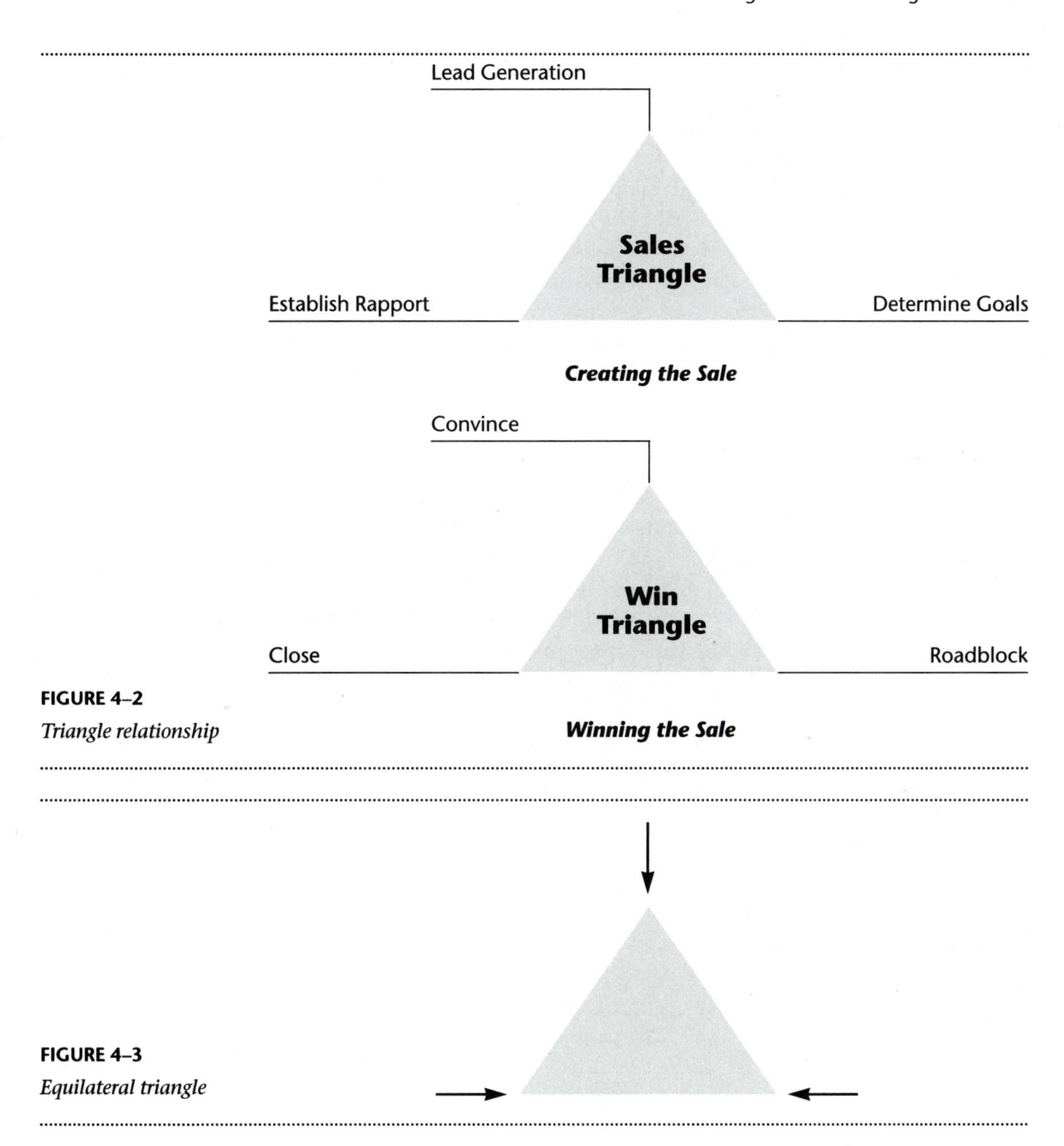


**FIGURE 4–2**
*Triangle relationship*

**FIGURE 4–3**
*Equilateral triangle*

The hotel sales triangle can apply to any of the three proactive revenue generation areas of a hotel, which are reflected in the points of hotel success triangle. Both transient and group room sales require an intimate understanding of the nature of generating business. The catering sales team in a hotel must also create business opportunities. While the goal of the catering sales effort is to sell meals and/or function space, not sleeping rooms, the sales triangle process applies.

This chapter begins with a review of the three main points of the sales triangle: lead generation, establish rapport, and determine goals. Within the discussion of each point of the sales triangle, additional triangles reveal themselves. These action triangles outline what a salesperson may encounter at each point of the sales triangle. The term *action triangle* is used to describe the action the salesperson must take at each point in the triangle. Action drives the process to the next step. Completing each part of the action triangle correctly compels the salesperson to move further in the process of creating a business opportunity. Each action triangle continues the concept of evaluating three distinct parts of one bigger whole.

## LEAD GENERATION

The most fundamental point in creating new business opportunities is the generation of interest. **Lead generation** is the process undertaken by potential clients or the hotel to generate interest. Interest in turn generates tangible business opportunities called leads. Leads are the starting points for all hotel business.

The action triangle within the lead generation point (Figure 4–4) reveals the three most prevalent sources of new business: client inquiry, solicitation, and third party (Figure 4–5).

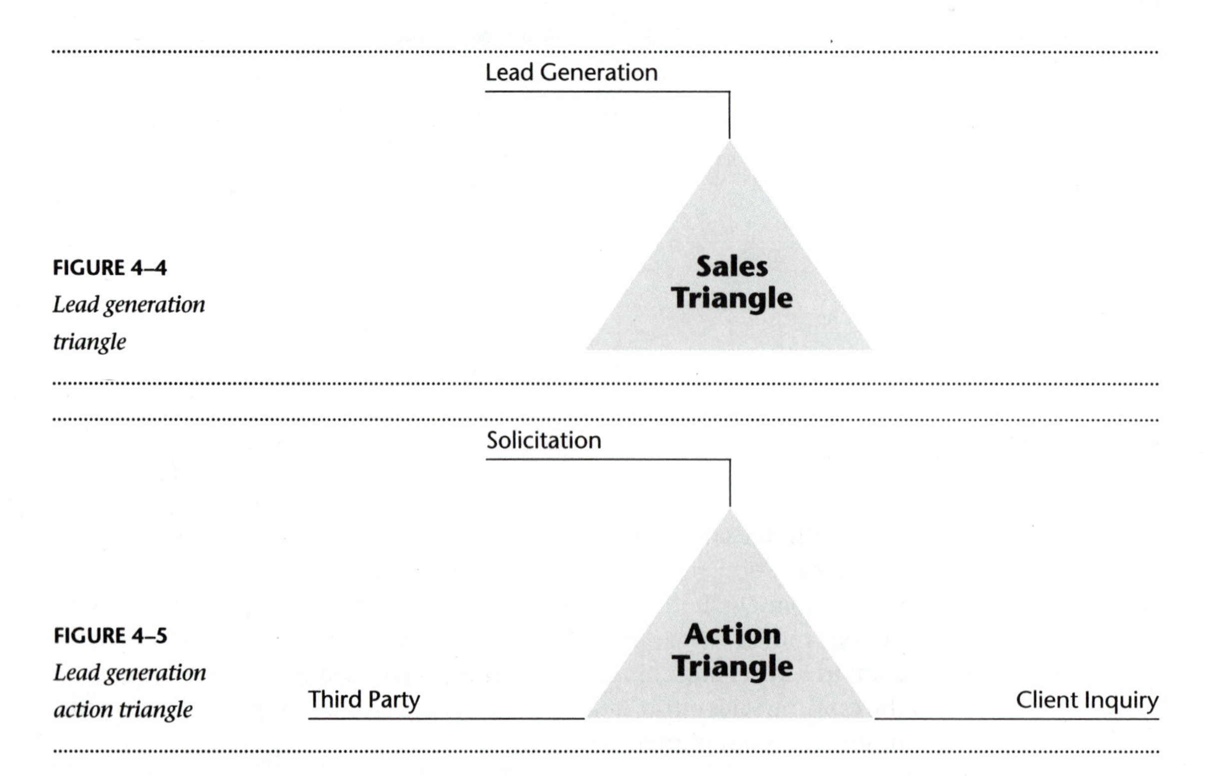


**FIGURE 4–4** *Lead generation triangle*

**FIGURE 4–5** *Lead generation action triangle*

## CLIENT INQUIRY

Hotel business most commonly originates from clients. When clients need rooms or function space, they inquire directly to the hotel sales office. An inquiry may come in the form of a phone call or a written **request for proposal (RFP)**. A preprinted RFP is an easy way for a client to gather information from many hotels at one time. Inquiries generated from Internet Web sites are also considered client inquiries, as are walk-ins, which are clients who walk into a hotel unannounced looking to book programs. Clients who book multiple programs at one time or programs that repeat year after year are also considered inquiry leads, because there was no proactive effort to book their subsequent business.

A client inquiry is not generated from direct actions taken by the hotel or salesperson (Figure 4–6). Every hotel has a certain inquiry volume. Certain successful hotels of differing product or location types may not need other methods of generating new leads because their inquiry volumes are so high. However, it is rare for most hotels to rely on the client inquiry exclusively.

## SOLICITATION

To solicit means to ask. **Solicitation,** therefore, is the process by which a hotel salesperson seeks new business opportunities through asking (Figure 4–7). The sources for new business opportunities are numerous. Hotels with low client inquiry volumes often rely on these sources to generate new business.

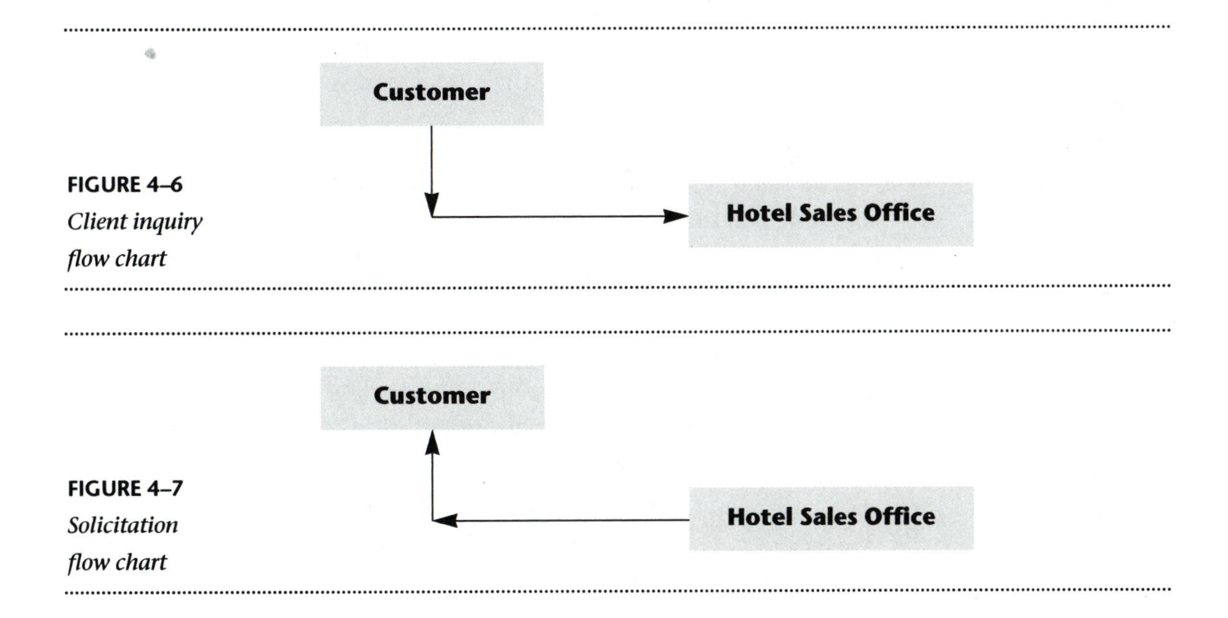


**FIGURE 4–6** *Client inquiry flow chart*

**FIGURE 4–7** *Solicitation flow chart*

Solicitation sources fall into four main categories: publications, trace files, readerboards, and sales blitzes.

**Publications.** Publications are any printed materials that identify organizations with potential hotel needs. Following are sample publications:

*Standard & Poor's* is a yearly report of the financial reports and data (e.g., assets, sizes, profits) of companies nationwide.

*Moody's Bank & Finance* resembles *Standard & Poor's*.

*Business Periodicals Index* is an index of all major English periodicals, including *Business Week, Fortune,* and *Money*. This is a great resource for articles on targeted businesses.

*Wall Street Journal Index* is an index like *Business Periodicals Index,* but it lists strictly articles in the *Wall Street Journal*.

*Who's Who* is a reference book on top executives and major figures in the U.S. marketplace. It often lists the names and phone numbers of top-level decision makers.

The local Chamber of Commerce directory is a listing of member organizations. It is a good resource for solicitation of specific market segments because organizations are often listed by industry.

Local business daily newspapers, which are usually available in large markets, are a great way to keep up on local and regional business events. They are a great resource for learning about new businesses in the area.

The local telephone book and telephone books of major nearby cities and/or feeder cities.

The local office building roster of tenants lists area tenants. If a roster is not available, a sales office can go to the major office buildings in the community and manually list their occupants using the directory in each lobby.

*Best's Insurance Guide* is a "Who's Who" of the insurance market.

*The Encyclopedia of Associations* is another type of "Who's Who" listing of valuable meeting information on various associations in the marketplace.

*The World Travel Directory* lists travel agents, wholesalers, and tour operators to help penetrate the tour and travel market.

*The National Directory of College Athletics* lists all college coaches, athletic directors, and decision makers in the collegiate sports market.

Membership directories of national organizations involved in the hospitality industry include:

**Meeting Professionals International (MPI)**
**Society of Government Meeting Planners (SGMP)**
**Professional Convention Management Association (PCMA)**

**American Society of Association Executives (ASAE)**
**Hotel Sales and Marketing Association (HSMA)**
**Religious Conference Management Association (RCMA)**

**Trace Files.** Trace files are customer files that come to the attention of a salesperson on a predetermined date. This date, called a trace date, is designated by the salesperson as a time when some action is needed. Trace files are collected daily by a sales assistant or appear daily on a salesperson's computer screen.

Trace files provide a tremendous amount of information as to a client's status, including information on the client's past bookings (i.e., history), budget environment, place of currently booked business, trends in specific meeting group types, and requirements. The hotel that keeps current on trace solicitation avoids missing opportunities to get involved in the client's early decisions.

The main purpose of trace files in solicitation is to stay in contact with clients. Groups who regularly book with a hotel may not need to be solicited, but groups who do not may. Trace files are the best tool for keeping current with a hotel's client base. Trace file systems must be implemented in such a way as to ensure the hotel contacts a client before the client chooses his or her next program and before another hotel contacts the client. The hotel must keep its trace file system current, because competing hotels also use trace files to contact clients. Hotels without computerized trace systems can use manual notations on a calendar for solicitation.

Trace files and trace dates are not strictly relegated to solicitation. For example, trace dates are useful for following up with groups regarding signed contracts, rooming lists, and so on. They remind the salesperson that something must be done. Trace file systems can also eliminate the files of groups that have gone out of business or are no longer valid to the hotel.

Hotels often designate trace files by category (e.g., catering, group sales, and transient sales). Each salesperson should endeavor to solicit only relevant files. Every salesperson must solicit within his or her knowledge base. If, in following up on a trace file, a salesperson finds the contact listed is no longer available, he or she must try to secure the name of another contact and note in the file whether that contact is the original contact's replacement or another meeting planner. This process of determining new sources of business within an organization, which is called **account penetration**, very effectively gains all business an organization has to offer.

Again, trace files cannot be the only solicitation tool used by a hotel. A typical file base shrinks 1 to 5 percent per year due to many factors (e.g., companies moving, takeovers, bankruptcy). A hotel finds, over time, that simply relying on existing business results in fewer and fewer opportunities.

**Readerboards.** The best way for a hotel to keep abreast of the competition is to know who is doing business with it. Most hotels and meeting centers post **readerboards**, which are daily event sheets or scrolling television monitors that tell meeting attendees the locations and times of their functions. Figure 4–8 shows a sample readerboard. Because they provide function information, readerboards are a great way to find out what organizations are booking at the competition. Competitive readerboards offer only new business opportunities for salespeople, because at that point the organizations are booked at other hotels.

It is imperative that a hotel's sales team, sales and catering, gather readerboard information on a timely basis. This duty can be divided among all team members. The results of this information gathering should be discussed with all sales team members. Hotels should make it a point to follow up on this information and to find out why groups are not booking with them. Two acceptable reasons for a competitor winning business are: (1) the hotel did not want the business (e.g., the business was inappropriate for the hotel's needs) or (2) the hotel could not accommodate the business (e.g., the hotel was too full or the group was too large).

There are more reasons why clients chose competitors (e.g., meeting quality, service levels, value). Readerboards allow the hotel to uncover the reasons, then take whatever corrective action is needed.

**Sales Blitzes.** The sales blitz is a unique tool that allows for blanket penetration of a geographical area. The sales blitz used by hotels is similar to the sales blitz used by manufacturers of food products. In major metropolitan areas, food manufacturers execute the sales blitz by hiring many individuals to stand on street corners and hand out free samples (e.g., candy bars or gum). The hospitality sales blitz is limited to the sales staff on hand and there are no free samples, but the concept of creating awareness is the same.

**Hotel Readerboard**
**Saturday, June 1st**

| | |
|---|---|
| Nelson Wedding | Salon One |
| ABC Company Meeting | Meeting Room 4 |
| Youth Sports Banquet | Salon Three |

**FIGURE 4–8**
*Readerboard*

A sales blitz in hospitality should be limited to the hotel's geographical sphere of influence. Sales blitzes are used primarily in the preopening or early stages of hotel sales offices. A **preopening sales office** is often put in place before the hotel is completed to generate community awareness and to book business for the hotel once it opens. A sales blitz can be a fun way for a sales office to create community awareness as a group. Existing hotels can incorporate sales blitzes into their marketing plans as well. Beyond preopening, blitzes can introduce new services or provide hotels vehicles for reentering neglected areas.

The sales blitz with the best results entails proper planning and direction. The sales team should first determine where to target and to whom. This is easier for downtown hotels, because they can saturate an office tower or a block. Regardless of location type, a hotel must determine where to blitz geographically. A good starting point is companies near the competition. Once the geographical area is determined, the hotel must decide what it wants to accomplish during the blitz. Sales blitz objectives can include:

- Announcing a new corporate meetings program
- Promoting value dates or discounted sleeping room rates
- Advertising new catering offerings (e.g., an "express" lunch menu that provides fast service)
- Highlighting a new off-premise catering service that services off-property food functions
- Announcing sleeping/function room renovations or enhancements
- Promoting contests or giveaways

Whatever the objective, its implementation should be classy and creative. A hotel should endeavor to do more than simply hand out brochures and menu packets. This old and tired practice wastes time and money. Instead, a hotel should distribute brochures while introducing a new product or service.

## THIRD PARTY

**Third-party leads** differ from the client inquiry and solicitation methods of lead generation in that another entity is included in the process (Figure 4–9). A third-party lead comes to a hotel from someone other than the client. This third party acts on the client's behalf in the search for an appropriate location for a meeting or another hotel need.

Third parties are becoming more and more prevalent in the hotel industry. Whereas at one time most organizations had in-house departments that handled meeting/travel needs, due to corporate downsizing and other factors, many organizations are looking outside their staffs for

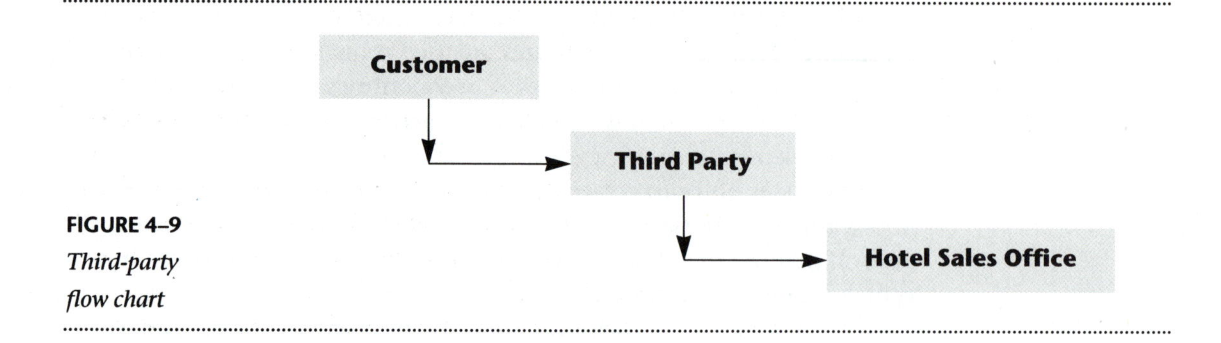


**FIGURE 4–9** *Third-party flow chart*

meeting and/or hotel planning services. These organizations are deciding to focus on their strengths and outsource ancillary functions. Outsourcing is the concept by which an organization focuses on its core product/service(s) and designates other organizations who specialize in ancillary functions to perform those functions on its behalf.

The outsourcing of meeting planning and/or travel services has given rise to organizations whose sole purpose is to help others select hotels, airlines, car-rental agencies, and other travel services. Following are some of the most common third parties today:

- Travel Agents—**Travel agents** are primarily used for transient business travel. The travel agent coordinates many aspects of a traveler's trip, including the hotel, the airline, and transportation. Some large travel agencies are adding meeting/group planning departments to handle the meeting/convention market in this era of outsourcing.
- Independent Meeting Planning Firm (or Individual)—The sole purpose of the **independent meeting planning firm or individual** is to conduct searches and help clients decide to and/or conduct meetings and conventions. In many instances with these third parties, the hotel has no contact with the guests until they arrive. This type of third-party lead is becoming very common. Some of the largest third parties in today's market, namely McGettigan Partners, Conferon, Krisam, and Helms Briscoe, account for a large portion of a hotel's group business.
- Convention and Visitor Bureau—The **convention and visitor bureau** (often abbreviated **CVB**) is another third-party lead generator. Most often used as an assisting service for meeting planners from outside of an area, the CVB determines the basic needs of the client and distributes that information to the appropriate hotels. The CVB helps save time for clients in that only hotels appropriate for the clients' functions are included.

Many CVBs put together calendars that list groups booked within the local community. Like readerboards, these calendars are a good place for a hotel to find city-wide conventions and other convention center–related business that has not booked with it.

- National Sales Office—The **national sales office** (often abbreviated **NSO**) is a third-party lead generator that is available only to medium to large hotel chains. An NSO is located in major cities like New York; Washington, DC; Chicago; and Los Angeles. These NSOs are staffed with salespeople who actively seek business for their chains. For example, an NSO salesperson stationed in Washington, DC, may call on national associations who have meeting needs throughout the nation and distribute those leads to their hotels in the appropriate locations. The NSO acts as an extension of a hotel's sales team.

With the lead generated, it becomes time for the salesperson to move forward in the sales process. At this point, he or she must take action to move to the next step. The next action is to establish rapport.

## ESTABLISH RAPPORT

Once a lead has been generated, it must be analyzed and qualified. The qualification questions reviewed in Chapter 3 apply here. Qualification begins the salesperson thinking whether to pursue or decline a business opportunity. Beyond simply asking qualifying questions from a preprinted list, the hotel salesperson must bring the contact into a comfortable, relaxed state of mind so that he or she can gather as much information from the contact as possible. Creating a sense of free and open exchange is called establishing rapport (Figure 4–10).

Rapport between a salesperson and a client creates an environment in which both parties reveal as much information as business guidelines

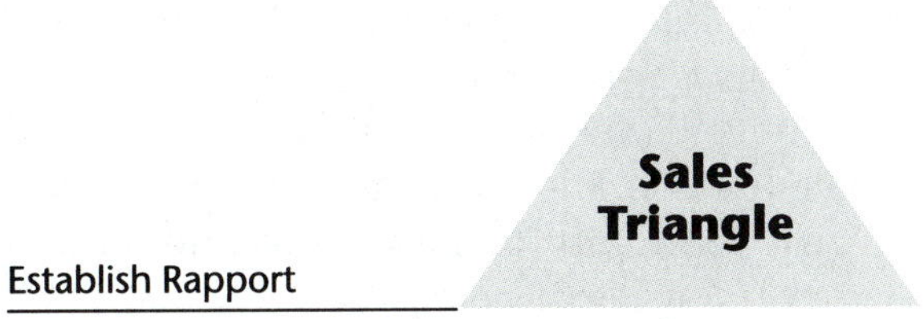

**FIGURE 4–10**
*Establish rapport triangle*

Establish Rapport

Sales Triangle

# *Industry Perspective*

## **"The Role of the Convention and Visitors Bureau"**

*John Pohl*
*Convention Sales Manager*
*Lexington Convention and Visitors Bureau*

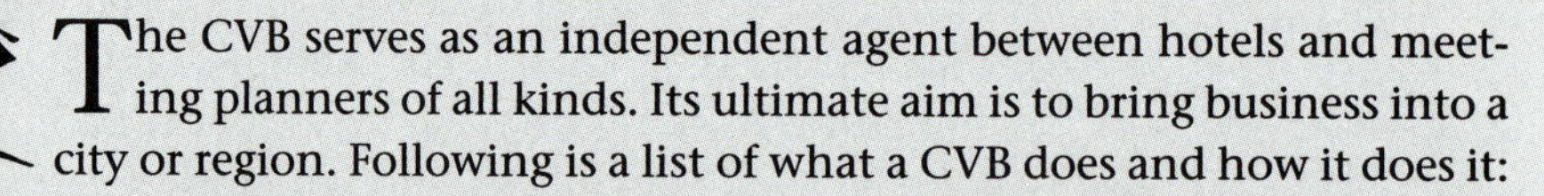

The CVB serves as an independent agent between hotels and meeting planners of all kinds. Its ultimate aim is to bring business into a city or region. Following is a list of what a CVB does and how it does it:

1. The CVB provides the meeting coordinator an avenue for sending convention RFPs to appropriate hotel facilities based on the room block, location, or meeting space requirements. These RFPs include detailed instructions for responses, past rate information, preferred dates, and historical information on the group room pickup. The CVB turns this RFP information into bureau leads, which are in turn sent to the hotels. These leads provide hotels with receptive organizations that are looking at their cities and/or hotels for future bookings.
2. The general aim of a CVB is to conduct an overall city sell. In responding to an interested meeting planner, the CVB provides information on attractions and facilities and other information that is pertinent to the planner's meeting needs. For example, the CVB often furnishes information regarding technical tours, golf outings, and field outings. The CVB represents the entire hospitality community, which may include restaurants, local arrangement companies, and transportation/bus companies. The CVB also provides the meeting planner information on local logistics, laws, and celebrations/events, as well as maps, assorted brochures, and quick answers that save the planner time and money.
3. Members of the CVB staff attend trade shows and exhibit-oriented events in an effort to promote their city and its facilities to interested planners. These exchanges occur throughout the year. Some of the larger ones include those sponsored by ASAE and MPI. Other big events are Spring Time in the Park and Destination Showcase. All these events give meeting planners an opportunity to review meeting locations they may have never considered before.

The NSO is funded by the hotel chain, and the CVB is funded by local taxes or membership fees collected from participating hotels. Third parties outside the NSO and CVB must charge for their services in some way. Travel agencies and independent meeting planners charge flat fees or book sleeping rooms at commissionable rates. A **commissionable rate** is understood throughout the hotel industry to include a 10 percent addition to the net room rate. This commission is paid to the travel agent or meeting planner once the guests pay for their rooms. In most cases, only agents and planners who have been issued identification numbers by the **International Association of Travel Agents (IATA)** are eligible for commissions.

permit. The feeling a client perceives when rapport is established allows for full qualification and analysis.

True rapport is established only when the three points of this action triangle are implemented: creating comfort, ensuring trust, and demanding confidence (Figure 4–11).

Establishing rapport begins by taking a mental inventory. A mental inventory is the set of specific personality traits and idiosyncrasies that relate to the contact or the organization. A hotel salesperson who is establishing rapport with a client must first determine the type of client or organization. Previous chapters outlined some of the differences between markets segments. The differences in the needs of a corporate client and an association client can be stark based strictly on the type of market segment of each and its inherent traits. The respective hotel needs will also differ.

Mental inventories of clients delve deeply into the clients' needs and wants, beyond established market segment traits. Through mental inventories, a salesperson discovers the reasons behind clients' buying decisions.

A mental inventory of a client begins with an examination of existing

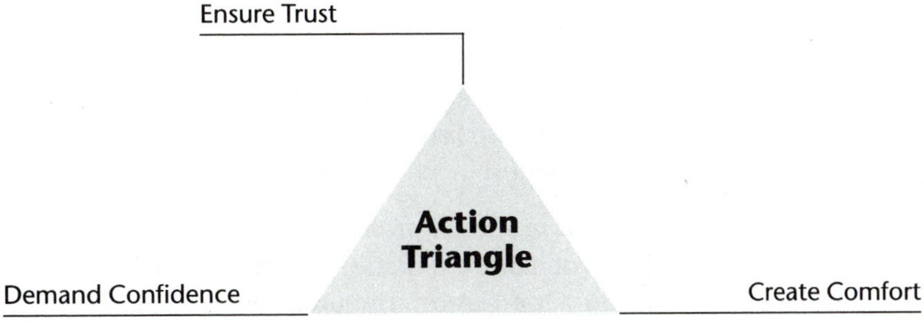

Ensure Trust

**Action Triangle**

Demand Confidence

Create Comfort

**FIGURE 4–11**
*Establish rapport action triangle*

sales file, if available. As was reviewed earlier, these files are often categorized by business type (e.g., group, transient, or catering). Each file is dedicated to an organization. Even if the hotel has never done business with the organization, the organization's file should include written correspondence with the contact and notes summarizing phone and E-mail conversations. These notes are often called a running call report. A running call report outlines the requests and specifics of all business opportunities an organization tried to bring to a hotel.

If contacts have been with organizations for substantial periods, a call report can give insight into those contacts. If certain contacts have asked continuously for specific considerations for themselves or their organizations, the requests are documented in call reports. The call report, combined with items like documented histories and sales contracts, indicates the specific traits exhibited by an organization. In combination these traits are called a customer profile. Whether computerized or manual, customer profiles commonly include:

- The organization may traditionally demand one or more components of the group sales equation (rates, dates, space) in its favor.
- The organization may be budget conscious, beyond room rates. Prices of banquet functions and ancillary activities (e.g., golf, tennis) may need to be discounted.
- Certain organization VIPs may require special accommodations (e.g., upgraded rooms, amenities in the room).
- Complimentary items are always requested. (Note: Hotels booking group business traditionally offer one complimentary room for every fifty group rooms. This is commonly called the "1 per 50" accommodation. Some groups ask for free suites or meal functions [continental breakfasts and receptions are most common]. Large conventions may ask that a hotel provide complimentary accommodations for planning committees or boards that convene at the hotel months before the conventions.)
- Transient customers on personal business may ask for discounted or complimentary rooms for themselves or their superiors.
- Catering clients may ask to sample the food being planned for upcoming meal functions before the functions to determine which items will be served. This is called a taste panel.
- Some clients may not respond to the hotel with requisite information in a timely manner.

The customer profile may be written into the call report, or it may be listed on a file cover sheet on the file. The cover sheet is intended to serve as an "at-a-glance" resource for the salesperson who must review customer traits quickly.

The mental inventory process continues with the qualifying questions that are asked with each business opportunity and the range of answers that are given. Open-ended questions extract information from clients and add to the salesperson's "database" of knowledge. This information lays the groundwork for establishing rapport.

## CREATING COMFORT

Taking time to complete the mental inventory discussed previously accomplishes more than simply uncovering information on customer traits. This inventory prepares the salesperson on how best to communicate with the customer. Creating a sense of comfort with a client begins at the most basic level of human interaction: communication.

Communication is defined as the process of transmitting a message from a sender to a receiver. Communication is vital to achieving countless goals, like selling, warning, enlightening, and entertaining. For a salesperson, making the most of communicating with a client creates comfort. Above all, this entails listening.

> *"Endeavor to listen twice as long as you speak."*
>
> UNKNOWN

Listening is the only way a receiver can hear the message a sender is transmitting. A salesperson cannot fully qualify or effectively create a mental inventory if he or she is doing all the talking with a client. The salesperson should hear the subtle hints and signals a client may give during communication. The salesperson should also create comfort by listening and getting to know the client. If the client prefers to discuss the weather or other less pertinent topics before discussing the program, the salesperson should follow the client's lead. In contrast, a client who is pressed for time should be allowed to address topics of interest quickly. Salespeople should avoid the trap of overusing hotel jargon. Terms like *block* or *slippage* may be unfamiliar to inexperienced meeting planners. Unfamiliar communication often becomes uncomfortable communication. A comfortable client provides a salesperson with much more useful information than an uncomfortable one. It is up to the salesperson to create that comfort level.

**UNDERSTANDING CLIENT COMMUNICATION**

| A client who states: | May mean: |
|---|---|
| "My boss will attend this meeting." | "I'm concerned with impressing my superiors." |
| "We want a relaxed general session." | "I picture a large, open meeting room with plenty of space." |
| "I can't sign this confirmation." | "I am not the decision maker." |
| "We need fast meal service." | "We prefer buffet-style meals." |
| "We prefer a late checkout." | "The hotel may consider 2:00 P.M. late, but I'm picturing 5:00 P.M." |

## ENSURING TRUST

Salespeople who position themselves as people who understand what is important to clients lay the foundation of trust. Ensuring that the client trusts the salesperson begins with comfort in the first stage. It builds with the words and actions of the salesperson. Trust is at the heart of the next step in the process of establishing rapport.

A salesperson can convey trust to a customer by adhering to two main rules: (1) use complete honesty and (2) conduct a thorough follow-up.

**Complete Honesty.** In the hotel industry, as in many others, clients often begin communicating with salespeople harboring certain preconceived notions. Whether justified or not, the image of a "salesperson" differs greatly from person to person. Some people in modern society distrust salespeople because they feel that to sell, salespeople must deceive in some way. In the vast majority of buyer-seller relationships, however, there is no deception and nothing is concealed. It is up to the salesperson to dispel all the client's preconceived notions as soon as possible. The only way to accomplish this is with complete honesty.

If a salesperson cannot answer a client's question accurately, he or she should say so immediately. Inaccurate answers do not build trust. Candid revelations of a hotel's weaknesses are always appreciated by clients. A hotel that cannot fully execute a customer's request should explain that up front. The hotel may suggest alternatives if they genuinely meet the client's need. The salesperson should be careful, however. Suggestions that do not approach a client's needs may be perceived poorly and erode trust.

**Thorough Follow-Up.** Trust is built with honesty and commitment. A salesperson must be as committed to the client as he or she is to booking business. Commitment is exemplified by thorough and complete follow-up of requests. When a salesperson is asked to send information, research the answer to a unique question, or return a phone call, he or she should do so immediately.

Follow-up applies to other members of the hotel staff as well. For example, a catering salesperson who is asked to secure sleeping rooms with the group sales department must be counted on to do so in a timely manner. The same can be said for the group salesperson who is asked to plan a last-minute dinner. Hotel salespeople make commitments on behalf of the entire hotel, and quick, complete follow-up on these commitments enhances the client's foundation of trust.

Once salespeople ensure that there is a solid foundation of trust between themselves and their clients, they can elevate the relationships. At this point, salespeople can move beyond the client-salesperson relationship to the friend-friend relationship. A client who feels comfortable and who genuinely trusts a salesperson returns again and again. No amount of marketing or advertising can buy what trust creates in a client: genuine customer loyalty.

## DEMANDING CONFIDENCE

At this point of the establishing rapport process, the salesperson must take charge. If comfort has been created and trust has been ensured, the client and the salesperson move to yet another level. Demanding confidence in an implicit way makes the client feel as if he or she would be remiss if he or she did not allow for continued action.

First, the salesperson should remind the client of what got the two of them to this point. Neither would be communicating in good conscience were it not for the reasonable reputation of the other party. A client would not continue negotiations if booking at the hotel was improbable. A hotel salesperson would not continue establishing rapport with a client who represents an inappropriate organization.

Demanding confidence adds more to the mental inventory of the salesperson by supplementing intuitive impressions with human markers. A **human marker** aids in the rapport-building process by revealing traits and insights that are not readily apparent. Human markers complete the picture of how and why clients react the ways they do. Markers like body language and discourse level are addressed here briefly. In-depth analysis can be found in advanced texts.

**Body Language.**

- A salesperson must be observant in face-to-face meetings with clients. In effect, the listening role moves from the ears to the eyes. Salespeople should ask themselves questions like:
    - How does this person carry him- or herself?
    - What expression does the person have? Is it one of a relaxed and trusting person, or is it one of an aggressive, confrontational person?
    - What is the person's mood or personality revealing? In the creating comfort stage, it can become apparent that a person is having a "bad day." An aggressive personality may want to take charge of all further discourse, while a timid person may defer to the salesperson.
- Arms crossed over the chest may indicate a defensive posture.
- A client who leans across a desk toward a salesperson may be aggressive.
- Strong eye contact indicates confidence.
- A firm handshake always makes a good first impression.

**Discourse Level.**

- The conversation between a client and a salesperson (both in person and over the phone) can reveal much about personality and mood. The voice is a tool; how the client chooses to use it is another marker.
    - Is the conversation often interrupted and the client distracted? The client could lack interest or time.
    - Balance the vocabulary level with the client whenever possible. This may mean minimizing jargon, as was mentioned earlier, or researching the client's organization or interests. It can be very impressive to a client when a salesperson takes the time to learn about the client's organization. Using terminology the client can appreciate or providing tidbits of news that apply to the client's industry can be dramatic.
- Written communication can add insight.
    - A client who favors handwritten notes to formal letters may have a less formal management style.
    - Intricate and lengthy RFPs may indicate that the client is concerned with each detail. Solid review of all aspects of a business opportunity is warranted in these cases.

These markers can all aid in the accumulation of a mental inventory. Thorough understanding of the client invariably leads to confidence. With confidence ensured, the action taken next moves the process to the crux of hotel sales. The next action triangle addresses the *what* of a client's needs and wants: determining goals.

## DETERMINE GOALS

Generating a lead and establishing rapport are solid first steps to creating a sale in hospitality. However, they do not, on their own, ensure a sale. The last action triangle addresses how a salesperson can virtually guarantee a sale. The process of determining a client's goals is crucial to cementing the need to buy in the client's mind.

**Determining goals** in a sales equation is defined as uncovering and addressing a client's buying criteria in such a way as to ensure the sale (Figure 4–12). After establishing rapport, the salesperson must first determine what the client is looking for in a hotel (goals). The next step is matching these goals to the hotel's features. The final step, or point in this triangle, is identifying the advantage created when the goals and features come together (Figure 4–13).

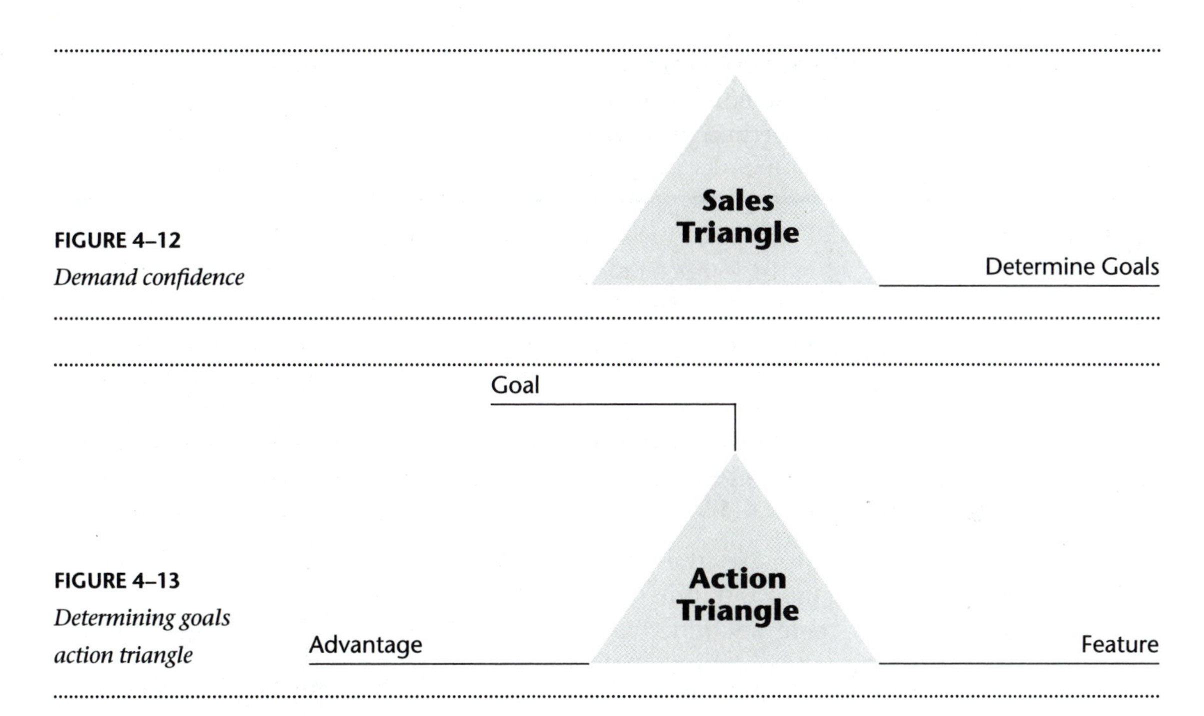


**FIGURE 4–12**
*Demand confidence*

**FIGURE 4–13**
*Determining goals action triangle*

## GOAL

A **goal** in the hotel sales process is simply an objective. The objective in pursuing a hotel for services can vary greatly from one client to another. Each client has some underlying goal or need that is driving his or her buying decision. Clients' motivation in selecting a product or service must be determined by a salesperson who desires to close the sale.

On the surface, it may seem that many consumers simply make purchases without underlying goals as motivators. That observation proves false when looked at closely.

The process of determining goals in the hotel client combines elements that were applied in the qualifying process and rapport building. For example, open-ended questions create comfort and ensure trust. A question like, "Why is quality for this program important to you?" might be answered with, "Well, we are looking to roll out a new product, and the perception of the hotel will reflect on us." This question uncovered two goals of the client:

1. The new product rollout is important to the organization, and the overall impression it gives its clients is tied to the location it chooses as the rollout site.
2. The salesperson understands the type of attendees and therefore the client's underlying goal. With quality as a goal, the salesperson immediately knows which areas of the hotel to use as function

space and thinks of questions regarding room upgrades and/or menu enhancements. Budget may be less of an issue to someone concerned with image.

**CASE STUDY**

## *Theoretical Buying Decision*

**QUESTION:** "What can motivate a consumer to choose one option over another?"

**BACKGROUND:** A consumer has an empty tank of gas. He or she is equidistant from two gas stations. One is on the left, the other is on the right (Figure 4–14A). Assume they are equally accessible.

What makes the driver choose the gas station on the right (Station B) over the gas station on the left (Station A) (Figure 4–14B)? Is it a whim or is there an underlying goal? What makes the consumer choose between two similar options?

This driver chose Station B for a reason, even if that reason is not readily apparent. The driver may not even be aware of that reason. The motivation, or goal, of this driver may have included one or more of the following:

- Value—The price for gas at Station B may have been lower than at Station A.
- Quality—The driver may have wanted the performance-enhancing options of Station B's gas.
- Service—Station B attendees may wipe windows or pump gas for the driver.
- Reputation—Word of mouth or other forms of advertising may have triggered the driver's decision.
- Other factors—The driver may have sought the convenience store in Station B, he or she may have known the owner, he or she may have gone there for years out of habit, he or she may have chosen it because it was brightly lit or closer to home, or many other possible reasons.

The preceding possible goals may have triggered the buying decision in the driver, or something else may have. The point of this case study is to prompt thought into the *what* or goal that consumers share when deciding on a purchase. Hotel consumers undergo the same process when deciding on a property.

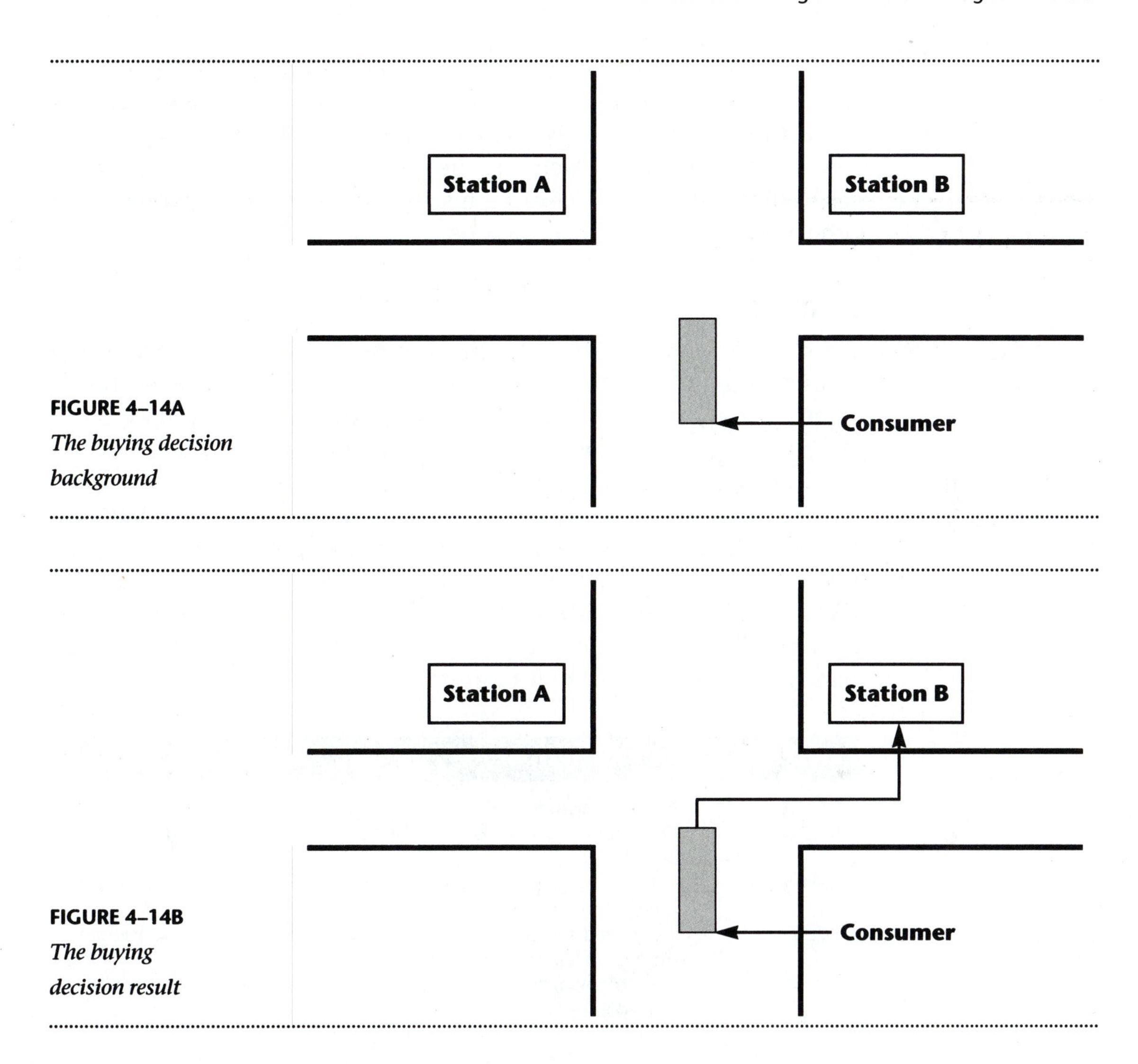


**FIGURE 4–14A**
*The buying decision background*

**FIGURE 4–14B**
*The buying decision result*

As goal determination continues, the salesperson should note the client's goals and the goals of any other organization members in the running call report and/or file cover sheet. As was reviewed earlier, market segments as well as organization members can exhibit traits and similarities.

In hotel sales, a client may express a myriad of possible goals. This chapter discusses four common goals that recur regardless of hotel product type:

1. Accessibility
2. Location
3. Value
4. Quality

A client's goals are not typically uncovered in one phone call or meeting. It may take several conversations to fully establish rapport and determine goals. Other resources that are available to the salesperson who is uncovering goals are research into the organization's file, discussion with sales office teammates for further insight and experience, and review of other events by similar organizations.

## FEATURE

Uncovering goals is the first step in ensuring a sale, but simply knowing goals does not further the sales process. Goals must be matched with the hotel's features for the sale to progress. A **feature** is a physical aspect of the hotel that can be shown, felt, or touched by the client in some way. A feature is not implied or promised. It is demonstrable.

If a client reveals that ease of access is a goal, the hotel's matching feature would be its location directly off a major highway. However, the salesperson who simply states that the hotel is easily accessible does not match a tangible hotel feature to the client's goal. The hotel's location near the highway can be shown and appreciated by the client, which makes that aspect of the hotel a feature.

**MATCHING GOALS AND FEATURES**

| Client Goal | Hotel Feature(s) |
|---|---|
| Accessibility | One block from Exit 4, near the Interstate, 10 minutes from the airport. |
| Location | Near many restaurants and nightspots, close to the scenic wharf drive and new water park. |
| Value | New need-period sales calendar offers reduced rates and menus during certain times of the year. |
| Quality | Industry awards like four stars or diamonds, testimonial letters from pleased clients. |

Done properly, matching goals to features lays the groundwork in a client's mind that a hotel can indeed meet his or her needs. A skilled salesperson can outsell a competitor in an identical hotel by matching goals to features, because this process makes a client believe one hotel is better suited than another. This is most advantageous in locations where there is little differentiation in product type (e.g., downtown or crowded resort areas), because the hotels may be quite similar.

A feature shows that a hotel can meet a goal with tangible attributes. It does not ensure that a sale will be made. That is done when the goal and feature are coupled with an advantage.

### ADVANTAGE

At this point in the sales process, the client has been shown that a hotel's features match his or her goals. The final step in creating a sale is to show a client how matching features to goals benefits him or her. Therefore, the salesperson must show the client the advantage of buying from the hotel.

An **advantage** is the result of matching a goal to feature and the benefit the client gains from their combination. An advantage can be expressed to a client in personal or intangible ways. As opposed to features, which must be seen or experienced, advantages can be implied. A picture in a client's mind of how a hotel's features meet his or her goals is an advantage. Combining goals and features to derive advantages cements the buying decision because the sale serves the client's best interest.

| Client's Goal | Hotel Feature(s) | Client's Advantage(s) |
|---|---|---|
| Accessibility | One block from Exit 4, near the Interstate, 10 minutes from the airport. | More people can attend more easily, which increases attendance numbers. |
| Location | Near many restaurants and nightspots, close to the scenic wharf drive and new water park. | Allows for off-site options to suit many tastes. |
| Value | New need-period sales calendar offers reduced rates and menus during certain times of the year. | Client may be able to afford levels of quality and service that were not possible before without exceeding spending limits. |
| Quality | Industry awards like four stars or diamonds, testimonial letters from pleased clients. | A quality property reflects well on the client. |

## WINNING THE SALE

The flow created between the three components of the hotel sales triangle ensures that a sale is generated, but the selling process does not end there. The sale must be closed, or won. As in any race, all the work that brought participants to the finish line will not matter unless the race is won. Without this final step in sales, all the salesperson's work will be fruitless.

Winning the sale is the ultimate aim of any salesperson. To do that, the goals, features, and advantages must flow from start to finish without detour. As the arrow shows in Figure 4–15, the win triangle takes over from the sales triangle after advantages have been matched to features and goals. The points in the win triangle, convince, close, and roadblock, ensure sale closure.

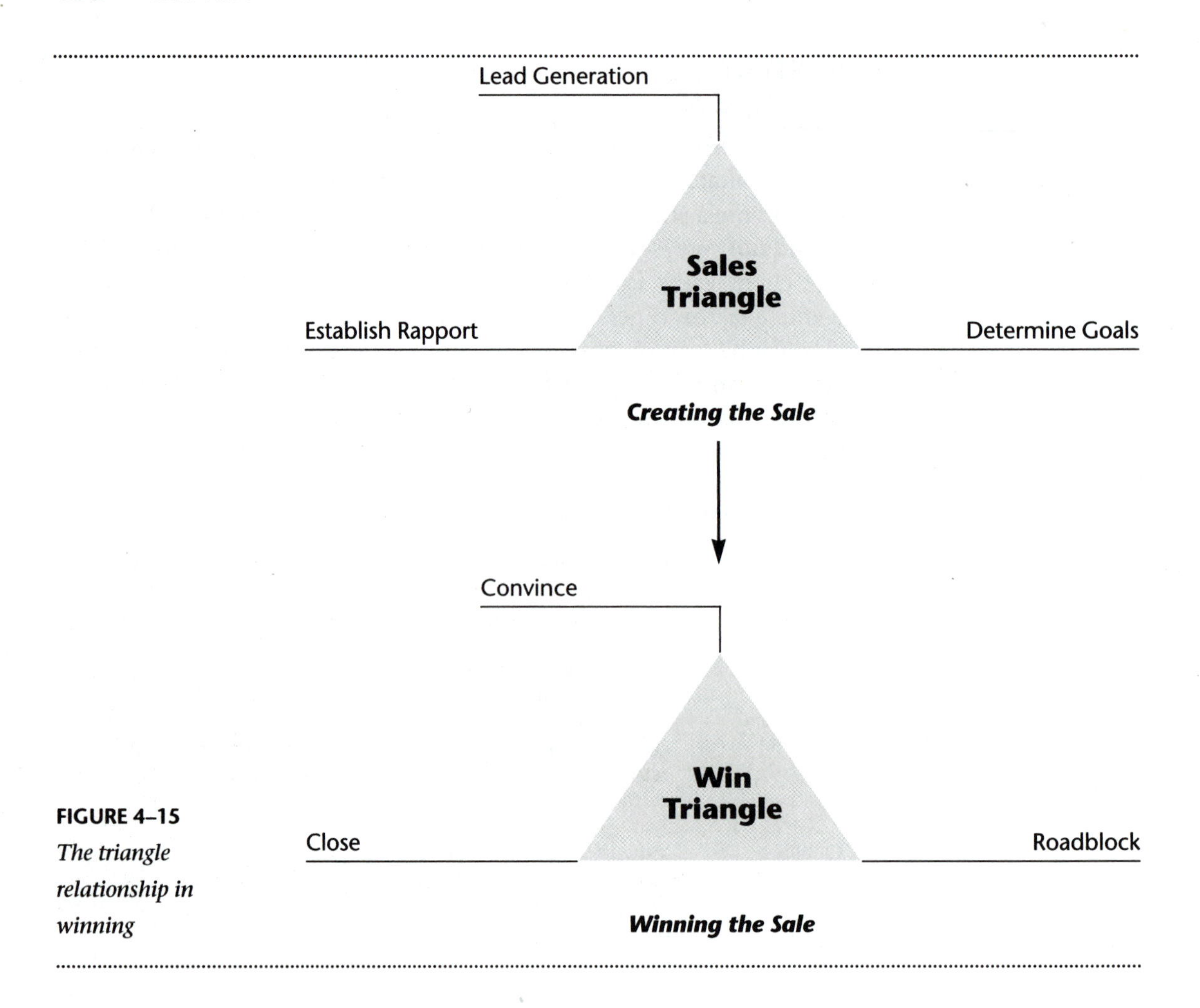


**FIGURE 4–15** *The triangle relationship in winning*

## CONVINCE

The convince step in the win triangle is in place for the salesperson to summarize and prepare for closure. The salesperson must review with the client the features and advantages that have been matched to the client's goals. Each can be reinforced by restating it to the client, if needed. The best result of reinforcement is affirmation by the client.

Gaining agreement, or affirmation, from the client that goals have been met by features and advantages is a useful sales device. Getting clients to affirm paints pictures in their minds that the best hotel choice is the one being discussed. A salesperson can simply ask the client to confirm that the hotel's features and advantages meet the client's goals. Statements like, "So, to make sure I fully understand your needs, you understand that our hotel is close to the highway, which makes for easy access for all your drive-in attendees. That fact addresses your initial goal of easy access, does it not?" An affirmation indicates that the client's goal has been met.

This process of review and affirmation can continue, if needed, goal by goal. If the client is overwhelmingly positive in his or her responses, the salesperson may decide that further affirmation is unnecessary. When building rapport, the salesperson should have gotten a fairly good idea of when the client is reacting positively or negatively. Affirmation brings the sales process to the next point in this triangle, the close. Negative reactions to all attempts at affirmation take the salesperson to the last point, which is roadblock.

## CLOSE

Affirmation that all goals are met or exceeded by the hotel's features and advantages predetermines the fate of the sale. The sale is made at this point. Salespeople are often prevented from closing sales because they fail to take the easiest step, which is to ask for the clients' business. New salespeople often forget that simply asking for the client's business formally ensures closure of the sale. Too many times, hotel salespeople go through the steps of building rapport and determining goals, only to stop. Assuming that a sale has been made does not close a sale. Affirmation may signal that the client is willing to close, but until the business is requested, the sale is not secure.

**CLOSING THE SALE**

| Sales Type | Statements to Secure the Sale |
|---|---|
| Group | "May I send you a contract?"<br>"Can we confirm this business?"<br>"How long do you need before I can expect a signed contract returned?" |
| Catering | "Let me start working on your final menus."<br>"At this point, should I turn away other groups interested in your function space?" |
| Transient | "Can I have your credit card number so I may give you a confirmation number?"<br>"What address would you like a confirmation sent to?" |

If the client does not offer all affirmations or meets business requests with indecision or, worse, indifference, the salesperson has hit a roadblock.

## ROADBLOCK

If, during the convince and close phases of the win triangle, the sale cannot be concluded, a roadblock has been reached. A **roadblock** can be anything, but most commonly it is an uncovered or a hidden client goal. A roadblock becomes obvious when there is no affirmation during the convince phase. A roadblock can also manifest itself when the business is asked for and the reaction from the client is indecision.

A roadblock cannot be overcome unless the salesperson attempts to uncover it. As Figure 4–16 shows, the salesperson must return to the determining goals action triangle and redetermine the client's goals.

In the hotel sales arena, there are numerous roadblocks that a salesperson may face. The exact nature of each depends largely on the client, the client's organization, the hotel, and the surrounding marketplace. Experienced salespeople find that certain roadblocks recur due to certain factors. Some common roadblocks are:

- Wrong Contact—A wrong contact arises when, during qualification, the salesperson fails to determine the correct decision

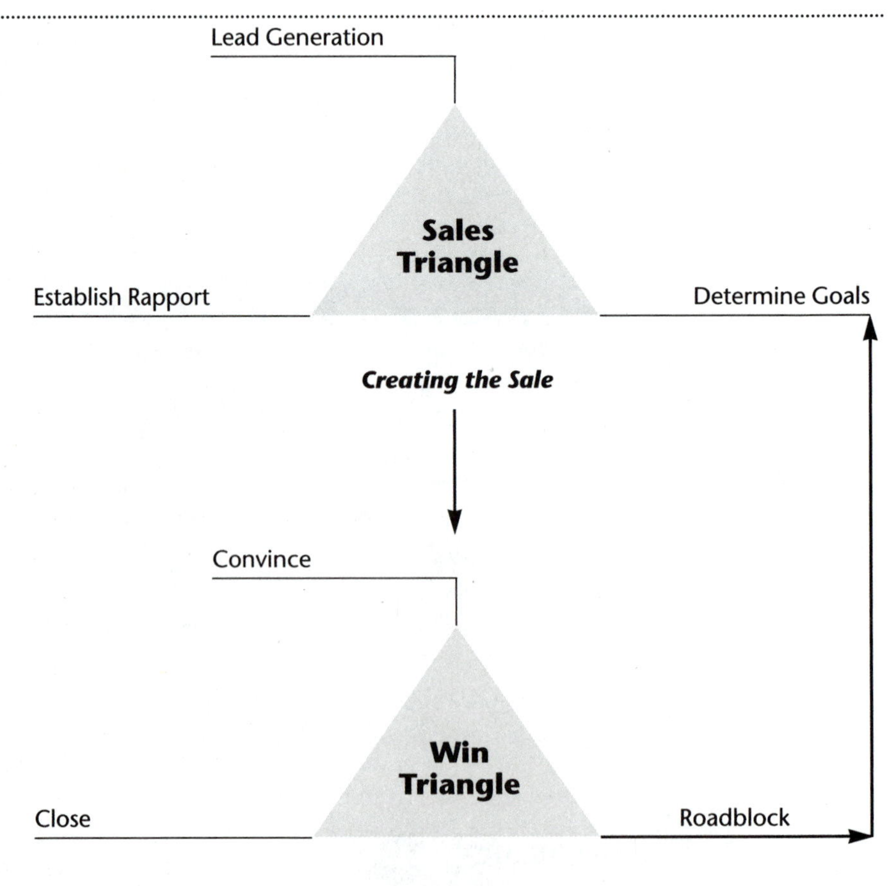


**FIGURE 4–16**
*The roadblock*

maker. A contact who is not authorized to make a decision cannot commit to a program, no matter how well needs are met.

- Rate Questions—If, during an attempt to close, the rate issue is raised, the salesperson should attempt to reinforce why the quote for a room is fair. He or she can also review the hotel's quality and service characteristics. If the time of year or citywide compression necessitate higher rates, the client will realize the hotel's quote is fair, because he or she will receive quotes from other hotels. If time permits, the salesperson could attempt to move dates into need periods to lower the client's rate.
- Room Rental—Room rental is viewed by many hotels as a pure profit revenue source. Others mandate strict adherence to room rental dollars per square foot of function space. A client who objects to a room rental due to the client education level or market tolerance may be placated with a room rental sliding scale. A sliding scale ties the room rental price to the group room performance. The more rooms that are used, the lower the rental.
- Catering Menu Prices—Roadblocks generated by high catering costs can be difficult to overcome. From the food cost analysis conducted earlier, it is understood that the hotel has minimal leeway in reducing food prices. If the total hotel impact of a business opportunity is high enough, upper management may allow for discounted menu prices. Many hotels also create special budget-sensitive menus for clients with cost concerns, although these menus are less substantial than regular ones. Often, small price reductions are viewed as signs of "good faith" by a client and major reductions will not be necessary.
- Function Space Size or Condition—If, in the course of negotiation, a client returns again and again to the amount of function space being offered, the salesperson must review the group sales equation carefully. If the amount of space being offered corresponds to the number of sleeping rooms being used (room-to-space ratio and space intensity), additional function space may be offered at rack rental prices. If no other space is available and dates are not flexible, a hotel could get creative in allocating space that a group may be able to use for its function. Large suites, meeting room hallways, and prefunction areas (open space in front of meeting rooms) may be designated as function space for a group if the business warrants. Meeting quality or condition, if less than optimal, can be overcome often by discounting rental or offering complimentary meeting packages. A meeting package can include popular food or beverage items

(e.g., continental breakfast, coffee breaks) or AV items (e.g., slide projectors, screens, flipcharts).

## CHAPTER REVIEW

### KEY CONCEPTS

Lead generation
Establish rapport
Determine goals
Solicitation
Third party
Client inquiry
Trace files
Readerboards
Sales blitz
Creating comfort
Ensuring trust
Demanding confidence
Customer profile
Goal
Feature
Advantage
Close
Convince
Roadblock

### REVIEW QUESTIONS

1. How can hotel sales triangle techniques apply to other industries?
2. What goals may a client have when looking to book at a hotel?
3. Name solicitation sources for hotel sales other than the ones listed in this text.
4. What goes into a salesperson's mental inventory?

## ROLE-PLAYING EXERCISE

With a sales teammate or classmate, practice implementing the different stages of the hotel sales triangle in a mock sales situation. Take turns playing the roles of salesperson and client.

Create the method in which the lead was generated. Determine the set of client goals, and have each person try selling. Use open-ended questions to qualify and establish rapport. Determine the goals of the other party and attempt to close.

Each person should have a hidden goal that becomes a roadblock to closing the sale. When finished, each person should critique the other's role as salesperson. Share the results with your sales team or class.

# CHAPTER 5

# *Sales Operations*

*“One’s word is only as good as its perception.”*

UNKNOWN

## INTRODUCTION

The intricacies of the day-to-day life of a hospitality salesperson are numerous. New challenges and opportunities arise each day that allow those involved in selling a hotel to learn and grow. These learning opportunities abound in all areas, not just the sales process. The duties of a hotel salesperson do not end with the booking of a business opportunity. To varying degrees, all hotels mandate certain levels of operational responsibility from their salespeople. The term used broadly to describe the duties and responsibilities salespeople can incur because of sales is *operations*.

**Sales operations** is defined as the functions/roles/duties a salesperson may engage in before, during, and after a sale. The daily responsibilities that arise in preparing to generate a lead, managing the lead once it is generated, and coordinating bookings within the sales office and with the hotel itself are all operational. Communication, networking, and management are all crucial components of the salesperson's operational skills.

Sales operations is a phrase used in the industry to describe the inter-hotel relationships a salesperson must build as part of his or her responsibilities. Salespeople must be able to rely on other hotel departments to deliver on the commitments they made on the hotel's behalf.

This chapter divides the major sales operational topics into three headings. The first heading outlines what is needed before applying the hotel sales triangle: preparing for the sale. The second discusses the operational skills that are needed once the opportunity is secured: after the sale. The third heading highlights the topics that are needed throughout the process: ongoing.

## PREPARING FOR THE SALE

In preparing for a sale, the salesperson must arm him- or herself with basic sales tools. The most fundamental tool in any sales discipline is knowledge of the product: the hotel. Knowledge of the hotel and what it offers is crucial before selling can begin. Another basic tool is familiarity with the competition. A salesperson must know what he or she is selling against. The other basic operational tools a salesperson must master in preparing for a sale include customer communication forms and hospitality sales tools.

### KNOWING THE HOTEL

Have you ever walked into a car showroom and asked the salesperson about a car and he or she did not know the answer? It can be frustrating to work with a salesperson of any product (e.g., a car, a piece of clothing, or a hotel) who does not know the product. For a hotel salesperson, the product is the hotel. The salesperson must know the hotel thoroughly before trying to sell it. Clients ask questions about the hotel that salespeople often do not expect and cannot prepare to answer. Other questions are common. The most important questions to answer in hotel sales are those regarding the hotel's products and services.

Every topic cannot be covered here, but fundamental knowledge of outlet hours of operation, meeting capacity, location, special services, and amenities are a must. The easiest way for a salesperson to begin knowing the hotel is by compiling a fact sheet or a personal binder to keep all collected information together and ready. The salesperson should start information gathering by approaching the managers of each of the hotel's restaurants, lounges, and room service departments and asking every conceivable question. For example, the salesperson should ask about unique situations and special setups they have seen. The managers will explain what they can and cannot do and help the salesperson avoid problems.

### QUESTIONS TO ASK THE HOTEL'S FOOD AND BEVERAGE OUTLETS

- Has the local food critic raved about the specialty restaurant?
- Do you offer buffets at set times or as demand warrants it?
- What are your hours of operation? Do these hours change during the week?
- What is your maximum capacity? Dress code? Average per person cost?
- What days of the week, if any, do you close?
- Do you offer "early bird" or "happy hour" price reductions?
- What are your signature food items? Which items are most popular?
- Which of your characteristics set your outlet apart from others?
- Does the chef prepare daily specials? What are some examples?
- Do holiday hours differ from normal hours of operation?

With the answers to these questions and information from managers, a salesperson can impress his or her familiarity with the hotel's outlets on a client and emphasize what the hotel team does best. With the proper knowledge, the salesperson can also avoid discussing what the hotel does not do well and steer clients from challenges before they settle on specific agendas.

Every hotel that has function space should have a detailed diagram of each function area and any other space for sale to clients. Each meeting space diagram should include a chart that outlines all possible setups and the capacities of the space in different configurations. Because this diagram is fundamental, it should be memorized. (See Chapter 3 for a discussion of setups.)

**QUESTIONS TO ASK ABOUT FUNCTION SPACE**

- How many classroom tables does the ballroom accommodate?
- How does seating capacity differ with rounds of 8 versus rounds of 10?
- How does rear screen projection affect the maximum theater-style seating?
- What are the capacities of all function rooms using common room sets and variations?
- How much turnaround time is needed to change room sets?
- Is a flambé dessert possible in the ballroom, or is it against the fire code?
- What is the maximum number of schoolroom tables that fit in the exhibit hall?
- What is the reception capacity of the prefunction area?
- How many tabletop exhibits fit in the ballroom?
- Are the airwalls in the ballroom soundproof?
- Where are the light and temperature controls in each room?
- When was the meeting space last renovated?
- Are all the function areas accessible? The Americans with Disabilities Act (ADA) requires buildings to be accessible to individuals with disabilities.

A client may ask any question without warning. Perhaps more than anything else in this section, the salesperson must know the meeting space and its flexibility.

**Accentuate the Positive.** Every hotel does certain things well and others not as well. Most salespeople are lucky enough to work at hotels that do more things well than not. Whatever the salesperson's situation, his or her hotel does some unique things. These things can include any number of amenities or services. Knowing the hotel aids the salesperson early in the sales process, because it allows him or her to distinguish the hotel from others. A hotel's distinguishing characteristics should be in its fact sheet.

**QUESTIONS TO ASK THE FRONT OFFICE MANAGER OR RESIDENT MANAGER**

- Do you have automatic turndown service for all guests?
- Do you have an automatic checkout billing system?
- Do you offer special meeting services or a business center and related services?
- Is your tennis court or golf course highly regarded?
- Do you offer complimentary coffee service or free newspaper delivery?
- Do you sponsor children's activities?
- Do you administer frequent stay programs and tie-ins to airlines and car-rental companies?
- Are your guest rooms newly renovated?
- What are your special in-room amenities (e.g., mini-bars, voice mail, work area, movies, toiletries, unique views, 24-hour room service, video games)?
- Do you have an express check-in service?
- Do you have an airport shuttle?
- Do you have concierge service?

Beyond understanding the hotel's outlets, function space, and special services, a salesperson should have a basic understanding of the hotel's administration and operations. The hotel's location type and surroundings are also important. The salesperson who is familiar with the hotel's location shows the client that he or she is aware of the surroundings and helps gain the client's trust. Remember, a hotel's location can be a selling point. If it is right off the Interstate or another major thoroughfare, the hotel can sell its accessibility. Accessibility is a goal for groups with large numbers of drive-in attendees. (In this case, the hotel's location by the Interstate is a feature, and ease for drive-in attendees is an advantage.)

**FACT SHEET OR HOTEL INFORMATION SHEET**

The fact sheet or hotel information sheet should include:

- Correct spellings of the general manager's name and other executive managers' names
- Total number of rooms and group ceilings as they relate to booking restrictions
- Breakdown of number of kings, doubles, suites, corner rooms, view rooms, business or concierge level, and so on.
- Roll-away, crib, and extra-person costs
- Banquet price averages for breakfast/lunch/reception/dinner and coffee breaks
- Secretaries club, frequent stay program, meeting incentives
- Activities (e.g., golf, tennis, pool) and their prices
- Nearby attractions and their hours and costs
- Nearby restaurants, nightspots, and so on
- Competitors, their phone numbers, their numbers of guest rooms, and their locations
- Major airlines servicing the local airport
- Major local thoroughfares and exits
- Hotel ownership, corporation, management, and corporate history, if applicable
- Mode of transport from the airport to hotel (e.g., taxi or bus) and its cost
- Specific directions from downtown (e.g., exit numbers)
- Length of drive to the ocean or next major city
- Distance from the convention center

Understanding the product is the first basic sales tool in the hospitality industry. The next important tool is familiarity with the competition.

## FAMILIARITY WITH THE COMPETITION

The salesperson's job would be much easier if there were no competing hotels. Clients who must book at the hotel pose a minimal challenge. Without challenge, salespeople can become complacent. Competition forces a salesperson to improve his or her selling skills. The strongest salespeople overcome their competition and make sales.

Whether it is a competing city or hotel, most salespeople have to face competition. Some salespeople may have no real competition in their areas, but those cases are rare. Market factors will drive salespeople to seize opportunities and face their competition. The salesperson must accomplish two basic tasks to overcome competition:

1. Know the strengths and weaknesses of all competitors; and
2. Gain the competitors' respect.

**Identifying Competitors' Strengths and Weaknesses.** There is a saying that goes "knowing is half the battle." When it comes to the competition, knowing is *most* of the battle. Salespeople who do not know what they face or how can they compete cannot beat their competition. In day-to-day sales activities, clients often say things like, "The XYZ Hotel is offering this," or "The ABC Hotel is just what we need." What should the salesperson do? Do they roll over and let the client accept the better sales job? (Obviously the other hotel did a better job of establishing rapport and determining goals). If he or she knows the competition, should he or she counter?

Knowing the competition's strengths and weaknesses puts the salesperson in a position of power. The salesperson's fact sheet on his or her hotel should include:

- Aspects the hotel does well
- Aspects the hotel does poorly
- Room average rates
- Number of rooms
- Group rates
- Typical group ceiling
- Function room square footage
- Quality of meeting space
- Outlet/ancillary options
- Banquet prices
- Hotel's location relative to its surroundings and other hotels

These things and more about the competitor are very important for the salesperson to know. Each time the salesperson moves to another city or another hotel, he or she must learn the strengths and weaknesses of all competitors in the area.

Senior hotel management should have gathered information for a competitive survey as part of the annual marketing plan. If this information is not current, it is easy to update. A good way to update competitors' information is to personally inspect the competitors while on overnight stays. If the hotel is in a highly competitive market, all team members should share this duty. Each salesperson should explore and ask questions. Staying at a hotel reveals what the hotel truly offers.

**QUESTIONS TO ASK WHILE INVESTIGATING THE COMPETITOR**

- What level of service does the competitor provide?
- How does the competitor's room service presentation look?
- Are the competitor's rooms in good or bad shape comparatively?
- How do the competitor's restaurants differ from those at the salesperson's hotel?

While staying at the competitor, each team member should examine the sets in the ballroom and other meeting rooms. Each should absorb all he or she can (e.g., the health club, the golf course, and so on). Team members must document all their observations and share them with the rest of the team.

After their stays, salespeople should meet formally with their counterparts at the competitive hotel. By doing so, the salespeople can gather information regarding the competitor's published rates, menu prices, standard amenities, and the like. Establishing rapport may enable the salespeople to gather more information from the competitor.

These investigative experiences, put together, can give a sales team a good look at what the competition in their area can and cannot do well. To supplement these experiences, the salespeople should solicit information from the CVB and any clients who have rapport with the hotel. As Chapter 4 mentioned, readerboard information is also valuable to understanding the competition, because it reveals the hotel's clientele. At the end of this process, each salesperson should be able to insert in his or her fact sheet binder a summary of every competitive hotel.

**Using Competitive Information.** What should be done with competitive information? The most important rule is to never disparage a competitor to a client. This is unprofessional and may lose the respect of the client and the competition. Instead, the salesperson should be magnanimous when discussing the competition. It is an unwritten rule in the industry. When the client presses, the salesperson should tell him or her what the competition does well. The salesperson should stress the positive in a competitor even if the client demeans it. The salesperson should not hesitate to recommend a competitor when the salesperson's hotel cannot or does not want to accommodate a group.

Knowing the competition and how to address the competition with clients comes into play when clients erect roadblocks. For example, a client may claim that a competitor offers a lower group room rate than the salesperson has quoted. Assuming the competitor is the same caliber as the salesperson's hotel, the salesperson should say, "Wow, that's a great price! It is wonderful that they can give you that high level of quality and service at that price. We would be bankrupt trying to keep our level of service and cover our costs at that price." By so doing, the salesperson puts doubt in the client's mind without appearing bitter or spiteful. Competitors have their own need periods and business cycles, so lower price quotes are inevitable. Knowing how to deal with these issues in busy times prohibits salespeople from lowering sleeping or function room quotes to secure business. In essence, if a salesperson really knows the competition and knows how to deal with any problems the competition may represent, he or she can overcome the competition.

**Gaining the Respect of Competitors.** The skilled salesperson does more than simply conquer the competition. He or she makes the competition work for him or her. This salesperson positions him- or herself as an ally, not an enemy. This is done easily by getting to know counterparts in sales offices that also handle the salesperson's markets or regions.

Getting to know counterparts is accomplished by networking and competition. Each salesperson who handles a market or region faces the same salespeople at competitive hotels. Competitors meet face-to-face at industry meetings and trade shows. The rapport-building process should be applied to salespeople as well as clients. Optimally, the salesperson becomes friendly with his or her counterparts and commiserates with them about the day-to-day challenges in the sales market. He or she may even share advice with them from time to time. Once rapport is established, a salesperson enjoys two things.

First, the salesperson can refer business he or she cannot book to a specific person. Clients appreciate being given a name, and it makes the salesperson look magnanimous and knowledgeable. Clients are more likely to call the salesperson first again if he or she is honest in terms of options. The foundation of trust increases in these instances, even though the business was not booked.

Second, the sales counterpart views the salesperson as someone who has the client's best interests as his or her ultimate concern. That impression rewards the salesperson with referrals from counterparts when those counterparts cannot or will not accommodate a group. Trust with counterparts in essence creates other sources for generating leads. These leads are prequalified and sent in time for the salesperson to pursue. If the competition does not want a piece of business, it does not mean the business is undesirable.

Therefore, the salesperson should pursue rapport building with competitors. When possible, competitors should be invited for lunch and a hotel tour. While they may accept to complete the competitive analysis discussed earlier, they present opportunities for making favorable impressions. Tours should be scheduled on days the hotel is at its best. If the hotel is putting on an extensive convention, for example, it looks impressive because all parts of the hotel are active. Showing the hotel in its best form reduces the sales tools a competitor can use to sell against it. The salesperson should not be afraid of admitting limitations, however. If the hotel cannot do a remote check-in, the salesperson should admit so. Referral business that does not apply to the hotel is of no value to the hotel. In the end, if a salesperson knows what the competition can and cannot do and has the competition's trust, he or she is at an advantage.

## CUSTOMER COMMUNICATION FORMS

The sales principles in this text must be communicated to book business. Transmitting a message from a sender (the salesperson) to a receiver (the client) is the basis of this communication. The tools used in effective sales communication are varied. A strong foundation in the basic ones allows the salesperson to apply them to any form of communication.

In hospitality, there are two basic types of communication. External communication, which is needed to communicate with clients and others outside the hotel, is reviewed in the following. Internal communication, which is used to inform and prepare departments within a hotel, are addressed in the section dealing with sales operations after the sale.

External communication forms are used in hotel sales to effectively and eloquently express the three points of the hotel sales triangle to clients. They are also used to communicate with competitors, third parties, suppliers, and vendors. The two main vehicles of external communication are hospitality sales letters and phone conversations.

This section first outlines the essentials of creating hospitality letters, including basic letter format and how it applies to different hospitality situations. Then the hotel sales triangle components are applied to external communication forms. Helpful hints for conducting phone conversations are also listed.

**Hospitality Sales Letters.** Letters come in various forms, each conveying a specific message. Today letters can be sent via computer (E-mail or the Internet). However, most business letters in the hospitality industry are still sent traditionally. Each method is a vehicle because it provides a means of communication. Whatever vehicle is used, the hotel salesperson should know how to compose the best letters. In every facet of hotel sales (group, transient, or catering), messages must be conveyed effectively and eloquently while adhering to accepted business letter–writing principles.

*Sample Letter Format.* Many books have been written on the art and styles of letter writing. A vast variety of letter styles and formats exist today. While most hotel salespeople do not type their letters (assistants usually take that role), it still is a good idea for them to understand how to compose well-written letters. Following is one of the most commonly used letter styles in today's business world: the block letter, which uses left justification. The left side is a sample using **block letter format**. The right is an outline of each part of the letter. This sample is not to scale. Actual letters have the correct number of spaces from the top of the page.

**EXAMPLE**

|  |  |
|---|---|
| 10/20/99 | Date (thirteenth line on page) |
| Mr. Joe Smith<br>President<br>ABC Hotels<br>123 East Lane<br>Gotham City, NY 12345 | Client's Name (sixth line below date)<br>Client's Title<br>Company Name<br>Address |
| | (Space) |
| Dear Mr. Smith: | Salutation (Dear Mr./Ms.): |
| | (Space) |
| Thank you for allowing me to write this sample letter. It is very kind of you. | Body of letter<br>• No indentation of paragraphs<br>• Space between paragraphs |
| I will follow up with you on effective letter writing in a few days. Practice those skills and you will succeed. | |
| | (Space) |
| Sincerely, | Complimentary close (Sincerely), |
| | (Space) |
| XYZ HOTEL AND TOWERS | Firm name (Your hotel's name, all capitals) |
| | (3 spaces) |
| Ahmed Ismail<br>Catering Manager | Signer (Ahmed Ismail)<br>Title (Catering Manager) |
| | (Space) |
| AI/ast | Reference Initials (AI/ast)<br>• Set the writer's initials in caps, the typist's initials in lowercase. |

The basic letter format is easy to read and flows logically from start to finish. The content of the letter always changes, but its form should remain the same. The following list highlights a few hints and ideas on how to compose effective and eloquent basic letters:

- In the salutation, only use the client's first name if you have been given permission (i.e., if the client uses only his or her first name with you or the client has directed you to use it).
- Sign just your first name in the closing if you wish. It is accepted practice in today's business world. Some people, however, do

not like it, because they feel it looks less professional. The choice is up to the individual. A close client-salesperson relationship merits first name only use in the closing.

- When signing off in the complimentary close, use an alternate to "Sincerely" or "Yours Truly" when applicable (e.g., "Happy New Year" or "Happy Holidays." Do not, however, use religious words like "Merry Christmas," because you may inadvertently offend someone.
- Personalizing letters for those with whom you have close relationships is acceptable. For example, congratulate someone on a personal or professional success. Add a birthday greeting to the post script (PS).
- Customize whenever possible. Avoid form letters that *look* like form letters. Remember, the experienced meeting planner may have several of your letters and other forms of communication. Avoid having the meeting planner notice several copies of the same form letter in his or her files. Changing a form letter, even slightly, makes it look new and fresh.
- Use phrases that induce positive and proactive feelings in the reader. For example, "Please do not hesitate to call" suggests that you feel the reader is undecided. Instead, use the phrase, "Please feel free to call."
- Avoid hotel jargon and unnecessary words. Do not use industry words the reader may not know. Words like *blocking space* and *rooming list* may mean little to an inexperienced meeting planner. Phrases like "Per our conversation" and "Per your request" sound overly formal.
- Close every letter with some type of action step. Let the reader know you will be calling or stopping by. If you can be specific (e.g., "I will contact you next Thursday as we discussed"), you will be actually setting up an appointment. Your contact will be expecting that phone call or those menus in the mail. Make sure you honor your commitment. You will look very unprofessional if you do not follow up.

**Variations of Hotel Sales Letters.** In written correspondence, as in verbal communication, clarity and accuracy are very important. A letter should invoke pride in its composer. In the hospitality industry, salespeople find themselves writing certain types of sales letters over and over. The many contingencies in sales cannot be addressed, but most can be highlighted so that the process of writing and the style of letter can be adapted universally.

As has been reviewed, the sales process allows salespeople to continuously learn and build their knowledge bases. Their learning curve applies to client relationships via the mental inventory process. The mental inventory can only be created through communication, which means every phone call and every letter teaches the salesperson more about the client and his or her personality traits. A salesperson also can learn about the client from his or her reactions to his or her own correspondence. Hence, all letters must be viewed as sales tools.

The five major types of sales letter forms in hospitality are: (1) introduction/good-bye, (2) confirmation, (3) cover, (4) proposal, and (5) thank you. Each has an infinite number of styles, but the basic shell of each and its objectives remain the same.

*Introduction/Good-Bye Letter.* In the **introduction/good-bye letter**, often called the "transition letter," the salesperson's relationship with a client is either beginning or ending. These letters are used often when a salesperson is starting work at a hotel, or when he or she takes over a group for another team member (also called a "turnover"). These letters are important because they are part of a client's first or last impression of the salesperson. Hotel promotions can also be good times to use these letters, because they can update clients on a salesperson's title and duties/markets.

Continuity is very important in the hospitality business, where personnel moves occur often. Before moving to other hotels, salespeople should always take the time to inform their clients of their departures and, ideally, who will replace them. Clients often feel better about continuing relationships at a hotel when the salesperson takes the time to notify them of anything that may affect them. (Note: Sales personnel who switch companies or go to work for the competition probably will not be allowed to inform their current clients because management likely does not want clients to move with the salesperson.)

## SAMPLE INTRODUCTION LETTER

Dear [client name]:

Please let me take a moment to introduce myself. My name is [salesperson's name] and I am your new contact here at the XYZ Resort and Towers.

While I know you have worked with us in the past, I look forward to personally continuing this mutually beneficial relationship. Rest assured, the superior level of service you have come to expect from the XYZ will continue with my tenure.

Again [client name], thank you for being a friend of the XYZ. I will be in contact soon. In the meantime, please feel free to call me directly at 123–4567 should you have any questions.

*Confirmation Letter.* A good **confirmation letter** confirms, or reinforces, what was mutually agreed upon. Typically, this letter is written following a phone conversation. It exemplifies what is referred to as, "Putting it in writing." Recapping what was agreed to, if applicable, and confirming the next course of action are the best uses of the confirmation letter.

## SAMPLE CONFIRMATION LETTER

Dear [client name]:

Thank you for taking the time to speak with me today. We here at the XYZ Hotel look forward to welcoming you and your attendees next March.

As we discussed, enclosed please find the banquet event orders outlining the details of your Regional Sales Awards Celebration. Simply look them over and return signed copies to my attention if all is in order.

Again [client name], thank you for choosing the XYZ. I will be in touch as the arrival date gets closer. In the meantime, should you have any questions, please feel free to contact me directly at 123–4567.

*Cover Letter.* Sometimes called a "transmittal letter," the **cover letter** may be used to prepare the reader (the client) for material being sent (e.g., brochures or menus). The cover letter may include the purpose of the enclosed material, reasons for developing the material, or the way in which the material should be used. It can also contain any basic message the salesperson wishes to convey. The cover letter simply tells the client why he or she should look at the material. It is intended as a quick, informal means of business communication. A sample first sentence could be, "Just a quick note to accompany the enclosed contract . . ." For its format, use the previously mentioned hints for letter writing. In today's business environment, the cover letter has been replaced in many cases with a fax cover sheet.

*Proposal Letter.* The secret to generating a lead is to create interest. This is the goal in submitting a proposal to a hotel client. A proper **proposal** includes (a) the proposal itself and (b) an accompanying proposal letter. The letter that accompanies the proposal is an integral part of that proposal. Because each hotel has a different proposal format, a discussion of proposal writing does not apply here. Instead, this section provides ideas on the accompanying letter.

Ideally, a proposal letter is no more than two pages and addresses the three points of the determine goals action triangle. In a proposal letter, the salesperson must address the client's goals and show how the hotel's features benefit the client. While the proposal addresses program specifics (e.g., banquet prices, room rental, cancellation policy), the proposal letter is the perfect vehicle to address the points of the hotel sales triangle.

As was shown earlier, in the qualifying of different clients, certain goals tend to be more common than others. This is not to say, however, that goals will be limited to those discussed here. New goals and combinations of other goals will be uncovered from clients on an ongoing basis. The following paragraphs discuss the four goals used throughout Chapter 4: accessibility, location, value, and quality. Chapter 4 showed how the four sample goals could benefit clients by using a hotel's features. The following section takes the four goals one step farther by applying them to a proposal. This permanent record compels the client to ponder the goals, features, and advantages while reviewing the correspondence. The best way to compose proposals is to dedicate each paragraph to one goal and its corresponding features and advantages.

- *Accessibility.* A central and convenient location is important for many reasons. Easy access to and from interstate roadways and a major airport nearby ensure ease of travel and accessibility. The XYZ Hotel achieves these objectives by providing an easily accessible downtown location 1 block from Exit 1 of Interstate 1, which is fewer than 10 minutes from Sky View International Airport.
- *Location.* A hotel's surroundings can contribute to the overall success of a meeting in different ways. With off-property features like restaurants, nightspots, and points of interest, attendees do not feel constrained to one location. The XYZ Hotel is within walking distance of over 100 restaurants and nightspots. The scenic Wharf Drive and Bill's Water Park, which are nearby, provide fun and excitement for the whole family.
- *Value.* In today's economy, value is more important than ever. To maximize the spending dollar, clients must ensure they get what they pay for. The XYZ Hotel prides itself on providing all our guests a meeting experience that exceeds monetary expectations. Our ability to provide you with discounted catering prices and our skill at working within your budget help you put a program together without exceeding your financial limits.
- *Quality.* As a meeting planner, your hotel selection inevitably reflects back on you. Organizing a program at a hotel that maintains a high standard of quality and service shows your attendees and your superiors you value their satisfaction above all else. The XYZ Hotel prides itself on detail-oriented staff and award-winning quality level. The hotel's list of satisfied clients only helps to show that your choice will be the correct one.

## PROPOSAL WRITING EXERCISE

Following are three more goals that can be raised by clients. Compose proposal paragraphs using these goals or others you come up with. This task grows easier with practice.

| **Goal** | **Feature** | **Advantage** |
|---|---|---|
| Attentive Service | The hotel's size allows only one major group to book at one time. | The group will have the entire staff's attention and focus. |
| Creativity | European-trained culinary staff and experienced catering personnel have worked with a wide variety of groups. | The staff create unique menus and room sets that attendees will appreciate. |
| Clear and Concise Billing | The hotel provides daily review of banquet checks and an easy-to-read master bill format. All charges are accompanied by documented backup. | The client is not surprised with unanticipated or incorrect charges. The hotel keeps budget numbers up-to-date while the client is in house. |

*Thank-You Letter.* A good **thank-you letter** shows a salesperson's appreciation for the client's business and asks for feedback on the hotel's performance. Many hotels have client comment forms that can be sent with thank-you letters. These forms are a great way for hotels to address problems before they worsen. They are also useful for identifying hotel employees who exceeded their duties for the client.

The thank-you letter is a good way for the salesperson to begin the resolicitation process. If the client had a terrific program recently, the opportune time to rebook him or her is when sending the thank-you letter, because the image in the client's mind is positive. In fact, the two best times to approach a client about booking with a hotel are (1) after a successful program at a hotel and (2) after an unsuccessful program at the competition. Use the thank-you letter to begin the process of bringing them back. A cover letter can be sent to a client finishing a program at another hotel and, if the experience was poor, the letter may prompt the client's future consideration.

## SAMPLE THANK-YOU LETTER

Dear [client name]:

On behalf of the staff and management of XYZ Hotel, I wish to personally thank you for allowing us to host your recent Regional Sales Awards Celebration. We appreciate the opportunity to serve you and hope your expectations were exceeded in every way.

Your thoughts and feelings about our performance are important to us. Please complete the enclosed evaluation form to let us know your overall impression. Input from our important clients, like you, allows us to continually improve our service as well as recognize the employees who helped us provide you with a quality meeting experience.

Again [client name], thank you for being a friend of XYZ, I will be in touch in the coming months to help you plan your next meeting. In the meantime, should something else arise, please feel free to call.

---

**Phone Conversations.** Written communication is important and requires skill, as was just seen. In today's busy world, salespeople may find that clients are pressed for time and need answers quickly. Some do not want to wait for letters or E-mail. They may prefer verbal conversations. In these cases, a salesperson may use the telephone much more often than any other communication tool. Because creating comfort and ensuring trust with a client may be accomplished over the phone alone, it is vital to make the best use of phone time. Following are a few basic insights and tips to using the phone effectively with clients:

- Cheerfully and immediately inform the client with whom he or she is speaking (e.g., "Good morning. This is John in sales and catering. May I help you?"). Starting the conversation with a relaxed and cheerful tone help sets the stage.
- Be candid. Always work to build the foundation of trust.
- Convey confidence. A positive attitude encourages the client to open up.
- Be courteous.
- Be direct and clear.
- Avoid long discussions.
- Avoid jargon.
- Compliment when appropriate.
- Appreciate other people's time. Always ask the client if the time is good to talk. People appreciate that you value their time as much as yours.
- Share information. Sharing fun or uplifting information (e.g., industry trends, personnel changes, sports news) is appreciated by the client.
- Provide enough information in messages or voice mail to allow the client to act or gather information for you. Avoid playing "phone tag."

## HOSPITALITY SALES TOOLS

External communication forms do not bring the salesperson and client face-to-face. It is the nature of many clients to want personal interaction with the salespeople they deal with prior to consummating a sale. In the hospitality industry, salespeople have at their disposal specific sales tools that bring them face-to-face with their clients. These tools are the site inspection and customer appointments.

**Site Inspections.** Client interest generated through written or verbal communication leads to another form of customer communication: the site inspection. The **site inspection** is used by potential customers to look at the hotel under consideration before purchase.

Most experienced meeting planners expect to visit hotels before booking. Inexperienced meeting planners should be encouraged to do the same. The site inspection is an opportunity for the salesperson to display the hotel. Especially for busy meeting planners or planners conducting city-wide convention searches, the site inspection may be the only opportunity for the salesperson to display the hotel. There are three stages to an effective site inspection: preparation, implementation, and follow-up.

*Preparation.* Once a site inspection is confirmed, the salesperson should inform other hotel personnel and departments. Senior management (e.g., DOM, resident manager, executive chef, general manager) should be made aware of the business impact of the business opportunity. The involvement of senior managers can be invaluable in helping the salesperson help the hotel put forth its best effort. Alerting key personnel in other departments (e.g., front desk, housekeeping, restaurants) helps create hotel-wide awareness. Preparing the entire hotel for an impending site inspection is necessary to ensure the hotel makes the best impression.

If possible, the salesperson should post in various hotel departments (e.g., the bell stand, the front desk, the restaurant hostess stand) a picture of the arriving client with pertinent information (e.g., name, group, date of site inspection). This way, employees can greet the client by name. This recognition technique starts the selling process before the client and salesperson meet. It can impress a client if the doorperson greets him or her by name as he or she arrives.

Once awareness of the client has been created, the salesperson should review the goals he or she wants to accomplish with the site inspection. These goals must correspond to the client's agenda. For example, a salesperson should not show a client an outdoor pool if the client only needs space for a half-day meeting. Review of the client's proposed meeting agenda ensures that the salesperson will only show relevant aspects of the hotel.

**QUESTIONS TO ASK BEFORE THE SITE INSPECTION**

- What does the client want to see when he or she arrives?
- Are the client's rooms/suites properly blocked?
- Does the client want to see food and beverage outlets?
- Does the client want to see back of the house?
- Does the client want to see the grounds? Parking?
- Does the client want to see shuttles?

Anticipating all possible variations and questions ensures the hotel can accommodate all possibilities. Whether the client is staying overnight or not, showing him or her various sleeping rooms is part of every group-related site inspection. The salesperson should personally check the client's rooms on the day of arrival to ensure they make the best impression. The salesperson should enter the designated rooms, open the shades to reveal the view, if any, turn on some lights and play a radio softly. The salesperson should create an inviting atmosphere.

Many hotels designate rooms as permanent show rooms. Show rooms can be deep cleaned, smoke free, and polished by housekeeping to make the best impression. These **show rooms** are considered "last-sell" rooms by the front desk, which means they are not released unless the hotel is sold out. Show rooms allow the sales team to know where the rooms are located. Knowing where the client will be taken allows the salesperson to begin preparing an agenda of where and when each area of the hotel will be shown during the site inspection. A few unscrupulous hotels have reportedly created special show rooms that are more nicely appointed than their regular rooms. These hotels renovate these show rooms more often and generally portray a false impression to their clients. A client may ask to see rooms other than those they have seen because they want an honest look at the hotel. An honest hotel will show any room. Again, clients appreciate honesty in all dealings.

In addition to show rooms, a client will likely want to see a hotel's meeting space. On the day of a site inspection, the salesperson should check the ballroom and other meeting space of interest to the client to ensure they are clean and orderly. An important piece of business might justify setting up the meeting room to reflect how it would look when the client's group is meeting.

*Implementation.* Once the client is on property, the next phase of the site-inspection process begins. An effective site inspection relates directly to its preparation. First, the salesperson should dress professionally and be well-groomed. Clients make first judgments of hotels based on the employees they meet. The salesperson's appearance and demeanor indicate the caliber of the hotel.

The site inspection should continue with a greeting in the hotel lobby, if possible. The client should be greeted like any VIP. If the client arrived the night before the inspection, the salesperson should set a time for the two of them to meet and an exact location in the hotel in which to do so. The sales office is a good place in which to meet a client. At this point in the site inspection, introductions of senior management (e.g., DOM or general manager) have their greatest impact.

Before touring the hotel, the salesperson should have a brief, sit-down discussion with the client. Reviewing where the two parties are sharpens the focus of each throughout the inspection. A summary from the salesperson of what he or she plans to show the client helps to ensure both parties achieve their goals for the inspection. A review of the determining goals triangle may be warranted.

If possible, this initial meeting should be held in a hotel restaurant over breakfast or lunch. This is another instance in which preparation can be beneficial. If such a meal meeting is arranged, the salesperson should secure ahead of time a superior server to handle the table. The rapport a salesperson has with familiar servers often translates into better service, which in turn reflects well on the hotel.

The site inspection should be well-planned in all aspects. The tour should flow from one stop to the next. The salesperson should backtrack as little as possible. Along the way, the salesperson should keep conversation going by continually establishing rapport. The client's personality will reveal itself early, so the salesperson will know quickly whether light conversation is desired or whether only strict business discourse is accepted. Areas in which the hotel could improve (e.g., renovations in progress, older meeting rooms, poor views) should be avoided, unless the proposed business is far into the future. In these cases, a renovation can be sold as a new feature of the hotel. For example, if during a tour a client notices the meeting space is being renovated and the proposed business opportunity is not due until after the renovation is completed, the salesperson could impress upon the client that the meeting space will be relatively new when his or her group arrives.

Selling is a constant element of this process, even if the salesperson is not speaking. The client notices every aspect during the inspection and judges the suitability of the hotel throughout. The site inspection benefits the salesperson, because it offers the chance to overcome roadblocks with visuals. Visuals are properties of exceptional quality or those with unique attractions. Often, higher rates or less desirable dates can be less important to the client if the client is overwhelmed by a top-notch facility. Like the new car buyer who completes a test drive, the client becomes enthralled with a hotel out of his or her price range.

*Follow-Up.* As soon as the site inspection is completed, the salesperson should recap it in the organization's file. While everything is fresh, the salesperson should write or dictate a follow-up letter. Using the hotel sales triangle as a guide, the salesperson should create a letter that addresses the client's goals using the features highlighted in the inspection. This type of letter is very powerful, because the salesperson and the hotel are now more than just a proposal. The client can now connect visually with what is written. The salesperson should thank the client for taking the time to tour the hotel and, most importantly, indicate the next action step (e.g., send a contract to book the business).

Overall, the site inspection can be a very powerful sales tool when conducted properly (with proper preparation, implementation, and follow-up).

**ITEMS TO NOTE AFTER THE SITE INSPECTION**

- Any additions or changes to the program mentioned by the client
- Prices quoted for rooms or services
- The availabilities of meeting rooms or suites in which the client expressed interest
- Any challenges should be documented now so they can be addressed later

**Customer Appointments.** The client's schedule may not always permit him or her to visit the hotel. This is especially true of clients who know the hotel under consideration. In these cases, it is often beneficial for the salesperson to visit the client in his or her office. This is uncomfortable for some salespeople in the hotel industry. Many feel awkward leaving their comfort zones. In reality, most sales professionals today make the customer appointment a staple of their sales tools. Those who are selling products, not services, must go out and show prospective buyers the products. The hotel salesperson who masters the ability to venture from the product (the hotel) and endeavors to sell it enhances his or her sales opportunities.

An appointment with a client who knows the salesperson through previous dealings is obviously easier than an appointment with one who does not. In either case, the salesperson must know that all clients value their time. If the salesperson does not respect a client's time, the client will not consent to see him or her again. Everybody wants to protect their time.

When visiting an office for a customer appointment, the salesperson should take a little time to inventory the surroundings. How is the office set up? Do employees speak in hushed tones, or is the environment more relaxed? Is the office new, modern, and efficient looking, or is it disorganized? This exercise gives the salesperson some idea as to how to interact with the client. However, the salesperson should not assume that the client is as disorganized as the office may indicate.

When the salesperson arrives at the office, approaching the receptionist's desk to announce him- or herself is important. The salesperson should be kind, courteous, and professional to the receptionist. Receptionists are often underappreciated, and a little kindness can be very appreciated. The salesperson should try to get the receptionist's name so the salesperson can address him or her by name on the next phone call. Some salespeople even direct thank-you letters to receptionists personally, so the receptionists will remember them. This familiarity could help the salesperson get a call through to a busy client.

A face-to-face meeting in a client's office can be as productive as a site inspection. Rapport-building skills in these instances are also effective. The salesperson must take in the surroundings visually. Are there letters from other hotels? If the client's message box is visible, is it full or empty? The salesperson should be prepared to adjust his or her approach if the client is clearly overwhelmed. The client's face and body posture reveal clues to add to the mental inventory. Is the client hurried? Is he or she pleased for the diversion from his or her routine chores? The salesperson must ask probing and open-ended questions to extract information from the client. The longer the client allows a salesperson to ask questions, the more the salesperson learns. If the client is a new contact, the salesperson should try to arrange a site inspection at the hotel.

While speaking with the client, the salesperson should keep eye contact strong and posture confident. This appointment may be the client's first contact with the hotel. The salesperson represents everything the hotel has to offer. If he or she appears negative in any way, the client will identify those negative characteristics with the hotel.

The salesperson should finish the customer appointment by asking the client for some type of next action. A phone call can be made in a few days to follow up. The salesperson should always send a note thanking the client for his or her time. Any action will make the appointment worthwhile. If some action results from each appointment, the salesperson has accomplished his or her goal.

A salesperson should not schedule too many appointments in one day. He or she will receive a few negative reactions, and he or she should not become discouraged. These guidelines will improve a salesperson's technique so he or she will enjoy more success.

## AFTER THE SALE

The first section of this chapter outlined the skills and techniques the hotel salesperson can use to bring the business opportunity from generation to close. After the close, the salesperson's communication and management skills become important. The operational skills that must be exercised once the opportunity is secured are unique to the hospitality industry. The hotel salesperson must first understand how to measure and compare his or her pieces of business with those booked by the rest of the sales team. Next, the salesperson must document the commitment. Finally, the salesperson must address internal issues with departmental relationships, internal documents, and customer service.

### BOOKING STATUS

Every salesperson quickly understands that every member of the sales office views each business opportunity he or she works on as his or her own. Each good salesperson takes ownership of his or her business. Knowing this, salespeople can judge other salespeople's work and understand where each is in the sales process. The hospitality industry has developed a way to qualify the status of every business opportunity. This status can be thought of as the "lifespan" of each business opportunity. From adoption to retirement, each piece of business changes and grows. Three descriptions of business opportunity status are pieces of the business lifespan: tentative (adoption), definite (adulthood), and actual (retirement).

**Tentative (Adoption).** The **tentative** status qualification describes a piece of business that is thoroughly qualified and determined that both the client and the hotel are interested in pursuing. All tentative business represents potential revenue. The term "adoption" is also used, because the lead at this point has grown past generation. The business opportunity was conceived (qualified) and "born" (put on the books). The tentative business has been adopted by the hotel. The salesperson wants to raise it at his or her hotel.

Some hotels further classify tentative business with letters or numbers that correspond to the strength or "sureness" of booking. Strong tentatives can also be called "first-option" business. Weaker tentatives are considered "second options." Usually, when business is classified as second option, the client is considering many sites and is not yet sure which to choose. In some hotels that use the first- and second-option designations, a second option may be as strong as a first option. The difference is the first option was booked before the second. A second option may be booked on top of the first option to ensure something is booked in that time frame. The second tentative thus becomes the hotel's second option.

## SAMPLE CODING FOR TENTATIVE BUSINESS

Using a scale from A to D, the following business opportunities are rated according to their potentials to sign contracts.

| Tentative Business | Classification | Reason for Classification |
|---|---|---|
| ABC Ball Bearings | A | A verbal commitment was given to book and a formal contract was requested. |
| Joe's Flower Shop | B | The group is very interested in the hotel but has not firmly committed yet. |
| Fancy Apple Farms | C | The group has narrowed its hotel choices to a few but the site inspection process has yet to begin. |
| 123 Hardware | D | The qualification and determining goals process is ongoing or the agenda has yet to be planned. |

For cases with first and second options, the first-option business has the right of refusal. The definition of the "right of first refusal" is that, if there is a second-option opportunity interested in the space, all first-option business must be approached before the second option and given the opportunity to sign a contract with the hotel. All second-option tentatives must be informed that they are holding second-option dates. No client should be led to assume that he or she can confirm second-option dates at his or her leisure.

**Definite (Adulthood). Definite** business has firmly committed to using a hotel. In its lifespan, it has grown fully. The industry standard is to only consider business definite when a signed contract is received. Some hotels allow definite classification for any business that has forwarded advance deposits or committed verbally, but this is not suggested. Without contractual assurance that the business is coming to the hotel, there is always a chance for something to arise and prevent the business from arriving. Most sales quotas are structured to reflect definite room nights on the books. Any cancellations by groups without signed contracts hurts the salesperson and the hotel.

Definite group room nights for the current year and future years are very important. All budgets and forecasts are measured with definite room nights. Keeping the numbers as accurate as possible allows for the most accurate prediction of hotel performance. Remember, the hotel success triangle is centered on a strong base of room sales. Inaccurate numbers give false information to the rest of the hotel's departments.

**Actual (Retirement).** Once the definite business has come to and gone from the hotel, it undergoes another change. At this point in the lifespan, the salesperson can see exactly how many rooms the group used and how many dollars it spent on catering and the rest of the hotel. These numbers are called **actuals** because they represent documented, true numbers. They are no longer the best guess of the salesperson or the client. Actuals are equated with retirement, not death, because actuals still play an important role in future business. As in real life, in which retired people continue to play important and productive roles in society, actuals contribute to the hotel long after the group has gone. Any repeat business from the group can be analyzed with real information contained in the actuals. At this point, actuals become history. Actuals are the foundations for future budgets, which can look to them for realistic production goals. Actual production figures over several years can show a pattern. A historical record is the best indicator of future performance for a salesperson as well as the salesperson's hotel.

## WRITING BINDING CONTRACTS

For a business opportunity to move from tentative to definite status, most hotels require signed contracts. A signed contract is, in most cases, a legally binding agreement between the hotel and the client. In it, both parties agree to stated prices and services. A signed contract should be the ultimate aim of a salesperson. Hotel policies and procedures vary so greatly that it is not possible to outline one way in which to prepare a contract. As is the case with proposals, most hotels have their own forms which are thoroughly reviewed by their own attorneys and senior managers.

Instead of dictating contract format, this section illustrates three widely accepted methods of how best to protect the interests of a hotel: standard cancellation fee, attrition clause, and sliding scale. Again, these concepts should not alter a hotel's contract format in any way. They can be adapted easily to any contract.

**Standard Cancellation Fee.** As was stated earlier, every contract should include something that ensures the hotel's interests are protected. What would happen if a group booked 2 years ago but decided 3 months before arrival that it could not come? Given that the group booking cycle of most hotels is longer than that, the sales office would be in a precarious position. The salesperson and the hotel would have held the space in good faith for 2 years and may have even turned other groups away because all involved expected the group to fulfill its contractual obligations.

A cancellation clause in any contract tells the signer, "If you cancel your program by X date, you are obligated to reimburse the hotel Y dollars." The key is to structure the cancellation clause in such a way as to keep the hotel in a positive but conservative light. The best way to set up the cancellation clause is to mirror it to the group booking cycle.

For example, a downtown hotel with a 4-year group booking cycle signs the ABC Company to a city-wide convention. The contract for the group, which is slated to arrive in 5 years, takes all available rooms in the group ceiling. The cancellation fee must be structured so that the closer the group gets to its arrival date, the more money it must pay to break its contract. Assume the contract has the group using 300 rooms for 5 nights, with a confirmed rate of $150 per night. In total this piece of business is worth $225,000 in room revenue (300 rooms × 5 nights × $150 per night). This revenue is what the hotel stands to lose if the group cancels and the hotel cannot rebook its rooms. Based on the hotel's booking cycle, if the group cancels less than 4 years out, the hotel may miss a substantial amount of business coming to the city. In this case, the hotel should have the stiffer parts of the penalty clause in effect from 3 and fewer years out. It might read this way:

Should ABC Company cancel its program in whole or in part within the following time frame, it agrees to reimburse the hotel based on the following stated schedule:

| Time Frame | Cancellation Fee |
|---|---|
| 5–4 years | 0 |
| 4–3 years | $22,500 (10 %) |
| 3–2 years | $112,500 (50 %) |
| 2–0 years | $225,000 (100 %) |

The hotel should base the percentages of total room revenue in each cancellation segment to reflect the booking cycle and what is potentially lost as the arrival time approaches. The preceding sample cancellation clause only considers the revenue lost in guest rooms. Due to potential revenue losses on the catering and outlet/ancillary sides of the success triangle, additional cancellation revenue may be included.

**Attrition Clause.** An **attrition clause** is similar to a cancellation clause in that the contract is structured to reimburse the hotel in the event that the business does not come to fruition. It is not intended to recoup losses from canceled business but rather to regain losses from lower-than-expected revenue. The difference here is that an attrition clause covers slippage (or lackluster group performance) of business that comes to the hotel.

If the ABC Company from the preceding example arrived with 150 rooms per night versus the 300 it contracted for, it would provide significantly less revenue than expected. Most salespeople anticipate 10 to 15 percent slippage, not the 50 percent slippage in this example. What can be done in this case?

An attrition clause imposes a scale of penalty that is relative to the slippage that may occur. Using the ongoing example, the ABC Company, which contracted for 300 rooms for 5 nights at $150 per night, arrives with 150 rooms. This means the hotel will lose $112,500 to poor group performance. An attrition clause like the following one will recoup the hotel's losses:

Should the ABC Company reduce its overall room commitment or utilization by more than 15 percent (every group should be extended 5–15% slippage as a professional courtesy), it agrees to reimburse the hotel X dollars.

The attrition clause can be set on a chronological scale that allows no penalty far from the scheduled arrival date and increases the penalty as the date approaches. The attrition clause can be explained to the client as a tool for tracking numbers. If the hotel allows the standard 15 percent slippage without penalty, the group could reduce its block far enough in advance so as not to adversely affect the hotel's booking cycle. In this example, the ABC Company contact could reduce the group's block by 10 percent 12 months out and by another 5 percent 6 months out. (These time frames may not be realistic for a hotel with a 4-year booking cycle, but they allow for small enough reductions far enough in advance that the sales office has time to recover somewhat. The salesperson must ensure that these two reduction deadlines are realistic for both the hotel and the client.)

To ensure full coverage for the hotel, the attrition clause must be used with, not in lieu of, a cancellation clause. Wary clients can be reassured that the hotel is giving them two opportunities to adjust their blocks without penalty.

**Sliding Scale.** The **sliding scale** is similar to the attrition clause in that its purpose is to protect the hotel from lackluster group performance. The sliding scale is intended to be used primarily with space-intensive groups. The discussions on space intensity and room-to-space ratio apply here. If a hotel's meeting space is completely booked, it cannot realistically add group rooms because group bookings usually have corresponding meetings. Therefore, to maximize rooms and space, a hotel might institute a sliding scale that ties group room performance to meeting room rental. To use the ABC Company example again, the ABC has booked 300 rooms for 5 nights, for 1,500 total room nights. The hotel has committed all its meeting space. (If, for the sake of discussion, the hotel's group ceiling is 300 rooms a night, this group would seem a perfect fit.) The sliding scale clause should look like this:

It is the policy of the XYZ Hotel to charge for meeting space. The room rental charge is based on your projected meal functions and room night actualization. The following scale applies:

| Slippage (Percent) | Total Room Nights Used | Meeting Room Rental (Per Day) |
|---|---|---|
| 15 | 1,275–1,500 | Waived |
| 20 | 1,200–1,274 | $ 2,000 |
| 40 | 900–1,199 | $ 8,000 |
| 60 | 600– 899 | $12,000 |

The numbers may seem high to a prospective client, but that is their intention. The preceding example shows the client that he or she is guaranteed free meeting space (if so agreed in the contract) only if he or she meets his or her commitment in sleeping rooms. This kind of scale often causes clients to reexamine their projections and guest room estimates. Clients might ask to reduce the blocks in their contracts. If so, the salesperson is obligated to reevaluate their business and their attractiveness based on the new criteria.

The salesperson's response to a client who chooses to reduce his or her room block commitment should be to inform the client that additional rooms are not guaranteed available should his or her numbers return to initial projections. Sliding scale amounts and slippage percentages differ based on the hotel's policy and booking cycle, but the aim remains the same: Hold the client as accountable as the client holds the hotel.

Catering contracts can use variations of the sliding scale that tie food and beverage performance to room rental. For example, if a group contracts for 5 days of meetings with breakfast, lunch, and dinner each day but only takes continental breakfast and coffee breaks, the hotel may lose considerable revenue. The hotel can set the sliding scale to correspond to scheduled food functions or estimated food and beverage revenue. A resort can also tie in proposed golf tournaments, tennis usage, and any other ancillary revenue source that stands to lose revenue due to lackluster group performance.

## DEPARTMENTAL RELATIONSHIPS

After completing a sale, the hotel salesperson's role changes. A salesperson becomes accountable to the client to whom he or she has committed a specific level of services on the hotel's behalf, as well as to the hotel to ensure that everything that was committed to the client is shared with the departments that must deliver.

The level of communication that is needed to establish rapport with external clients (those who purchase a hotel's products or services) equals the communication that is needed to establish rapport with internal clients (those who deliver on the sale). Hotel salespeople (group, catering, and transient) must understand that without a solid comfort and trust level with both types of client, they will fail.

For a hotel, communication skills are as important internally as they are externally. Each salesperson has a certain level of mandated internal operational responsibility that is based on his or her sales discipline and hotel type. The successful salesperson communicates a group's needs to the rest of the hotel effectively. This communication begins with the sales office. The process of transmitting the needs of a group to the hotel begins when a group salesperson communicates with a catering or a convention service person. The documents used to spread the group's "message" throughout the hotel are called internal operations documents.

**Communication within the Sales Office.** Chapter 1 examined the three ways to deploy a hotel sales office. The three-tiered, two-tiered, and two-tiered-modified methods of deployment each requires different operational responsibilities from the salesperson. To review, Figure 5–1 illustrates the flow of a piece of business from booking to arrival.

Two-tiered deployment (Figure 5–2) exists in hotels with no convention service departments. In these hotels, the catering department assumes the servicing and menu-planning roles of all group business, as well as the booking of all local catering.

The modified two-tiered deployment method (Figure 5–3) employs both the catering and convention service departments. However, the catering department does not play a role in group servicing. The convention service department does all the menu planning and group servicing, while the catering department works strictly on local catering.

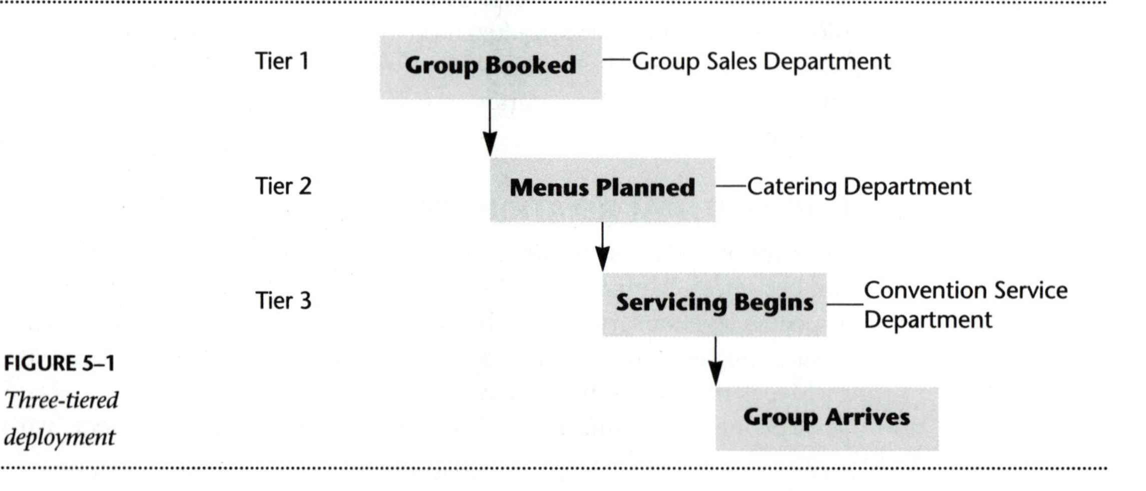


**FIGURE 5–1**
*Three-tiered deployment*

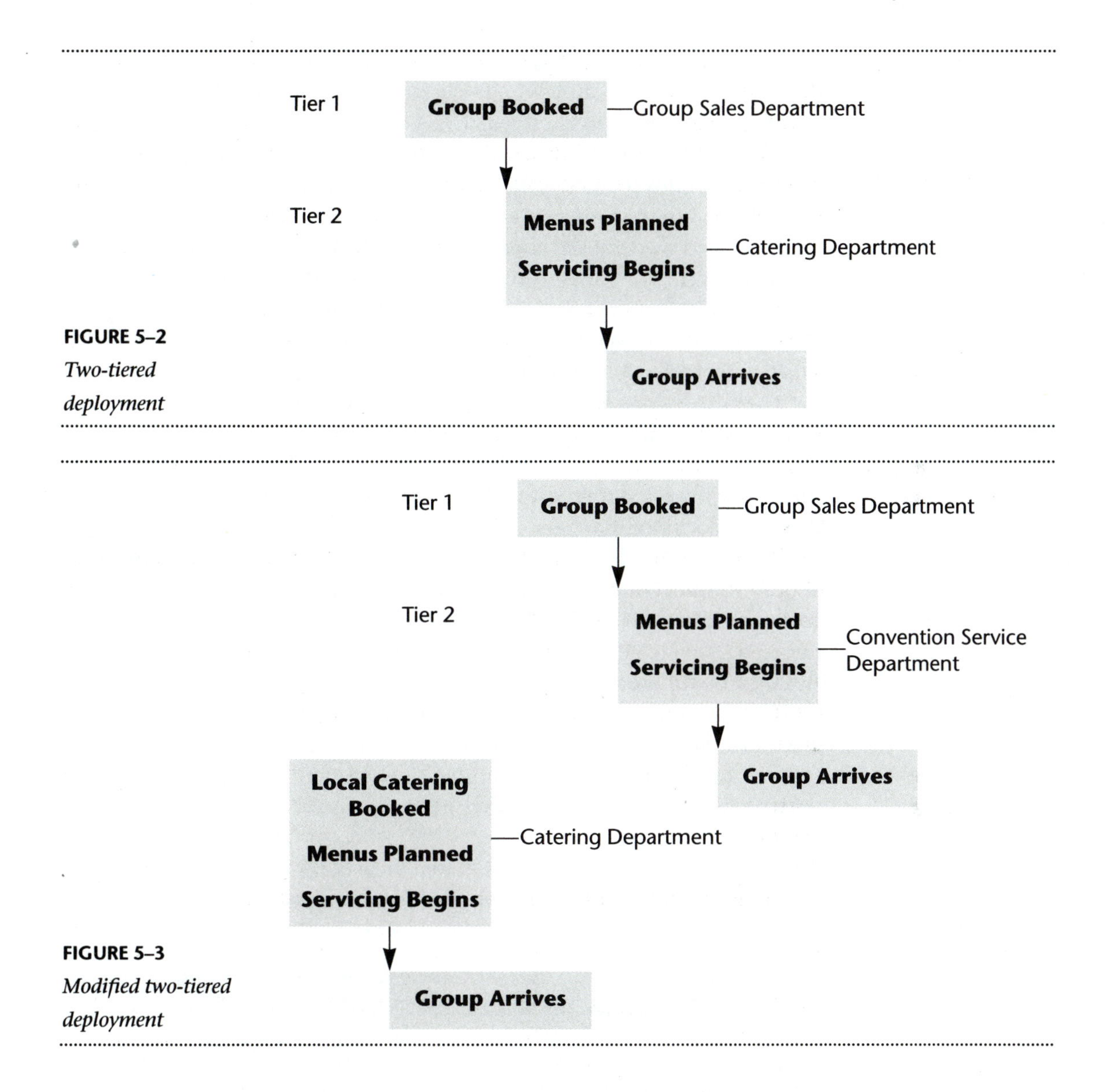


**FIGURE 5–2**
*Two-tiered deployment*



**FIGURE 5–3**
*Modified two-tiered deployment*

As each of the preceding figures illustrates, the hotel sales office must effectively communicate within itself before involving other hotel departments. The most important interoffice relationship is that of group room salesperson to the catering or convention service person. The communication process begins with the group turnover, which was looked at earlier. Again, to review, the management of group servicing at any hotel begins with a process of communication between the room salespeople and the catering and/or convention service department regarding specific group details. This method of communication is called "turnover." **Turnover** is the process by which a group salesperson makes the catering and/or convention service department aware of the details of a group. Because the salesperson who is involved in selling rooms is most often the first hotel employee to communicate with a group, and thus knows more about the group than anyone at the hotel, the turnover process must be as complete and as detailed as possible. Group turnover is the method by which a catering or convention service manager becomes aware of a particular group, and the details of their program to that point. Properly done, the turnover gives an "at a glance" look at where the group is at this point, as well as valuable information on the client and contact(s).

The turnover process should be completed with ample time for the catering/convention service manager to prepare. A large convention should be turned over no later than 1 year out. This time is needed to coordinate the hotel's efforts on a group as well as to manage the catering/convention service manager's slate of upcoming groups.

The responsibilities of the group salesperson within his or her office are important in that nothing happens within a hotel if this communication and rapport are not established first. Most internal operational documents, which are addressed in the next section, are generated during this initial turnover process.

The catering and/or convention service people who handle a group after turnover hold the success or failure of a program in their hands. Beyond group turnover, the interface between the group side and the catering/convention service side contributes to the success or failure of a program.

*Sales Office Interface.* The antiquated view of the interface between the group side and the catering/convention service side of a sales office incor-

**KEYS TO FOSTERING THE INTEROFFICE SALES PARTNERSHIP**

**Group Sales**

- Group turnover documents should be completed in a timely and detailed fashion.
- If food and beverage needs are known (i.e., meal preferences or budget), communicating them will save the other person time.
- Group salespeople who can make themselves available to help coordinate a group while they are in house will relieve some pressure from their partners.

**Catering/Convention Service**

- Unexpected decreases in sleeping room usage should be communicated as soon as possible.
- If function space needs change, or if they were not correctly blocked initially, the catering/convention service person should attempt to rectify the situation quietly.
- At the conclusion of a successful function, the catering convention service person should start the resolicitation process for the group salesperson.

porated an "us" versus "them" mentality when communicating to and about a group. Because of the differing priorities of each, the industry nicknamed the two "foodies" and "roomies" respectively.

Aside from the obvious differences in job roles, the ultimate goals for both are the same. If the clients are happy, both sides win. The best interests of a client are served when the catering/convention service managers can get their sales partners to work together.

Understanding the concerns of both sides of the sales office goes a long way toward dispelling stereotypes. A group salesperson may know group details that are not included in a turnover. The catering/convention salesperson may discover details that were never revealed to the group salesperson. If the two sides can achieve a level of comfort and trust in each other, they can foster a relationship that can evolve into a partnership.

## INTERNAL OPERATIONAL DOCUMENTS

The operational responsibilities of a group salesperson do not end with the sales office. Because most of a group's hotel details are uncovered during the qualification process, the total hotel impact of a group salesperson can be extensive. A typical group booking impacts many different departments (Figure 5–4).

Each department relies on the message communicated from the sales office to understand its role in the success of a group. As was just reviewed, the message is first relayed to a catering/convention service person. That person, in turn, relays the message throughout the hotel. The documents used to transmit this message are called internal operations documents.

In most cases, except for meetings managers who handle both the sales and catering aspects of small groups, group salespeople do not create the internal operations documents. Some hotels, however, require their salespeople to retain the responsibility of transmitting some of the groups' details through internal operations documents. It is important for all salespeople, whether they create the internal documents or not, to be able to read and interpret these documents to ensure their understanding of the group (from qualifying) is being transmitted properly. These documents include banquet event orders, group resumes, and internal memos.

**Banquet Event Orders.** The **banquet event order (BEO)**, sometimes called the "banquet prospectus" or the "catering event sheet," is an important document in that it deals with all the nonsleeping room needs of a group. It is a fundamental document that communicates to a hotel's internal departments the details of any function. Every aspect of a function, from the name of the group to its meal choices, times of events, and prices all must be spelled out to ensure that what the salesperson and the client have agreed on is communicated.

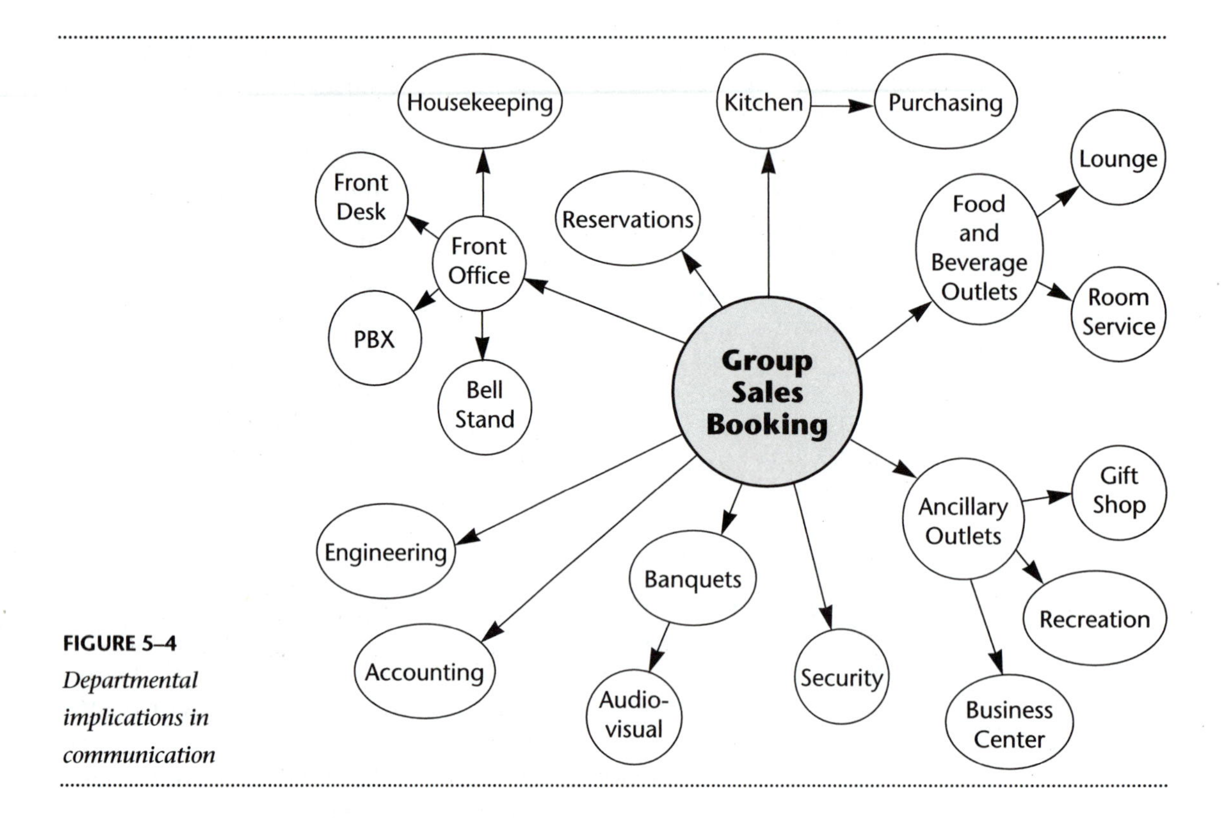


**FIGURE 5–4**
*Departmental implications in communication*

The BEO format differs from hotel to hotel. Its function can also differ from hotel to hotel. In most hotels, the BEO also serves as a contract, thereby becoming an internal and an external form of communication. These hotels require the client's signature on the BEO as a confirmation of the details it contains. Other hotels use a separate catering contract, or letter of intent, to confirm the program in question.

The BEO should be completed in ample time for the internal departments to prepare. The departments must allow enough time for the kitchen to purchase all the food and ensure that kitchen staff have no questions or menu suggestions. The banquet floor managers must schedule appropriate staff levels. Early completion of BEOs can help avoid double booking of function rooms and even allow all the catering/convention service managers time to move rooms for efficiency. As a general rule, BEOs should be completed at least 3 weeks before function dates, further supporting the need of the salesperson to complete the turnover in a timely fashion.

When the BEO is completed, it is ready for distribution. A BEO should be distributed to the appropriate operational departments at the 3-week point. These departments can include:

| | |
|---|---|
| Kitchen/Executive Chef | Director of Food and Beverage/ Director of Catering |
| Banquet Manager/Captains | Purchasing |
| AV | Stewarding |
| Accounting/Credit Manager | Engineering |

The BEO should also be distributed to a central catering office file that is broken down by day so that the salesperson can look at upcoming functions.

Every hotel that uses the BEO for internal communication uses some type of daily review meeting to discuss upcoming BEOs. Some combination of department representatives on the distribution list and the catering/convention service managers responsible for the upcoming BEOs get together to review the BEOs and anticipate any possible challenges. The meetings often review the BEOs for the following 2 days; Fridays review 3 days. This means that most BEOs are reviewed twice, but all details are scrutinized.

Whatever external uses a hotel has for the BEO, the internal function remains the same: communication. Figure 5–5 is a sample BEO that highlights areas with which all hotel sales personnel must be familiar.

**XYZ Hotel and Towers**
**Banquet Event Order**

**BEO 1234**
**DATE SUBMITTED:** 12/5/98

**SALES FILE NA555**
**CONV. SERV. FILE 1232**
**CATERING FILE 0001**
**PAGE 1 of 2**

**FUNCTION DAY/DATE:** Sunday, February 14, 1999
**ORGANIZATION:** Gotham City Valentine Couples Group
**POST AS:** Valentine's Day Dance

**BILLING ADDRESS:** 123 Lovers Lane, Gotham City, NY 01234
**BOOKING CONTACT:** Ms. Jane Doe
**ON-SITE CONTACT(S):** Mr. John Q. Public
**PHONE:** (202) 555-1521
**FAX:** (202) 555-1522
**SALES MANAGER:** Mike Smith **CONV. SERV. MANAGER:** Andrew Jones
**CATERING MANAGER:** Janet Hill
**ATTENDEES EXPECTED:** 275 **GUARANTEED:** 290 **SET** 305

**FIGURE 5–5**
*Banquet event order*

**BEO Continued on Next Page** **PAGE 1 of 2**

**BEO 1234 Continued from Previous Page** **PAGE 2 of 2**

| **FUNCTION TIME** | **FUNCTION** | **ROOM** |
|---|---|---|
| 3:00 P.M.–6:00 P.M. | Room Set Up | Ballroom |
| 6:30 P.M.–7:30 P.M. | Reception | Ballroom Foyer |
| 7:30 P.M.–12 midnight | Dance | Ballroom |
| 3:00 P.M. | Room Set Up<br>**No Food or Beverage Needed** | Ballroom |
| 6:30 P.M. | 3 Host Bars* | Ballroom Foyer |

House Brand Liquor @ $3.00 ++ per serving
Premium Brand Liquor @ $4.00 ++ per serving
Top-Shelf Liquor @ $5.00 ++ per serving
House White/Red Wine @ $2.50 ++ per serving
Premium and Imported Beer @ $4.50 ++ per bottle
Assorted Soft Drinks @ $2.00 ++ per serving
*Bartender fee of $35.00 + assessed per bar, should sales not exceed $300.00 each

International and Domestic Cheese Display
Garnished with Fresh Fruit and Served with Assorted Crackers
@ $4.50 ++ per person

"Sweetheart" Dessert Station to Include:
Mini Raspberry Cheesecake, Chocolate-Dipped Strawberries
Assorted Valentine Candies
Heart-Shaped Cookies with Red, White, and Pink Icing
Freshly Brewed Coffee, Decaffeinated Coffee, and Tea Service
@ $10.00 ++ per person

| | | |
|---|---|---|
| 7:30 P.M. | Valentine Dance<br>**No Food or Beverage Needed** | Ballroom |

| | |
|---|---|
| **Note to Banquet Captain:** | The theme for this evening is Valentine's Day. All appropriate decorations should include red and white. |
| **Note to Banquet Kitchen:** | Please ensure food items are replenished continually. |
| **Reception Setup:** | Cocktail Lounge-Style Seating<br>Skirted Buffet Tables<br>3 Banquet Bars with Bar Backs<br>Valentine-Themed Decorations and Props |
| **Dance Setup:** | Skirted Disc Jockey Table in Center/Front of Room<br>Dance Floor |
| **Decorations/ Special Arrangements:** | Additional Decorations Supplied by Client<br>Disc Jockey Provided by Client |
| **AV Requirements:** | Please supply power cords and outlets for disc jockey.<br>Please adjust ballroom lighting. |
| **Room Rental:** | Waived |
| **Billing Arrangements:** | Advance Deposit Received<br>Incidental Payments at Conclusion of Function |

++ Indicates 20% Service Charge and 10% Sales Tax Will Be Added
\+ Indicates 10% Sales Tax Will Be Added

**Approval Signature:**
*If the Preceding Meets with Your Approval, Please Sign One Copy and Return.*

**FIGURE 5–5 (*cont.*)**
*Banquet event order*

This sample BEO shows a fictitious Valentine's Day dance function. The layout and order of topics may differ from hotel to hotel, but the same fundamental details will be included.

**XYZ Hotel and Towers**
**Banquet Event Order**

| | |
|---|---|
| **BEO 1234** | **SALES FILE NA555** |
| **DATE SUBMITTED:** 12/5/98 | **CONV. SERV. FILE 1232** |
| | **CATERING FILE 0001** |

*BEO Number.* This number should serve as an internal control number for all BEOs. Each BEO should have a unique number. It is useful for tracking purposes.

*Date Submitted.* The date the BEO was created and distributed should be marked so that all the appropriate internal departments know it was submitted in a timely manner.

*File Number.* Here the listings of group file numbers serve a few purposes. First, at a glance, anyone would know if this BEO applied to local catering or a sleeping room–related group. In the example, the function was a convention group because the all three file numbers were listed. This hotel uses the three-tiered deployment: the sales, catering, and convention service representatives are listed. The other purpose for listing the file numbers is to give the manager in charge a little backup. If the representatives were not available for some reason, another manager could pick up the appropriate file and find out what he or she must know about the group.

| | |
|---|---|
| **FUNCTION DAY/DATE:** | Sunday, February 14, 1999 |
| **ORGANIZATION:** | Gotham City Valentine Couples Group |
| **POST AS:** | Valentine's Day Dance |
| **BILLING ADDRESS:** | 123 Lovers Lane, Gotham City, NY 01234 |
| **BOOKING CONTACT:** | Ms. Jane Doe |
| **ON-SITE CONTACT(S):** | Mr. John Q. Public |
| **PHONE:** | (202) 555-1521 |
| **FAX:** | (202) 555-1522 |

*Function Day/Date.* Shows the day of the function.

*Organization.* Lists the name of the organization that booked the function.

*Post As.* Often, as in this example, the group that booked the function wants to post the name of its function differently. Posting is the act of naming the group throughout the hotel. The readerboards in any hotel list the daily events as the groups want them posted. Attendees often look for the posted name on readerboards.

*Billing Address.* Lists where the final bill is to go. It is listed here so that the banquet captain who prepares the bill at the conclusion of the function can include the appropriate information.

*Contact Names.* Informs the internal departments about who is in charge of the event. Many times, the person who booked the function is not the same as who is on site during the function. The hotel staff look much more efficient if they know for whom to ask.

**SALES MANAGER:** Mike Smith **CONV. SERV. MANAGER:** Andrew Jones
**CATERING MANAGER:** Janet Hill
**ATTENDEES EXPECTED:** 275 **GUARANTEED:** 290 **SET** 305

*Managers' Names.* Similar to listing the file numbers, this section of the BEO has a dual purpose. First, it lists the manager(s) who booked the group. The hotel can tell here if the BEO applies to local or group catering functions by which type of salesperson is listed. In some hotels, the salesperson who created the BEO (either a catering or convention service manager) will initial by his or her name to approve the BEO and authorize it for distribution.

*Attendees Expected.* This figure represents the initial number of people for whom the function was booked.

*Guaranteed.* The "guarantee" for a function is very important in the hotel industry. Every full-service hotel requires some type of advance notice from a group as to how many people it guarantees will attend. This guarantee is reinforced by the fact that most hotels bill the client for this number of attendees as a minimum. Most hotels require a guaranteed number of attendees from a client 48 to 72 working hours before the function. This is vital for food purchasing and staffing levels. If a group came into a hotel with significantly more people than expected, the guarantee gives the hotel some time to accommodate drastically different numbers.

*SET Number.* The set number serves a contingency purpose. Because many intangibles affect the turnout of a function, most hotels set functions for 5 percent over the guaranteed number. This is to accommodate any last-minute attendees the client did not expect. Typically, the room will be set for, and the kitchen prepared to serve, this extra 5 percent. The banquet captain in charge of the function will do a "head count" once everyone is seated so he or she can inform the kitchen if that extra 5 percent or more of food is needed. Hotels should never bill for this overset, as it is sometimes called, unless the numbers of attendees dictate.

| FUNCTION TIME | FUNCTION | ROOM |
|---|---|---|
| 3:00 P.M.–6:00 P.M. | Room Set Up | Ballroom |
| 6:30 P.M.–7:30 P.M. | Reception | Ballroom Foyer |
| 7:30 P.M.–12 midnight | Dance | Ballroom |

*Summary Information*. This area provides an at-a-glance look at the BEO and its contents. Each function, time, and room is listed in chronological order. This information is usually posted with the "post as" name of the group on the hotel's readerboards.

The middle section of the BEO is called the body, or agenda specifics. This is where the BEO creator must clearly and articulately list *everything*. Again, in chronological order, each food item and service requirement is listed as it applies to the event. This is where prices and amounts are spelled out.

If an event does not need food (as in this example for the dance setup and the dance), it should be noted on the BEO as "No Food or Beverage Needed." The kitchen and/or banquet staff are trained to correlate functions and their possible food needs with the BEO information. By using this disclaimer, the BEO informs the appropriate operational departments of the client's questions and need or desire for food and/or service. This disclaimer reassures hotel staff that there will be no last-minute changes.

If the BEO is longer than one page, as is the example, it should be noted on both pages like this:

**BEO Continued on Next Page** **PAGE 1 of 2**

and

**BEO 1234 Continued from Previous Page** **PAGE 2 of 2**

Noting that the BEO continues on the next page triggers readers to look at the attached page. It also helps them to remember to complete all BEO requirements. The notation on the second page tells the reader who may pick up the second page of the BEO only that he or she is missing the first page. Listing the BEO number helps readers find the corresponding first page.

**Note to Banquet Captain:** Please note the theme for this evening is Valentine's Day. All appropriate decorations should include red and white.

**Note to Banquet Kitchen:** Please ensure food items are replenished continually.

*Notes*. In this area of the BEO, the salesperson in charge takes the time to highlight certain details that he or she wants specific individuals or departments to address. The example included "Notes" to the banquet captain and the kitchen that were important to the success of the function or to the client. BEOs can include notes to any department or individuals who are part of the BEO distribution. These notes should be followed up by catering/convention service person and again in the BEO review meeting to ensure everyone understands the point the hotel staff are trying to make.

*Event Setup.* Here, the BEO speaks to the banquet floor staff directly. This area should list the specific room set requirements for each event listed earlier in the summary information on the BEO. The example BEO listed setup requirements for the reception and the dance because they were included on the same BEO. The room setup (at 3:00 P.M.) required nothing from the hotel, so the BEO did not need to dictate setup.

The BEO should be thought of a functional document. The BEO creator should write it as if he or she were doing the setup. The BEO should be read over to ensure it can be read and interpreted by anyone.

*Decorations/Special Arrangements.* This section is sometimes called the "etc." section. This is where a salesperson makes everyone aware of any outside additions to the function. If the client was to use any outside vendors, or if the client brings special additions, like decorations, as in the example, the BEO would list them here. This section should list everything the hotel is not supplying, like a disc jockey (DJ), production company, musicians, florist, or some other service provider of whom the hotel should be aware.

*AV Requirements.* This area is important in that the AV department usually does not look anywhere else on the BEO. Nothing else on the BEO applies, unless a "Note" is addressed to the AV staff. All relevant details and requirements are listed here.

**Room Rental** Waived

**Billing Arrangements** Advance Deposit Received
Incidental Payments at Conclusion of Function

*Room Rental.* This is the part of the BEO where the hotel lists the charge for the use of the function room. Sometimes called "Set Up Fee" or "Function Space Charge," the room rental can contribute a lot to the profitability of a function. In this example, the rental was waived because the group was spending a large amount on the function in terms of food and beverage.

*Billing Arrangements.* This section is arguably the most important in that it involves what the hotel is in business for: money. The salesperson wants to inform all interested parties, namely the banquet captains who make up the bills, the accounting department that processes them, and the clients who must pay them, of their understanding of the billing process. There are typically only three options available to a client in terms of billing: direct billing, advance deposit/prepayment, and payment upon conclusion of function.

Direct billing involves sending the bill to the client for payment, assuming the accounting department has approved the client's credit history. With advance deposit/prepayment, the client sends money ahead of time to cover the expenses of the function. Sometimes this method is used because the client/organization's credit history is so poor that the controller denied them direct billing. The only drawback to this payment method is that it does not cover incidental or unplanned charges. It should be used exclusively in instances where the purchased food/beverage amounts are fixed. It can, however, be used with other payment methods if costs are not fixed. In the example, the group sent in an advance deposit, but the BEO states that the food is to be replenished continually and there are hosted bars. Therefore, there is no way to know the exact total charge ahead of time.

The group in the example supplemented its advance deposit with the third payment method: payment upon conclusion of function. Here, the total unpaid charges are settled after all amounts are tallied. Most often it is the banquet captain's job to ensure the bill is correct and the money is collected. It should be stressed again that the billing requirements must be accurate. If the banquet captain read that the group should be direct billed and the salesperson mistakenly omitted the need to collect at the event's conclusion, the hotel could go unpaid.

++ Indicates 20% Service Charge and 10% Sales Tax Will Be Added.
\+ Indicates 10% Sales Tax Will Be Added.

*"Plus/Plus."* A common practice in the industry is to add a service charge and tax to the prices of food/beverage and some services. Most hotels outline this policy by adding one or two "pluses" after each quoted price. The term "plus/plus" indicates that the price must have both the service charge and the sales tax added. If a price were to be quoted with only one plus, only the tax was added. Percentages differ from hotel to hotel. The opposite of this pricing strategy is to quote prices inclusively. Inclusive pricing simply means that the salesperson has built the service charge and tax into the listed price. Some clients prefer to have all costs outlined up front, without the need to add further charges. If a hotel uses plus/plus pricing, it should be explained on the menus and the BEOs clearly.

---

**Approval Signature:**
*If the Preceding Meets with Your Approval, Please Sign One Copy and Return.*

*Signature Line.* The last detail applies only if the BEO is an external confirmation document. If BEOs are sent to clients for approval, the signature line should indicate that signing this document indicates agreement with its contents. A signed BEO prevents clients from saying they "didn't expect this menu" or "these are not the agreed upon prices." If signed BEOs are required, clients should receive copies for their records.

# *Industry Perspective*

## "Group Billing and Its Impact on the Hotel"

*Dawn Hill*
*Assistant Controller*
*Marriott Corporation*

The importance of group billing, that is, the method of payment by which a group pays for its rooms and/or banquet functions, is often misunderstood by salespeople. Hotels are in business to make money, just like all other for-profit enterprises. Timely and complete payment of group accounts is vital to the financial health of any hotel.

A hotel has costs and financial obligations, just like the organizations it books. Cash flow, that is, the incoming and outgoing measurement of revenue, dictates how well a hotel meets its obligations. These obligations can include labor costs, food costs, insurance, taxes, ownership payments, capital improvements, supplies, advertising, franchise fees, and others. The incoming cash flow, or revenue due a hotel, is called accounts receivable. Accounts receivable play the most important role in meeting the preceding financial obligations. In any given hotel, the bulk of accounts receivable is made up of group and/or catering accounts. It is for this reason that the billing of these accounts is so important.

The most common method of payment for groups is direct billing. This option extends credit to a group under the assumption that the group will pay all hotel costs it incurs in a set time frame. For this credit to be extended, the client must complete the direct billing application thoroughly. It is the salesperson's job to make sure that all information is provided and relayed to the accounting department in a timely manner. For example, hotel references and bank references must be checked by the hotel before extending credit. An organization with a history of poor payments at other hotels, or one with too little money in the bank to cover the upcoming function, may be denied credit. The salesperson must not be timid in determining the method of payment early in the qualifying process. If billing problems are addressed early enough, other arrangements can be made. The most important thing to remember when determining direct billing status is that credit is a privilege, not a right. Groups who have direct billed at other hotels should not automatically assume that credit will be extended.

The group salesperson should understand that booking groups who do not pay well affects the accounting department. Most hotel accounting departments are measured on how quickly they make payments. The age of the accounts receivable (an average of the time all receivables have been outstanding) is an important measurement of cash flow performance.

In summary, salespeople who book groups without sufficiently considering the groups' payment abilities may hurt rather than help the hotel. A salesperson can book a record number of groups, but if the groups do not pay, they are of no use.

**Group Resumes.** When discussing internal communication forms, an important document that pertains exclusively to groups, the group resume, should be reviewed. Earlier in this section, it was mentioned that some hotels require the group salesperson to create some of the internal operational documents. The **group resume** is typically that document, because it incorporates the sleeping room component of a group.

The group resume, sometimes called the "group profile" or the "group cover sheet," serves a purpose similar to that of the BEO in that it communicates to other hotel departments specific information regarding a group. The biggest difference between the two is that the group resume is distributed to all departments, not just those concerned with executing functions and events. Departments like housekeeping and the front desk are included.

The group resume informs the hotel of the size of the group, the number of overnight rooms, the number of on-property functions, and so on. It should be completed far enough in advance of the group's arrival (like the BEO) to ensure that all affected departments have time to staff and prepare appropriately. Many hotels review the group resume in meetings of departmental managers. The preconvention meeting or **precon** is similar to that of the BEO meeting in that all departments review the information at hand. The biggest difference is that the precon is dedicated to one group resume and group clients often attend to review the upcoming events with the hotel.

Group resumes are vital to predicting occupancy as well as revenue numbers. The resumes help departments that deal with guests on the "front line," like the front desk, because they can provide answers to many questions.

The format of the group resume differs from hotel to hotel, as does BEO format. The main document of the group resume should contain as much information about the group as possible. Ideally, the resume should be no more than two pages. Because the group resume contains sleeping room information and catering function details, portions of it often look like portions of the group turnover document and the BEO. At minimum, the group resume could contain the following information:

---

**XYZ Hotel Group Resume** Today's Date:
Group Name: Dates of Function:
Contact Name: Address:
Telephone: Fax:
**SALES MANAGER:** **CONV. SERV. MANAGER:**

**Room Rate:** ___ Single ___ Double ___ Triple ___ Quad ___ Suites

**Group Billing:** ___ Sign All Charges ___ Room/Tax to Master
___ Individuals on Own

---

The preceding three lines take a quick look at the room rate structure and room billing.

---

**Current Room Block: ____ (date)**

| Day/Date | Day/Date | Day/Date | Day/Date | Day/Date | Total |
|---|---|---|---|---|---|
| ____ | ____ | ____ | ____ | ____ | ____ |

**Pick Up As of Today: ____ (date)**

| Day/Date | Day/Date | Day/Date | Day/Date | Day/Date | Total |
|---|---|---|---|---|---|
| ____ | ____ | ____ | ____ | ____ | ____ |

---

Here the resume shows the room block and room pick up of the group at the time the group resume was generated.

---

| VIP | Arrival | Departure | Room Type | Billing | Amenity |
|---|---|---|---|---|---|
| M/M Jones | 2/2/99 | 2/4/99 | Suite | Sign All Charges | Yes |
| Ms. R. Smith | 2/3/99 | 2/4/99 | King | On Own | No |
| Mr. A Willis | 2/3/99 | 2/4/99 | Twin | On Own | No |

---

This section of the resume is important in that it lets the hotel identify the VIPs of the group. Typically, the VIPs in this listing are the on-site contacts, speakers, and assorted "important people" who are deemed important by the group. It is a good idea to send these VIPs amenities or some other type of welcome gift upon their arrivals.

*Agenda Summary.* Here the group resume should list briefly the catering function agenda of the group in a way similar to the "Summary Agenda" format of the BEO. The difference here is the resume should not provide more detail than a summary of events. Menu selections and other function-related information are reflected in the BEO. The agenda summary might look like this:

Monday, February 15, 1999
8:00 A.M.–5:00 P.M. Meeting
6:00 P.M.–7:00 P.M. Reception

Tuesday, February 16, 1999
8:00 A.M.–12:00 P.M. Meeting
12:00 P.M.–1:00 P.M. Lunch

Some hotels attach all BEOs to the group resume because they adhere to the notion that there is no such thing as too much information. While some argue that departments like housekeeping do not need BEOs, others insist that the more people in the hotel who know what is going on, the more attention the group can receive from the total hotel.

The rest of the group resume should provide each hotel department with any specifics it needs. Most resumes do not have pertinent information for every hotel department, however. Which departments require notification depends largely on the nature of the group. The following shows what each department might see in different scenarios:

Front Desk
- Major arrival time: 6:00 P.M., scattered departures.
- Bus arrival on second night at 3:00 P.M.
- Please key pack and preregister all VIPs.

Reservations
- Expect last-minute calls due to slow pickup.
- Please be aware of the suite reserved for M/M Jones.

Housekeeping
- Turn-down service each night for all attendees.
- Please make sure all rooms are ready for the bus arrival on the second night.
- Please deep clean the suite for M/M Jones.

Banquets
- Hang banner during meeting.
- Store materials for presentations in Security.

Room Service

- Please note amenity delivery for M/M Jones.
- Expect late-night orders on first night as the group will return from activity without eating dinner.

Restaurants

- Late-night dinner possibilities on first night.
- Please set up breakfast buffet on second morning as the group has no meal scheduled.
- Many group members are vegetarians. Suggest vegetarian daily specials.

Kitchen

- See preceding notes for restaurants.

Hotel Operator

- Wake-up calls each morning at 6:30 A.M.
- Expect high volume of messages during the meeting.

Security

- Please deliver materials being stored to Banquets before meeting starts.
- Valuable presentation equipment is being used in meeting room. Please check on it in the evening.

Accounting

- Please note billing requirements.

**Internal Memos.** A viable form of internal written communication that covers topics not related to BEOs or group resumes is the internal memo. The memo can play a vital part in getting a salesperson's job done effectively. Memos can be used to follow up on verbal conversations. The memo is also useful in reinforcing issues addressed in other documents, like BEOs and group resumes. Special items of interest to other departments can be highlighted with a memo. A memo is also a good form of communication to use with sales office peers and superiors for documentation purposes. Announcements, policy changes, and other important bits of information can be shared with a memo.

The easiest way to write a memo is to organize thoughts using the following three-step formula:

1. Communicate the purpose.
2. Relay the supporting circumstances.
3. Suggest the proposed action, if appropriate.

These steps translate into three paragraphs that begin with these, or similar, phrases:

"I am writing because . . ."
"The facts are . . ."
"I propose that we . . ."

This approach works well, because it is nearly impossible to complete the phrases without stating the memo's purpose, the circumstances, and the action needed. After writing the first draft using the three preceding phrases, the writer may want to tailor the phrases to his or her style. Hotel staff should avoid using the memo as a substitute for personal communication. As has been reviewed, the memo is a terrific follow-up to an initial personal contact, but many in the hotel industry employ the "management by memo" philosophy, which entails communication almost entirely via memos. The latter can lead to ineffective communication, because an overwhelming number of memos from one person tend not to be reviewed with the same scrutiny as others.

Memos should not be used to voice opinions or invoke change. Memos should not serve as barriers. If someone does not have the courage to state something to another face-to-face, it probably does not belong in a memo. Following is a common memo format:

XYZ HOTEL MEMORANDUM

Date: (Today's date)
To: (Addressee)
From: (Individual or group name)
Re: (Subject of the memo)
cc: (Names of those to be copied on this memo)

[Body of the memo]

Memos typically do not end with signature lines, so they are not signed at their bottoms. Instead, most individuals who generate memos initial next to their names on the "From" line to indicate that they approve of the memos and their contents.

An effective method for ensuring that important messages are communicated internally is the three-layered approach. If upcoming operational requirements are intricate or out of the ordinary for a hotel, a salesperson would need to guarantee that the message is communicated, understood, and completed. The three-layered approach employs different methods of communication, but the end goals are the same.

The first step in this approach is to contact needed personnel/departments by phone. The salesperson should communicate clearly what is needed and when. Written messages or voice mail should not be left for operational personnel, because large operational departments often have many different people coming and going throughout the day and night.

The salesperson should try again and again by phone until the right person hears the information.

The second step is to follow up the phone call with a memo or E-mail. The salesperson can more easily recap the conversation and highlight important issues when the receiver has the memo in front of him or her. To add a level of impact for the receiver, the salesperson can "cc" or copy the receiver's immediate supervisor. While the issue may not impact the receiver's boss, the recipient may give the issue more attention knowing his or her boss is aware of the issue.

The third step is to personally follow up as the due date approaches. A few days before a major group arrives, or a large dinner function is held, a salesperson should visit the operational departments that will be called upon to perform. These face-to-face meetings will cement commitments and help avoid misunderstandings.

## CUSTOMER SERVICE

All people in the hotel industry must continually remind themselves that, without satisfied clients, they would be out of work. The notion of customer satisfaction in the hotel industry must evolve into a notion of exceeding customer expectations. This goes beyond simply achieving a client's goal, as was discussed in Chapter 4. Exceeding a client's expectations entails incorporating all the salesperson's skills in communication and rapport building.

All consumers can name a few stores and restaurants that they go back to again and again. These are places where the consumers are confident they will be pleased. Most consumers can also name a few establishments where they swore they would never return. These are common experiences for consumers.

> *"Eighty percent of your business comes from 20 percent of your customers."*
>
> ANONYMOUS

The question of what exactly happened to cause someone to be so satisfied or dissatisfied is at the root of exceeding a customer's needs. In most cases, when expectations are exceeded, loyalty is instilled in the consumer. This loyalty is worth more than any advertising. Salespeople must instill in themselves and their hotels that all the work they do to book groups is lost if their hotels cannot create on-property experiences that create client loyalty. The business that returns to a hotel again and again makes up a much greater portion of total revenue than do new pieces of business. Client loyalty ensures that business will return again and again.

As was learned earlier, hotels often sell in locations that are very similar in terms of product type and service level. Most sleeping rooms are very similar (e.g., each has a bed, television, phone, window). Many hotels in the same location have meeting rooms of comparable sizes and dimensions. Loyalty drives the client's repeat buying decision between similar hotels.

A repeat sale is the easiest one a salesperson will ever make. Repeat customers typically return because they have become loyal to the hotel. If a salesperson has a loyal customer base, he or she will have more time to solicit and seek new clients. Salespeople in all industries seek to combine increased repeat sales with more time for solicitation. The best way for a hotel salesperson to instill customer loyalty is to take ownership actions.

**Ownership Actions.** **Ownership actions** are defined as the acts or services performed by a salesperson to help ensure the success of a group. A salesperson can take ownership of a group by undertaking these actions. Because the hotel industry is service based, the value clients place on the product is a direct result of the service they perceive they receive. A client's perception begins with the salesperson's initial greeting and ends with the thank-you note or call. In between, the client experiences various service levels from everyone at the hotel they contact. A client's service perception can begin with the hotel doorperson and end with the credit manager.

Any salesperson can contribute to the overall service perception after the group is booked. By taking ownership actions, salespeople can communicate to their clients how important those clients are to them.

Taking ownership actions has the dual advantage of reflecting well on external customer (the client) and the internal customers (the hotel) staff. If a salesperson shows both groups how badly he or she wants to exceed expectations, he or she will win the respect of his or her peers and foster customer loyalty. Ownership actions can be taken in three distinct stages: (1) before the group arrives, (2) while the group is in house, and (3) after the group has departed.

*Before the Group Arrives.* Throughout this text, the notion of planning has been stressed. Salespeople who do not properly plan ahead lose efficiency. For a hotel, advance planning is crucial to ensuring that a group's needs are taken care of. The best way a salesperson can make his/her hotel aware of a particular group is the preconvention meeting.

- *The Preconvention Meeting (Precon).* The precon, as was reviewed earlier, is typically the venue through which the client meets the other managers in the hotel and reviews with those managers the group's meeting agenda. The precon shows the client that the entire hotel team is committed to the success of the client's program. The team of hotel leaders should introduce themselves and explain what they do and how they will help the program succeed. At the precon, the group resume is reviewed. The precon is most often run by the convention service manager a few days before a large meeting or convention starts. The salesperson should also attend the precon, because the client may feel most comfortable with him or her due to rapport building. The salesperson's role in the precon is minimal, but most clients perceive his or her presence as necessary.

*While the Group Is in House.* Salespeople must not assume that their job is finished once a group arrives. The act of selling continues throughout the duration of a group's stay. Salespeople should employ differing customer service tools while a group is in house to reinforce this ongoing selling concept. Each of the following tools focuses on personal interaction and visibility of the salesperson to and with the client.

- *"Meet and Greet."* A simple, but often overlooked, customer service tool is the act of greeting clients when they arrive for their functions. It is important for a salesperson to be at the front desk to welcome clients whenever possible. If possible, the salesperson should go to the client's registration desk and meet with the client briefly during the function. If the on-site contact differs from the person who booked the function, the salesperson and on-site contact might not have spoken before arrival. Therefore, it is a good idea for the salesperson to try to spend some time establishing rapport with the new contact.

  To increase the client's service perception, the salesperson can bring the general manager when meeting and greeting clients. Even if the client met the general manager at the precon, the general manager's presence will impress on the client how much the hotel values his or her business.
- *Check Rooms.* The salesperson should, of course, be very familiar with a group's agenda. Whenever possible, he or she should check the scheduled function rooms before start times. The salesperson can visually check the rooms as if he or she were the client. If everything is not set up properly, there should be time to rectify any problem.

  In many hotels, the banquet/floor managers and the catering/convention service people check rooms. It is their primary responsibility. If the hotel is very busy, however, the floor managers may be occupied. The salesperson can fill this need as well as show clients his or her hands-on dedication. The servers, house staff, and other line personnel will also see that the salesperson is involved and cares about groups. The salesperson will gain their respect.
- *Be Visible and Available.* As much as possible, the salesperson should try to give the client the impression that he or she is available whenever needed. This should be the salesperson's main priority while the group is in house. Without neglecting his or her selling duties, the salesperson should greet the client when the client stops by the salesperson's office. Clients may stop by unannounced during their

programs. If possible, the salesperson should suspend his or her current task and address the client's needs or delegate the duty. The client should never get the impression that the salesperson is too busy to see him or her.

When a client approaches a salesperson for help, the salesperson must take ownership of the problem. This is not to say that the salesperson must personally change the meeting room set or whatever else needs attention, but he or she should direct the client to the right person. The appropriate staff should handle any problems; the salesperson should simply act as overseer. The salesperson should follow up to ensure everything turned out the way the client wanted. Clients remember this type of ownership action, because it shows that the clients' needs are always paramount.

- *Management by Walking Around.* "**Management by walking around" (MBWA),** the theory that the best managers are visible and accessible, has generated interest recently in the hospitality trade journals. No manager can be effective if in his or her office behind closed doors. MBWA simply reinforces the ownership actions employed while a client is in house. The MBWA concept applies to both internal and external clients.

**INDUSTRY EXAMPLE OF MBWA**

A well-respected general manager in the Midwest uses his own version of MBWA. He uses the term "walkabout" to describe basically the same thing. Each day, he walks throughout the hotel personally checking on groups, empty function space, the outlets, sleeping rooms, and so on. He carries a small notebook on these tours and writes down anything he finds. He addresses these items with the appropriate managers later. The impact on clients and individual guests is powerful. This general manager makes people feel important while keeping himself in touch with the hotel's workings. Not all general managers employ this management philosophy. Some find it difficult to make the time to employ MBWA.

*After the Group Has Departed.* The time between the major departure of a group and the actual departure of the group contact is another opportunity for the salesperson to continue selling. Often, this time is taken to recap the hotel's performance, review billing, and address performance issues. Later, once the contact has returned home and he or she has had time to hear from attendees, the salesperson should incorporate a formal performance evaluation into the thank-you letter.

- *Postconvention Meeting (Postcon).* Ownership actions continue after the group departs. Often, a large group contact or convention client may request a **postcon** at the conclusion of his or her function. The postcon is a useful tool for the client and the hotel. It should be run by the person who conducted the precon, and the client should meet with the leaders who attended the precon. Instead of reviewing a group's resume, the postcon often examines a postcon report, which summarizes the group's activities at the hotel.

The postcon report (Figure 5–6) highlights the number of used rooms and the average rate. It also lists each group function in banquets and outlines the number of attendees (covers) and revenue. Comparing this information to initial projections is useful. The salesperson who booked the group should be interested to learn

**XYZ Hotel Postconvention Report** — Today's Date:
Group Name: — Dates of Function:
Contact Name: — Address:
Telephone: — Fax:
**SALES MANAGER:** **CONV. SERV. MANAGER:**

**Room Rate:** ___ Single ___ Double ___ Triple ___ Quad ___ Suites

**Group Billing:** ___ Sign All Charges ___ Room/Tax to Master
___ Individuals on Own

**Actual Rooms Used**

| Day/Date | Day/Date | Day/Date | Day/Date | Day/Date | Total |
|---|---|---|---|---|---|
| ____ | ____ | ____ | ____ | ____ | ____ |

**Actual Average Daily Rate**

| Day/Date | Day/Date | Day/Date | Day/Date | Day/Date | Total |
|---|---|---|---|---|---|
| $ ____ | $ ____ | $ ____ | $ ____ | $ ____ | $ ____ |

**Catering Activity Summary**

| | Event | | | | | |
|---|---|---|---|---|---|---|
| **Day/Date** | Brkfst | Breaks | Lunch | Dinner | Reception | **Totals Per Day** |
| Number of Covers | | | | | | |
| Revenue | | | | | | |
| Number of Covers | | | | | | |
| Revenue | | | | | | |
| Number of Covers | | | | | | |
| Revenue | | | | | | |
| Totals/Event (Covers/Revenue) | | | | | | |

**Comments:**

______________________________
______________________________
______________________________
______________________________

**FIGURE 5–6**
*Hotel postconvention report*

how the rooms picked up on the group's departure. The salesperson can also use this document to better evaluate the business opportunity in the future. The postcon report can become part of the salesperson's actuals information.

In the postcon, fresh impressions and suggestions are meaningful. Compliments or criticisms directly from clients mean more to managers. The postcon is also a great opportunity for the credit manager to review the master account with the client before it is sent out. The bills for large conventions can be very involved, so any opportunity to examine them with the clients who will be paying them lessens confusion and reduces errors.

**Customer Evaluations.** Customer evaluations in the hotel industry are similar to the "rate our service" cards found in many restaurants. The evaluations for hotels are more involved in that they address quality, cleanliness, and satisfaction issues for each hotel department. When the client takes the time to complete the customer evaluation, it is useful in evaluating how a hotel performed relative to the client's expectations.

A salesperson should always send a client evaluation form with his or her thank-you letter. Evaluations are a valuable tool for the client to use in praising other departments or employees who may have exceeded the client's expectations. Whenever possible, it is desirable to share these positive comments with the employees who are mentioned. Negative comments are also valuable learning tools. With them, challenges can be corrected before they become chronic.

Some hotel chains generate client evaluations at the corporate level, so salespeople at all hotels may not send clients evaluations. If the salesperson feels comfortable with his or her level of rapport with a client, he or she may ask the client to write a letter complimenting the service and the hotel. Positive client letters are called testimonials. Testimonials can strongly impact prospective clients because other clients, not the salesperson, are extolling the virtues of the hotel. Testimonials can be framed and posted in the sales/catering reception area for people to read while waiting. A hotel can also keep testimonials in a binder, often called a "brag book," for potential clients to peruse.

## ONGOING

The operational aspects of sales that deal with bringing a group to a hotel and ensuring quality service for that group while in house are crucial to master. Sales operations skills need not be tied strictly to booking and servicing groups, however. Other operational concepts are the management and self-preparation issues in which hotel salespeople must be well-versed. This section covers a wide range of the issues that salespeople should address on an ongoing basis.

For example, every business professional should be cognizant of time management, because the operational and sales demands on a hotel salesperson's time mandate that he or she manage time in the best ways. Another important topic is networking. The sales profession is people oriented, so preparing to and meeting people through a network of related organizations and industry gatherings furthers a sales effort. Managing a salesperson's career and positioning best for growth and advancement within the industry merits continuous study. The final point in this text is the rapidly changing world of technology and its applications to hotel sales.

## TIME MANAGEMENT

Many busy professionals today claim there are too few hours to accomplish everything. For hotel salespeople, time management is crucial to effectively completing the duty of selling and its related operational demands. The two most important time-management issues in sales are prime selling time and prioritizing.

**Prime Selling Time.** In certain hours of each work day, the hotel salesperson should focus on selling. In others, he or she can address operational issues if needed. Whenever possible, operational issues and related paperwork should be completed around prime selling time. Prime selling time dictates when one should prioritize the hotel sales triangle. **Prime selling time** is defined as the specific hours during the day when the salesperson has the best opportunity to reach current and prospective clients (Figure 5–7). The optimal selling hours of hotels differ slightly based on the hotels' time zones.

In general, prime selling time runs from 9 A.M. to 11 A.M. and 1 P.M. to 4 P.M. each day, because these are the times when most people are in their offices. Salespeople calling from any of the four continental time zones (Eastern, Central, Mountain, and Pacific) have slightly altered sets of prime selling times, especially if they are deployed by regions of the country. For example, a salesperson who works on the West Coast may start his or her day earlier because his or her contacts are on the East Coast and already well into their day. Similarly, the salesperson working until 7 P.M. on the East Coast, has an opportunity to reach most of his or her contacts on the West Coast.

Outside prime selling hours, the salesperson can concentrate on paperwork and other pressing issues. This is not to say that selling cannot be conducted at any time of day, but the processes of lead generation and customer rapport building have the best chances of success during these outside times.

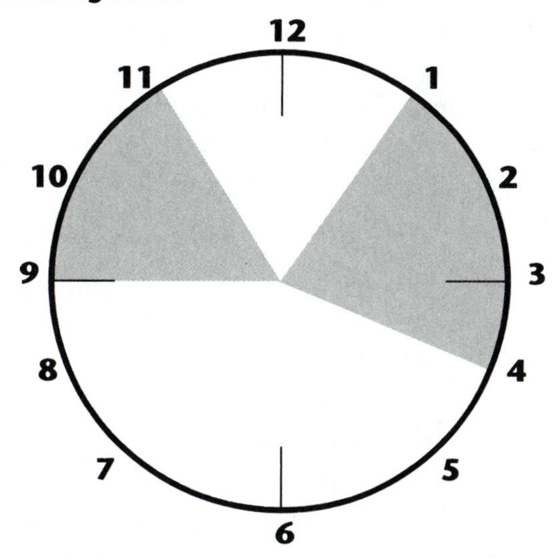


**FIGURE 5–7**
*Prime selling time*

**Prioritizing.** Being able to judge what must be done first and what can wait are important for a salesperson if he or she is to make the best use of the workday and take full advantage of prime selling hours. The ability to prioritize helps salespeople regulate workflow and stress level, which increases productivity.

Efficient prioritizing of a workday begins with purchasing a "day planner" or mastering a computer datebook planner. The next step is to instill a habit of reviewing and updating this planning tool consistently. Such tools are of no use if they are not used consistently.

In these planners, everything must be written down. Items and notes of importance, like appointments, site inspections, due dates, trace dates, special follow-up dates and others, should be included. These planners should be used to follow up on proposals and contracts. Salespeople who are assigned special projects by their managers should plot the projects in their planners, including when and how they will complete the projects. Salespeople should use planners to track mileage to sales calls, expenses on sales trips, and any other items they find beneficial.

On a day-to-day basis, planners should serve as salespeople's "prioritizers." Viewing a day's schedule at a glance ensures that appointments are spaced evenly with ample time between for preparation and follow up. If the planner has a "to do" area, items in the area should be prioritized with numbers.

For example, if a salesperson uses a priority scale of *1* to *5*, with *1* the highest, an item with a *1* must be done immediately. In contrast, a *5* can wait until later. At the start and finish of each day, this list should be reviewed carefully. If the day ends and a salesperson still has a *1* on his or her priority list, he or she should stay and do it. A combination of *4*s and *5*s on the list may not require immediate attention, but the salesperson should transfer them to the next day's "to do" list. In so doing, the salesperson must increase the priority levels of these items by at least 1. For example, a *5* becomes a *4* the next day. This is important because otherwise salespeople could allow themselves to avoid indefinitely things they do not want to do.

At the start of each day, the salesperson should make it a habit to review the agenda for that day as well as the next. That way, he or she will not be surprised with a due date or an appointment.

## NETWORKING

Because the sales profession is people oriented, it is logical to assume that the more people a salesperson contacts, the more sales opportunities he or she finds. Lead generation and rapport building require interaction with people. The hotel industry makes available a network of related organizations and industry gatherings to enable salespeople to meet other salespeople and potential clients. Networking, or meeting and talking with these different people, furthers a sales effort.

Many different types of organizations and events provide sales and catering teammates opportunities to network. Different areas have more organizations, or fewer. In any case, the following list highlights some of these groups and what they intend to achieve:

Hotel Sales and Marketing Association (HSMA)

- Usually a local grouping of hotel/motel managers and executives who meet to share ideas and network.

Society of Government Meeting Professionals (SGMP)

- A grouping of local hotel and meeting facility salespeople and various government meeting planners. A good group to work with if the government is a major local player or the hotel wants to focus on this market segment.

American Society of Association Executives (ASAE)

- National umbrella organization made of state chapters. Each state chapter alters the name somewhat (e.g., KSAE is Kentucky Society of Association Executives). Like SGMP, this group combines association decision makers, hotel representatives, and other vendors. In some states, ASAE can be a powerful government lobbying body that can have a major impact on the hotel community.

Meeting Professionals International (MPI)

- Perhaps the most recognized and well-run organization of its type in the country and now the world. MPI is unique in its basic structure. For a hotel salesperson to join, he or she must bring a meeting planner. This balance of planners and suppliers (hotels are suppliers) allows for equal influences and direction. (Note: Most local chapters help hotel salespeople find planners if they want to join.) MPI organizes national meetings and regional seminars and even has an informative newsletter. Look for them on the Internet.

Religious Conference Management Association (RCMA)

- Another nationally recognized organization that focuses on planning meetings and conventions for religious groups of all kinds. The RCMA national meeting is a must for tapping into this large meeting potential.

Convention and Visitors Bureau (CVB)

- Each city or region and/or state has designated a locally funded (usually from the hotel community's occupancy tax or dues) organization to attract convention group business and promote tourism. This is a very important entity for a hotel, because CVBs often sponsor events, familiarization trips, and trade shows in which all interested hotels should participate.

**National Association of Catering Executives (NACE)**

- An organization of hotel catering and convention service personnel who meet to share ideas and network.

Other local organizations can provide networking contacts that may pay off in different ways. These organizations include:

- Chamber of Commerce
- Better Business Bureau
- Kiwanis/Elks
- Rotary Club
- Downtown or waterfront development commissions
- City hall/state capitol
- Sports commissions
- Nonprofit organizations (e.g., Red Cross and YMCA)
- "Business Builder"/"Business After Hours" networking receptions

Networking in these and other groups helps the hotel in intrinsic ways. The more a salesperson talks to people, the more those people remember the salesperson. When at lunches, dinners, or receptions for any of the preceding organizations, the salesperson should make it a goal to meet at least five new people each time. He or she should bring plenty of business cards and distribute them when appropriate. Some people are not comfortable at these events, but salespeople must think of them as sales opportunities. After a while, salespeople will have address books filled with names that may be helpful. In turn, the people in the address books feel as if they have viable hotel contacts and may pass salespeople's names to others.

## CAREER MANAGEMENT

Sales, catering, and transient careers can be very rewarding. A hotel career must be fostered just like the sales skills learned in this text. This section analyzes two components of career management: beginning and fostering a sales career.

**Beginning a Hotel Career.** Hotel careers are not limited to sales and catering. Opportunities abound in accounting, food and beverage, human resources, engineering, retail, and customer service. The hotel industry is unique in that it brings differing disciplines under one heading.

Educating oneself is a very important first step to entering the hotel world. Students of hospitality often wonder which paths into a hotel sales position are best. Without experience on a resume, how does one enter the hospitality world?

Without hotel sales experience, beginning a sales career in a hotel may require some work. However, hotels of every size, location, product type, and service level are always looking for new employees. Some large chains employ staffs of several individuals whose sole purpose is to visit the country's higher-learning campuses seeking talent. Small chains and independent hotels must use other means. The current state of expansion in the industry makes working at a hotel a very real possibility. There are several ways to enter this field, but each requires initiative and perseverance.

To get into the sales and catering department, a prospective candidate can take advantage of hotel management training programs, internships, volunteering, or cross-departmental experience.

*Hotel Management Training Programs.* Most large hotel chains offer extensive management training programs for recent graduates. Hyatt, Marriott, Sheraton, Hilton, and Westin, to name a few, each has a prearranged training program that lasts from 6 months to a year or more. Each program candidate works in most or all the hotel departments to gain experience in all facets of operations. Upon completing the program, the candidate is often assigned a junior management or supervisory role at a hotel. Some management training programs conclude in candidates' departments of choice. Permanent positions may not be available in the sales office of the hotel providing the training, but candidates are eventually placed at hotels. The most prevalent entry-level position in hotel sales is meetings manager.

*Internships.* If a management training program is unavailable, interested candidates may be able to seek paid internships. While not as formal as management training programs, internships are often focused on providing broad-based exposure to the hotel's departments. Repeated internships during the course of education (e.g., summers) allow candidates to focus on particular disciplines. Sales offices have many marketing and promotional projects that require no more than 3 months' work, which makes them perfect for summer interns.

*Volunteering.* If formal training opportunities at a hotel are not available, volunteer meeting planning may be the road into hotel sales. Nonprofit organizations and charities of all kinds are always looking for help planning fund-raisers and other events. Experience working with a hotel from the other side (planning) may catch the eye of a director of sales.

*Cross-Departmental Experience.* Recent school graduates may find themselves frustrated with a lack of sales opportunities at their hotels of choice. If other departments are offering training or internship programs, job seekers should explore them. It is common knowledge that most hotels prefer to promote from within. Therefore, a housekeeping supervisor or an assistant front desk manager finds the chances of gaining entrance to sales much greater than does an employee outside the hotel. Directors of sales also look for operational experience gained from other hotel departments. For example, the assistant front desk manager brings customer rapport skills gained from guest interaction, as well as in-depth knowledge of the front office.

**Fostering a Hotel Career.** Whether a salesperson works for major chain or an independent hotel, he or she must always think about how best to enhance his or her career. Assuming the salesperson enjoys what he or she does, what are the keys to long-term success? The best approach to fostering a career is to predetermine the career path as much as possible.

A good starting point is to map long-term career goals. A list or chart should be made to detail where the salesperson hopes to see his or her career 1, 5, and 10 years in the future. Does the salesperson envision him- or herself as a general manager eventually? Does he or she want to rise through the sales ranks and lead a team as a director of marketing or a director of sales? Perhaps the salesperson is content and feels good doing his or her current job. Whatever the specific goals, yearly plans should reflect where salespeople want to be and how to get there.

*The 1-Year Plan.* The 1-year plan should reflect the salesperson's most recent job evaluation or review. A yearly plan should focus on areas in

# Industry Perspective

## "Thoughts on Hospitality Sales Careers"

*An interview with:*
*Ric Nicholson*
*Director of Sales and Marketing*
*Hyatt Regency, Bellevue, WA*

**BACKGROUND:** Mr. Nicholson began his hospitality career over 20 years ago by undergoing formal culinary training in the San Francisco area. He was introduced to hotel sales as part of a work-study program and never looked back. He entered the management-training program with Hyatt and proceeded up the sales ladder by relocating to different hotels and taking on different markets. Mr. Nicholson left Hyatt to direct the sales and catering office at Harrah's Casino in Reno. After 12 years in various senior management positions, he relocated to the Seattle area and returned to Hyatt. In his current capacity, Mr. Nicholson is responsible for the sales and marketing effort. His experience and insight into the skills and education that are needed to start and further a career in hospitality sales are invaluable.

Q: "What qualities and characteristics do you look for in new sales candidates?"
A: "Currently, I do not take on any individuals without some level of real-world hotel sales experience. That applies to the vast majority of the positions on my staff. I am willing to look at interested candidates from within other departments of my hotel. Managers and supervisors of the front desk, catering, restaurants, etc., bring valuable operational knowledge to the table. Even those candidates will only be considered for very entry-level-type positions. Individuals working for other hotel companies may be considered if their experience warrants. I don't have the time to sit down and teach someone how to be a salesperson. I can show them our systems and introduce them to the intricacies of my hotel, but I have to have someone who can 'hit the ground running.'"
Q: "Once in place, how can a salesperson best ensure advancement?"
A: "Being as flexible as possible is key. When I was offered a new opportunity, I took it. No debate. It was difficult for me and my family, but that is how you got ahead back then. Relocatability was, and still is, crucial. Flexibility is not just limited to relocation. I must be honest and to the point here. Salespeople should not be afraid of switching

hotel companies. The notion of working for one company for a lifetime isn't realistic anymore. Don't burn bridges along the way, but the financial benefits as well as the experience gained from learning a new way to do things may further a career faster. The current environment in our industry seems to be leaning toward less mobility and less flexibility. Quality-of-life issues are more important now, which is fine, but that may limit one's ability to grow."

**Q:** "Do you advocate working at different hotel types and different market segments throughout a career?"

**A:** "It makes sense to get as much experience as you can in as many different areas as possible. Because, ultimately, later in your career you want to be able to 'call the shots' somewhere. It doesn't matter if it is in this industry, or another, but all the experience that you've gained puts you in a much better position. A salesperson handling the corporate market at an airport property for 20 years will know their market inside and out. But what do they know about associations? What about the transient demand at a resort? The more broad the experience, the better off you are. However, it also depends on what your career goals are. If you want to be a general manager, it may not be as important to understand all the intricacies of sales, but you will want to know what goes on in your sales office and be able to speak their language."

**Q:** "What is the realistic career progression for salespeople in today's hotel environment?"

**A:** "It goes back to the second question. If somebody has the buy-off of spouse and family coupled with true desire, the sky's the limit. Obviously, they would have to have some smarts and a ton of drive. If they were good at what they did, and made it known they could move, they could go as far as they wish. It matters, of course, what the size and scope of the company they currently work for can offer. A smaller chain may not have the opportunities that a larger one has. Crossing over into other departments should not be discounted if the end goal is senior property management. Again, you don't have to stay with one company. The cream will always rise to the top."

**Q:** "If a salesperson's end goal is marketing, what opportunities exist and how does one get there?"

**A:** "Big-time marketing, and by 'big time' I mean corporate direct mail, national newspapers, guest loyalty programs, etc., are handled by small numbers of people. Even at large chains, these departments aren't big. Many of the top-level marketing folks at different hotel companies now haven't ever worked at a hotel. Our industry currently looks to other industries for top-level marketers, unlike a few years ago, when all the top executives of hotel companies started out as front-desk clerks and bellpeople. Most marketing opportunities exist at the property level. Directors of sales and marketing typically handle the marketing at hotels. That, in itself, dictates moving up the sales ladder and proving yourself as a salesperson in order to get involved with marketing. If marketing is your end goal, you may be better suited to another industry."

which the manager feels the salesperson needs improvement. This plan is most useful when set up as an "action plan" for the salesperson to act on right away. The action plan should specify the areas for work and the best ways to do so. A supervisor's input is vital, because he or she controls the salesperson's short-term career destiny. The supervisor's input on the action plan helps the salesperson understand the specific expectations of management and how best to fulfill them.

*The 5-Year Plan.* The 5-year plan should be a blueprint of the salesperson's next desired position. If salespeople are content with their careers, they must still prove to themselves and to management that they will stay productive for many years. Do they want to become senior sales managers or move into transient sales soon? The 5-year plan should be written. To move up the sales ladder, the salesperson must map how to get there. He or she should start immediately by asking his or her superior how the superior got to his or her level and the time it took. Positioning oneself as a leader and a team player in day-to-day activities is a very good step. Exceeding sales goals consistently is a must. If possible, the salesperson should take on extra projects and responsibilities whenever possible. Being the first to address a difficult situation enables a good reputation. Always supporting management and sales teammates positions the salesperson as one whose only interests are those of the hotel. The salesperson will find that consistency over 5 years puts him or her in a position to dictate his or her next position.

*The 10-Year Plan.* The 10-year plan is essentially a rough career outline. Salespeople may have greater or fewer options depending on the types and sizes of their companies. If a salesperson works for a chain and wants to be promoted quickly, he or she should be open to relocation. Human resources managers at large chains have career profiles on management staff at other hotels. These profiles outline salary, performance history, company, experience, education, management suggestions or career path, and relocatability. Often, other hotels look at these profiles before employees learn of the opportunities.

**CAREER-MANAGEMENT TOOLS**

A good ongoing career-management technique for salespeople and students interested in the sales field is to keep abreast of hotel trade journals. Publications like *Hotel & Motel Management, Meetings and Conventions, Events,* and *Hotels* cover a wide range of topics that are timely and relevant. Association newsletters from groups like ASAE and RCMA can give the salesperson the planner's point of view of the industry. Individuals interested in the food and beverage side of hotels should seek *Restaurant Business, Cuisine,* and *Hotel Restaurant* magazines for similar insight. Other magazines and newsletters can provide resources for research, career opportunities, and networking. Some can be very specialized, as shown in the following:

**Corporate Market Segment**
Corporate & Incentive Travel
Corporate Meetings and Incentives

**Transient**
Business Travel News
Tour & Travel News
Travel Age
Travel Agent

**Other**
Insurance Meeting Management
Medical Meetings
Midwest Meetings

**General**
Meeting News
Hotel & Travel Index
Event Solutions

Salespeople should review their profiles periodically to ensure they are accurate and to make changes to reflect where they want to be. Marriage, new families, and other changes in personal status may necessitate changes in employee profiles.

If a salesperson lives in an area where his or her company has more than one hotel, he or she may have career opportunities without having to relocate. Called cluster cities, these areas allow for career movement from hotel to hotel in the surrounding region. Large cities like New York, Chicago, and Los Angeles are often considered cluster cities because hotel chains regularly build more than one hotel in them.

Whatever a salesperson's career goals, he or she must remember to enjoy the job and have fun.

## TECHNOLOGY AND HOTELS

Today's hotels differ greatly in their levels of modernization. Not long ago, hotels had manual systems. These manual hotel systems had no computers to help them run their departments. A manual hotel typically had some type of display board at the front desk, called the "room rack," that it would use to manually update the status of each room. Sometimes color coded, this system would let the front desk agent know at a glance which rooms were occupied, dirty, vacant, or ready for occupancy. A cash register and a large drawer of metal keys made up the bulk of the front-desk area. Some hotels had registration books that guests would sign upon checking in. All accounts were updated by hand. Some hotels still use these systems.

**Hotel Operating Systems Today.** Most hotels today take a more modern approach. The **property management system (PMS)** ties different operational departments together. Through it, housekeeping, accounting, reservations, and the other various departments are connected to the front desk. The PMS system allows the front-desk agent to see at a glance what rooms are available, check the status of a guest's or a group's account, and so on. The outlets on property can post charges from the restaurant, golf course, room service, and anywhere else, without anyone having to go to the front desk. The several PMS systems on the market accomplish virtually the same goal.

Reservation departments in today's hotels are also very often computerized. A global network has been created to allow travel agents direct access to specific hotels or chains. This **global distribution system (GDS)** also ties airlines and car-rental companies together. The purpose is to allow travel agents to book entire vacations or travel itineraries at once. A hotel's reservation department manages the hotel's inventory and pricing strategy by updating this system to reflect the property's goals (e.g., yield management).

Most hotels have separate on-property reservations systems that interface with the hotels' PMS systems and their GDS systems. The GDS system feeds the hotel reservations from outside sources. Therefore, the group salespeople should understand how their rates and availabilities display on their GDS systems.

Inconsistencies between the rates offered to GDS and the rates the sales department is selling can arise. Problems can result when a salesperson quotes a group a high rate due to city demand but group members making their reservations via travel agents or travel-management companies receive a lower rate. As has been reviewed, the travel planner's job is to always book the lowest rate possible for his or her clients.

The most widely used GDS systems go under the names of Apollo and Sabre. The only drawback to the current GDS systems is that they do not interface completely with the various hotel systems. There is yet to be a fully accepted operating system that will tie all travel-related service providers (hotels, airlines, car rental agencies) together.

Another facet of technology that greatly impacts transient demand and, by extension, group demand, is the central reservations desk or **central reservations office (CRO)**. The CRO is becoming more and more important in the global community because it serves as a "clearinghouse" for individual reservations. Hotels with toll-free numbers typically route their calls through central receiving centers that are staffed 24 hours a day. These CROs can be owned outright by hotel companies or they can serve as surrogate agents that are working on hotels' behalfs.

The CROs receive their room-pricing information from one of the GDS systems, or they tie directly to a hotel's reservation system. Large chains maintain expansive call centers that can staff from 10 to 100 full-time agents. Whatever system a hotel uses, the demand created by the CRO provides a vital transient demand source. Some hotels may even find that group leads are generated (or relayed) to their sales offices from CRO agents. This occurs when clients mistakenly call the toll-free number to book groups. Some large-chain CRO centers have national sales staff to help prequalify calls before they reach the hotels. Figure 5–8 shows the paths the transient client can take to reach a hotel. The paths available to the group client were covered in Chapter 4.

**Operating Systems Interface.** Hotels of any sizes, product types, and service levels have several different operating systems that interface directly or indirectly with each other. These systems can be so varied that some hotels have information systems departments to continuously maintain and upgrade these systems. In addition to the PMS and reservation systems, hotels may have integrated sales/catering programs and **point of sale (POS)** systems. The POS systems tie the registers at outlets and ancillary revenue sources to the main PMS system. The sales and catering systems must communicate their sleeping room needs to the reservations system for the hotel's sleeping room inventory to reflect accurate availability figures.

Many modern hotels use data storage vehicles that store all relevant guest history and financial data on digital laser disks, thereby eliminating the need for storing vast amounts of paper. Voice messaging from the **hotel switchboard (PBX)** must be tied into the PMS system for guest

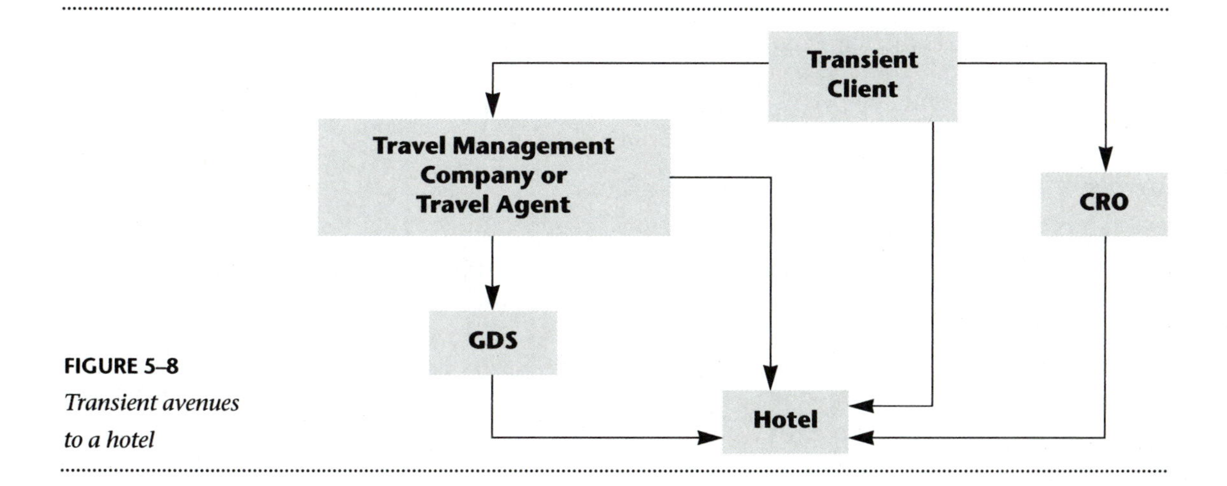


**FIGURE 5–8**
*Transient avenues to a hotel*

access. These systems must all be tied together for them to interface properly. Figure 5–9 shows the basic interface configuration.

**Sales and Catering Technology.** Currently, only a few of the largest hotel chains with significant financial resources have been able to computerize both their sleeping room and function space availability displays internally for sales and catering use. Creating standard, chain-wide programs for these two important functions can be cost prohibitive for many hotels.

Ready-made sales and catering software packages are available. The most well-known is Delphi. Another, similar program is Miracle. Whatever system a salesperson has access to, he or she should endeavor to learn all its features and applications so he or she can make the most of it.

The most important technological tool for the sales and catering office is the database. While not a new phenomenon, the database is an extremely useful resource. Extracting historical data from a database is sometimes called **data mining.** Mining data in such a way as to extract information within set parameters allows a sales office to use its resources effectively. Data extracted from databases can identify trends or supply specific information regarding new sales initiatives. The most common database searches used in sales yield history reports, lost business reports, and customer demographics.

*History Reports.* A database search of group history at a hotel can yield valuable information. The history search can be used as a lead generation source or a trend identifier. A pattern in these history reports may indicate that changes are needed in pricing strategy or deployment. The leads generated from history are like those generated from the efficient usage of a hotel's trace files.

The biggest benefit the history database search offers is the ability to tailor to specific needs. History reports can be used to find out who has

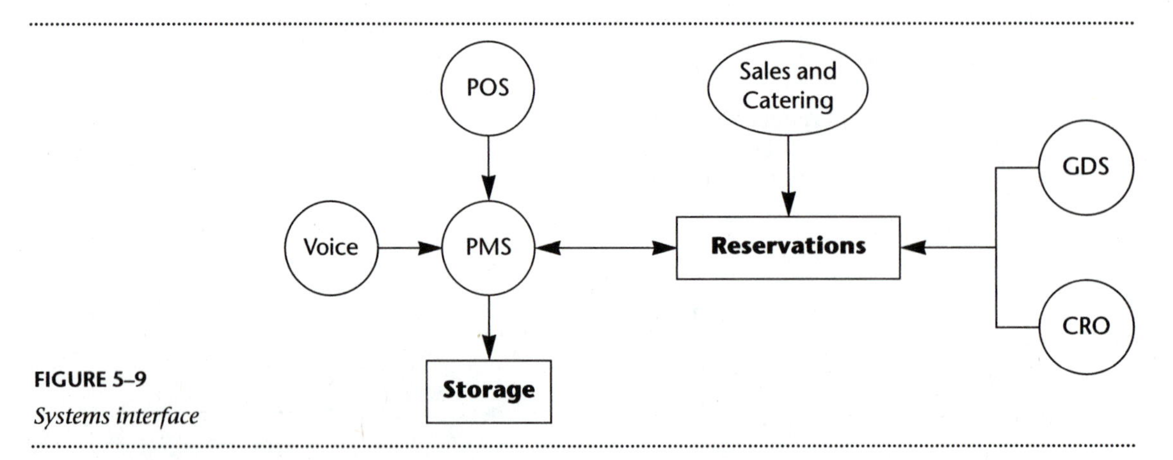


**FIGURE 5–9**
*Systems interface*

met at a hotel in specific time frames, which is useful information when soliciting business for need periods. Searches can be conducted to reveal information on specific market segments. For example, if a hotel wants to do a promotion for the insurance industry, the database can search all specific groups within that segment. A search like this adds to the impact of a promotion, because the people sent information know the hotel. Such receptive targets are more likely to consider the information because they have purchased the hotel's services in the past.

Broad-based history reports (those with few parameters) can help senior management determine budgets. An annual marketing plan is more realistic when expectations are based on past performances.

*Lost Business Reports.* A **lost business report (LBR)**, is a listing of business opportunities that did not book at a hotel. These opportunities may have been lost to a competitor or turned down by the sales team because they did not fit the hotel's strategy. LBRs should be routinely entered into a hotel's database and accessed like history reports.

The LBRs can be used to augment a hotel's solicitation efforts. They can be used to solicit for need periods as history reports are used. Because of today's ever-changing business environment, something that was lost or turned down previously may look more appealing later.

The LBRs can also be used to identify trends. If a sales office is routinely losing or turning down business due to rate strategy or catering prices, a combination of LBRs can reveal the common reasons. These reports may justify a reevaluation of the sales strategy. Also, the loss of business due to the condition of the hotel (e.g., worn sleeping rooms or function space) may be reflected in the LBRs. Senior hotel management and owners may expedite the release of renovation funds if business is being lost as a result.

The LBRs can be used by the director of sales to monitor a salesperson's ability to close a sale. Individuals who have not yet mastered the hotel sales triangle may find that they are losing business at the same points in the sales process. The LBR serves as a sort of "report card" on a salesperson's habits and technique.

*Customer Demographics.* Demographics help determine target markets. The ability to identify consumers based on their buying criteria is important to many industries. For example, in television, the analysis of an audience's demography identifies which groups watch which shows. With that information, advertisers can buy commercials that reach their targeted demographic groups.

In hospitality, using demographics as a parameter in a database report allows a hotel to search for specific group types, market segments, and their respective buying habits. From the previous discussions, it is understood that certain groups share similar traits, such as space intensity, peak night room size, and budget consciousness. A demographic report allows a hotel to search its database for one or more of these traits. Parameters can be set to search for specific tentative, definite, and actual status groups on the books. If the database is set up for it, LBRs can also be included.

For example, if a hotel wants to increase its average rate during a certain time frame, it can set the parameters of the demographic report to search for all groups that have paid as much or more than the targeted rate. The sales team then has another set of receptive customers who can be solicited. The same applies to searches for groups who have specific catering budgets. The transient sales effort can be augmented by searching the transient database (often called the guest history) for guests who have met at certain times or paid certain rates. The more sophisticated systems allow a hotel to search by geographic region, zip code, area code, feeder city, and other parameters.

A good rule to remember when working with all the preceding reports is that database reports are only as good as the information they receive. Therefore, salespeople should always strive to be complete when supplying database information.

**OTHER TECHNOLOGICAL TOOLS FOR GROUP SALES**

- Computerized trace file programs
- Database searches from lead suppliers (e.g., PCMA, MPI)
- Group profitability programs
- GDS searches of competition for rate analysis
- Readerboard database analysis
- STAR reports for competitive market share
- Computerized account management programs

## THE FUTURE OF THE GROUP SALES OFFICE

The preceding sections looked at some of the most prevalent technological aspects of the modern sales office. As new computer applications are developed, hotel salespeople will gain insight into how to do their jobs better. While some argue that the hotel industry lags behind other industries in the advancement of technology, most agree that change is occurring rapidly. At some point in their careers, salespeople will have the opportunity to experience, and maybe even further, this technological advancement. Following are some highlights of the cutting edge in technology as it relates to the hospitality industry, items in the developmental pipeline, and a few untapped possibilities.

**The Internet.** The growing importance of the Internet can be seen everywhere. Most advertisements now include Web site addresses where more information can be found on a product or service. E-mail is becoming the communication method of choice for many. The hospitality industry, for the most part, has not yet fully tapped the potential of this medium. That fact, however, is changing.

Most hotels, large chains and small alike, have created Web sites that highlight their properties. Many more sites are in development. Some small chains and independent hotels have teamed up with interested parties (e.g., local/regional governments, convention bureaus, entertainment attractions) to use the Internet to package areas of the country as destinations. Also, online providers, like America Online (AOL) and Microsoft Network have developed and packaged tour/travel areas any user can access.

Currently, the vast majority of Web sites are information-only resources. The technology needed for individuals to get online and book all facets of a vacation are still largely in development. The encryption technology needed to address the security issues of credit-card numbers must also be resolved.

The Internet has begun to serve as a lead generation source for hotels, because Web sites generate consumer interest. The Internet may eventually take direct bookings into hotels, thereby bypassing the reservations department entirely. Like the "ticketless" travel trend in the airline industry, hotels may soon be able to let their guests make reservations online and indicate their room preferences. An unstaffed front desk may simply require a credit-card swipe to release a room key.

The full potential of the Internet, especially as it applies to hotel sales, is yet to be realized. The following technology ideas may contribute to hotel sales/catering and the hospitality industry in general.

*Internet Links.* Imagine if a hotel chain linked each of its properties via the Internet. The sales applications could be remarkable. If each hotel could share its database with others in the chain, it could make sales decisions more effectively. For example, if XYZ Company has met at three other hotels in a chain and is now looking at another at which to hold a board meeting, a chain-wide database search on the demographics of the XYZ Company could yield information on its:

- Rate history
- Size
- Dates
- Space requirements
- Client goals and how they were met with features and advantages
- How expectations were exceeded

Such an Internet setup would create, in essence, a company-wide client profile. Hotels with these setups would have a tremendous advantage over the competition. Their clients would feel that the hotels in the chain are attuned to their needs and would return to the hotels again and again, thereby creating company-wide client loyalty. These links would allow hotels to share other information as well, namely LBRs and histories. Hotels could search other hotels for information on groups that would fill their need periods. A search by group name, size, or home city would be simple.

**The Future Hotel Salesperson.** With further advancements in technology, the role of the salesperson will evolve into mobile, adaptable account manager. The salesperson will take his or her laptop computer on sales calls to keep in touch with the hotel and check availability, download account profiles, and so on. Soon salespeople will book pieces of business in clients' offices.

In essence, group sales will be more client focused. Salespeople will be able to give contacts instant information. The rapport building possibilities are tremendous. Salespeople who work for chains will be able to book directly into sister hotels as clients' needs arise. Eventually, the need for national sales offices will be eliminated. If an account is large enough, a salesperson could represent its entire company and sell exclusively to it.

Regardless of how the group salesperson evolves, the principles of selling will remain paramount to success. Adapting them as technology advances will enable salespeople to stay ahead of their competition. However, salespeople should not let their sales abilities become compromised by the advancement of technology. Salespeople should keep the hotels sales triangle in the forefront whether dealing online or in person.

**The Hotel of the Next Century.** Changes in technology will affect all hotel departments. As was just discussed, most hotels today have computer systems. The major chains currently use different operating systems in each of their departments. These departments (e.g., sales/catering, front office, reservations, accounting, human resources, engineering), operate computer systems that typically cannot interface with the others. If all departments were tied in a network and each was running the same format, the hotel would immeasurably increase efficiency. Redundant labor would drop. Check-in would be achieved with the point and click of a mouse.

A network should be set up in real time to allow everyone with access to the network to interface with other users at the same time, without any download delay. For example, in real time someone in the sales office could access a guest's account at the front desk to make sure the guest was being checked into the right room. A salesperson could access a group's payment history in accounting while discussing a possible meeting with that group. The salesperson could even check the maintenance history of a room he or she wants to use as a site inspection room to find out if the room was renovated recently or if its toilet has a history of overflowing.

On a real-time network, each manager would have access to other departments according to his or her seniority and need to know. For example, the general manager would have access to every system, while a restaurant manager would not have access to group profiles.

The following outline (A) shows various hotel departments and the functions that could be enhanced or eliminated using this application.

**EXAMPLE**

**OUTLINE A**

Each department must have real-time access to its functions as well as to all others via network and multiuser workstations.

**Accounting**
Accounts payable/receivable
Group credit/individual advance deposit
Payroll
Computerized timecards
Departmental budgets
Daily/monthly reconciliation
Monthly/period-end reports
General cashier/individual cash banks
International currency exchange

**Sales/Catering**
Group room forecasts
Rate/room restrictions
Rate/rooms history
Meeting space availability online
Catering forecast (daily, weekly, monthly)
Catering service/set up labor forecast
Groups checks, door cards, readerboards
Food cost/purchasing forecasts
Sales group files online (connected via Internet to all hotels)
Call reports
E-mail capability (inter- and intrahotel)
Letters, reports, interhotel paperwork

**Human Resources**
Employee profiles
Performance reviews
Chain-wide/hotel staffing levels
Awards/recognition

**Front Office**
Day of demand strategy
Room status management
Check-in/-out (individual/group)
Housekeeping forecast
Bell stand/valet forecast
PBX forecast
Outlet posting

**Engineering**
Room maintenance history
Preventive maintenance forecast (sleeping/meeting rooms, common areas)
Heat/light/power history and forecast
Grounds maintenance
Recycling efficiency
Amortization

**Outlets/Ancillary**
Food and beverage outlets
Golf/tennis/recreation
Gift shops/newsstand

**Reservations**
Total hotel rooms forecast (rate, occupancy)
Yield/strategic management
Competitive demand analysis
Individual advance deposit
Rooms packages

## CHAPTER REVIEW

### KEY CONCEPTS

Knowledge of the hotel
Familiarity with the competition
Customer communication forms
Internal versus external communication
Hospitality sales letters
Phone conversations
Site inspection
Customer appointments
Booking status
Contracts
Interdepartmental relationships
Internal documents
Customer service
Time management
Networking
Career management
Hotel operating systems
Sales and catering systems

### REVIEW QUESTIONS

1. What types of information must a salesperson know for his or her hotel?
2. Explain how a competitive analysis is conducted.
3. What other types of hospitality sales letters can you think of, and how are they used?
4. How does a site inspection differ from a customer appointment?
5. Explain the difference between first- and second-option tentatives.
6. How does a sales booking impact the rest of the hotel?
7. What makes internal operational documents so important?
8. Define *networking* and its importance to hotel sales.

## VIDEOTAPE EXERCISE

Conduct a role-playing exercise with one person playing the salesperson and the other playing the client. Videotape each participant. When finished, review the tape with the sales team or classroom. Videotape different sales scenarios, such as:

- Competitive analyses
- Customer phone conversations
- Site inspections
- Customer appointments
- Contract negotiations
- Pre-/postcons

This is a good opportunity to tie all chapters together by taping each step in the sales process. Begin with the hotel sales triangle steps and continue to the final guest's arrival. Rotate participants in each role, and have them critique each other. Videotape reveals unexpected things.

# *Glossary*

**account penetration** Process of determining new sources of business within an organization.

**actual business mix** Analysis based on data accumulated over a period; running account of all customers who have stayed at a hotel. Market factors like economic slowdown/expansion, corporate relocation, national emergency, and weather play important roles in determining the actual business mix of a hotel.

**actuals** Status of hotel business that has come and gone. These documented numbers represent the foundations for future history research.

**advance purchase reservations** Reduced rates for reservations booked far in advance. Advance purchase reservations induce transient guests to get their reservations on the books ahead of time.

**advantage** Result of matching a goal to a feature. The benefit gained from this combination is the advantage.

**all-suite hotels** Hotels targeted to the consumer looking for a hotel experience rivaling that in upscale and luxury hotels. A suite can appeal to more consumers. All-suites typically have two or more rooms per suite, a varying service level, limited on-site food and beverage facilities, and complimentary receptions and breakfasts. Breakfast-inclusive rates appeal to many. The staffing levels at all-suite hotels are generally leaner than those at upscale or luxury properties. The reduced staffing levels enable the rates at all-suites to be more affordable than those at upscale or luxury hotels.

**American plan** Package that includes three meals a day with the room rate.

**American Society of Association Executives (ASAE)** A national umbrella organization made up of state chapters, this group combines association decision makers, hotel representatives, and other vendors.

In some states this can be a powerful governmental lobbying body that can have a major impact on the hotel community.

**amplifier** Equipment piece with some type of audio source that allows the sound to be enhanced or, more often, intensified before presentation.

**assistant controller** Coordinates the day-to-day activities of the accounting office. The members of the accounts payable and receivable teams as well as the credit manager report to him or her. The general cashier and the night audit staff also report to the assistant controller. Financial reporting and compliance issues are a big part of the assistant controller's responsibilities.

**attrition clause** Contractual hotel clause that covers lackluster group performance. Its aim is to reimburse the hotel for dishonored room commitments.

**audio monitor** Equipment piece that is useful in any setup with a live music source. It is usually a small speaker in a stand-alone configuration near the mixer that "listens" to something throughout the audio system.

**audio source** Any device or entity that creates a sound to be fed into an audio presentation system. It can be a presenter, speaker, live band, and so on.

**average daily rate (ADR)** Composite average of all rates booked at a hotel on a given night.

**banquet event order (BEO)** Fundamental document that communicates to internal operational departments the function specifics of a group. The BEO is relevant only to departments concerned with executing an event or a function.

**banquet manager** Person who coordinates the staff in charge of setting up function rooms, serving meals, and cleaning up. The banquet manager works with the catering and/or convention service departments to ensure all service sides of a program are completed correctly. He or she is often the manager closest to the client during a program, so his or her customer-service skills should be well-developed. The banquet manager is sometimes called a banquet maitre d'.

**block letter format** Common letter form that is left justified.

**boom microphone** Microphone attached to some type of extension. This is used to capture the audio source when you cannot get very close.

**brand loyalty** Institutionalized preferences of a consumer for a product or service based solely on a brand name or logo.

**breakfast** Typically a sit-down meal in the morning that serves traditional breakfast fare. The breakfast, as a food function, is usually held in a room separate from the meeting.

**breakout room** Room designed to allow attendees of a general session to "break" into smaller groups for more intensive discussion. A breakout room is generally much smaller than the main meeting room. The need for breakout rooms is common among larger groups.

**business opportunity** Occurs when an organization and a hotel communicate in some fashion regarding sleeping rooms and/or meeting space.

**cable** Generic term for all types of connecting cables used in most AV equipment. Sometimes called coaxial or "coax," cables comes in various lengths and gauges to perform various tasks.

**captive audience** Customers staying at the hotel who will, for convenience and lack of other options, partake in the hotel's outlets. A captive guest eats in the restaurant, uses the business center, and participates in a meeting at the facility.

**cart** Sometimes called an AV cart; used to make portable AV devices like monitors, slide projectors, and overhead projectors.

**central reservations desk, or central reservations office (CRO)** The CRO serves as a sort of "clearinghouse" for individual reservations. Those hotels with toll-free numbers typically route their calls through a central receiving center that is staffed 24 hours a day. These CROs can be owned outright by a hotel company, or they can serve as surrogate agents working on the hotel's behalf.

**coffee break** Food function designed to break up attendees' day. The coffee break can be set up inside or outside the main meeting room. It allows attendees to stretch their legs and network between sessions. Coffee does not have to be served, but it often is during the early and mid-morning breaks. Afternoon breaks can include any type of beverage and snack. These breaks can be themed to match the mood and feeling of the planner and attendees.

**commissionable rate** Ten percent industry addition to the net room rate. This commission is paid to the travel agent or meeting planner once the guest(s) pay for their room(s).

**compression of demand** Theory that the need for hotel rooms in a city or geographical region remains fairly constant despite occupancy levels. In effect, if one part of an area is sold out, the demand for rooms compresses in such a way as to drive those looking for rooms elsewhere. This compression often occurs first with downtown and convention hotels. A city-wide convention may take up all rooms in the downtown area, while the normal or average demand for transient and other group rooms remains fixed. People then have nowhere to go but outward from the downtown area. This compression leads to increased occupancy for hotels not normally affected by the demand in the downtown area.

**confirmation letter** Letter that reinforces or confirms a mutually agreed upon action.

**continental breakfast** Lighter version of the sit-down breakfast that serves cold food items and hot/cold beverages. The continental breakfast can be served in a separate room but most often is served in or around the central meeting room. It is a common starting event at which attendees congregate and get to know each other before the program begins.

**continental plan** Package that includes continental breakfast and a room.

**convention and visitor bureau (CVB)** Third-party lead generator that is most often used as an assisting service for meeting planners from outside an area. The CVB determines the basic needs of the client and distributes the information to the appropriate hotels.

**convention center** Locally funded or privately owned structure that caters to large groups and conventions.

**corporate marketing** Effort of one or more hotels working alone or in unison to position themselves as the consumer's first choice. In most cases, this is exemplified in the national and regional marketing efforts of medium to large hotel chains that promote their products as one whole.

**cover letter** Sometimes called a transmittal letter, it prepares the reader for what is being sent with it.

**customer rapport** Level of communication between a client and a salesperson. Customer rapport means the client and salesperson feel comfortable with each other and exchange useful information.

**data mining** Extracting data from a database.

**decorations/props** Items used to enhance the visual appeal of a function room.

**definite** Business opportunity that has firmly committed to a hotel to sign a contract.

**department head** Typically reporting to a member of the executive committee, the department head is the manager most directly involved with a department's day-to-day operation.

**Destination Management Company (DMC)** An organization that assists meeting planners with function logistics. DMCs organize transportation, off-site activities, recreation, and other details.

**determining goals** In a sales equation, the method by which a client's buying criteria is uncovered and addressed by the hotel in such a way as to ensure the sale.

**dimmer switch** Light control device that is often mounted on function room walls to control the intensity of house lights. It can be connected to remote switches to allow light control from the podium or somewhere away from the function room wall, or it can be a stand-alone control for portable lights.

**dinner** Last formal food function type possible in a given day. It can encompass several courses and menu items. Dinner can lead to formal business presentations or less structured events. Dances and celebrations that are scheduled after dinner are not classified as food functions because their focus is activity, not food.

**director of catering (DOC)** Person responsible for the catering side of the sales effort. He or she must be able to direct all local and group catering efforts on property. Typically, the DOC oversees the catering sales staff as well as the operational catering staff.

**director of food and beverage (DOFB)** Runs each department that sells, buys, or makes food and beverage products for guests.

**director of group sales (DOGS)** Person solely responsible for the group room sales effort. The DOGS is personally responsible for key/focus group accounts that have important and/or long-term impact on the hotel. Reporting to the director of marketing, the DOGS is accountable for achieving group revenue targets. He or she often works very closely with the director of transient sales and the director of catering.

**director of marketing (DOM)** Oversees the sales and marketing operation and directs the group sales strategy while maximizing transient revenue.

**director of operations** Combines the responsibilities of DOFB and resident manager. Room-related and food and beverage departments report to the executive committee member.

**director of restaurants** Person responsible for the staffing, quality, and cost control of all food and beverage outlets in a hotel. Reporting to the director of food and beverage, he or she works closely with the executive chef's staff to ensure restaurants and lounges meet standards.

**director of services** Viewed as the "behind-the-scenes" version of the front office manager. He or she is responsible for the housekeeping, laundry, and, often, recreational services of a hotel.

**director of transient sales (DOTS)** Person responsible for the transient sales effort at a hotel. Working with his or her team of reservationists, the DOTS attempts to maximize the potential revenue of the transient market. In coordination with the DOGS and members of the executive committee, the DOTS is the one most responsible for properly implementing yield management. He or she is sometimes called the director of reservations.

**displacement** Impact when rooms taken by a group piece of business exceed the group ceiling. Displacement can also be measured in the analysis of rates.

**display tables** Tables used inside a function room to display materials and other items. Several display tables drastically reduce seating capacity. Six-foot tables are most commonly used for displays.

**dissolve** Process by which two or more projection units are faded in and out together to create a seamless presentation.

**dubbing** Process by which recorded audio is transferred from one recording to another.

**effective marketing** Marketing a service, a product, or an idea in such a way as to invoke the perception of benefit to the consumer.

**equalizer** Audio device often used with an amplifier and/or a PA system that allows for adjustments in bass, treble, and midrange frequencies. It can be employed when the audio source lacks sound quality or the acoustics of the room are less than ideal.

**European plan** Commonly mistaken for a package but no meals are included. It is another way of asking for the room rate only.

**event functions** The vast majority of groups a salesperson books at a hotel will require function space for a meeting or convention of some sort. These are classified as event functions because the focus is on the event itself.

**executive chef** Person responsible for the overall food production effort. He or she must control food cost while ensuring that the hotel's level of food quality is maintained. More of a manager than a hands-on chef, the executive chef monitors the food production of the restaurants, lounges, catering/banquet functions, and in-house employee cafeteria.

**executive committee** Made of senior-level managers who direct one or more facets of a hotel's operation. Reporting directly to the general manager, the executive committee sets specific revenue goals and operational targets. Sometimes called the leadership or operational committee.

**exhibit/display space** Area near the general session for displays and exhibits from various providers. Often called a trade show, this space is designed to provide attendees an avenue for mingling and networking with vendors. Academic groups may provide display space for attendees to share new ideas with each other.

**exhibits** Vary in dimension. Large exhibit displays should be set up in a separate area whenever possible, because they reduce seating.

**extended-stay hotels** Provide their guests with the services, amenities, and facilities they want or need to facilitate long-term stays in one location. To varying degrees, these services/facilities can include stove and/or microwave, refrigerator, dishes and kitchenware, limited housekeeping services, grocery shopping service, and, occasionally, business services. The cost of a room is often less than that of a room in an all-suite hotel. A guest can rent a room by the day, week, or month. These hotels rarely have on-site food and beverage outlets, but they are often built in locations that have restaurant options nearby.

**feature** Tangible aspect of a hotel that can be shown, felt, or touched by a client. A feature is demonstrable.

**feedback** High-pitched squeak or squeal that is caused when audio from the speaker system recirculates through a microphone.

**flipchart** Large pad of paper mounted on a tripod or another type of easel that is used to illustrate a point. Useful in teambuilding, brainstorming, and other types of meetings.

**food cost** Purchase price/menu price.

**food function types** Center around meals.

**freeze-frame** One frame of video or motion picture that is stopped for display.

**frequent stay incentive program** Offers repeat guests the motivation of earning points that can be redeemed for some type of reward. Similar to programs offered by airlines and car-rental companies, these rewards can result in free room nights, vacation packages, and other perks for the loyal customer. Most programs grade the customer based on volume of usage. The top-level grades offer lower rates, upgraded rooms, and other amenities for each stay. Some business travelers become so loyal to a chain's frequent stay program that they pay higher rates or stay at less-than-top-notch facilities to earn points. Frequent stay programs are also called guest loyalty programs.

**front office manager** Person responsible for a large portion of the most visible aspects of a hotel's operation. He or she directs the day-to-day activities of the front desk, bell stand, and concierge staff. Some hotels include the PBX (internal switchboard or operator) staff in the front office manager's line of authority.

**front projection** Style of light projection that uses a standard front reflective screen of any size. The light source (often a projector of some kind) must come from the front only.

**full-service hotels** Provide their guests the services, amenities, and facilities they want or need for a full hotel experience.

**gateway cities** Traditionally those located in areas that make them first practical stops for international flights coming to the United States. Seattle, San Francisco, and Los Angeles are considered gateway cities for Asia and the Far East. New York, Boston, and Washington, DC, are gateways to Europe and beyond.

**general manager** Individual ultimately responsible for the hotel. The general manager may report to a regional manager in a chain or to the hotel owner. Sometimes referred to as a managing director or general director, the general manager directly or indirectly (via other managers) coordinates the hotel's operational and sales effort.

**Global Distribution System (GDS)** A global network that has been created which allows travel agents direct access to a specific hotel or chain. The GDS also ties airlines and car rental companies together. The purpose is to allow the travel agents to book entire vacations or travel itineraries at one time.

**goal** Client's buying or motivating objective.

**group block** Allotment of rooms for a group.

**group catering contribution** Catering business acquired by a hotel that has all, or a major portion of, attendees staying at the hotel. All functions that result from this group (all breakfasts, lunches, dinners, receptions, and so on) become group-related catering functions. The group-related functions contribute to greater catering revenue.

**group ceiling** Number of rooms the group sales department is expected to sell as part of the total rooms sold at the hotel. With the transient sales effort, the group rooms must bring the hotel as close to sold-out status as possible.

**group reservation methods** Ways in which group reservations come into the hotel. Most hotels offer group attendee three ways to make reservations for an upcoming event: (1) individual call-in; (2) rooming list; or (3) registration cards.

**group resume** Fundamental document that communicates to all departments the specifics of a group. All food/beverage, sleeping room, and ancillary details are communicated via the resume to each operational department.

**group rooms** Reservations that bring more than one guest into the hotel. Group rooms comprise a series of bookings that correspond to specific functions. These functions can be conventions, meetings, or other events at the hotel or nearby. Most hotels categorize a booking of 10 or more rooms per night as a group booking.

**group sales equation** Rates = Dates + Space; Dates = Rates + Space; Space = Rates + Dates.
Rates—Group sleeping room rates
Dates—Dates of the group function
Space—Function space needed in the hotel

**group turnover** Method by which a catering or convention service manager becomes aware of a group and the details of its program to that point. Properly done, the turnover gives an "at-a-glance" look at where the group is, as well as valuable information on the client and contact(s).

**guaranteed reservations** Reservations made by a transient guest who wishes to ensure that a room awaits him or her upon arrival. A reservation is guaranteed by a cash deposit or credit card. A guest must cancel a guaranteed reservation by a specific time on the day of arrival (usually 4 to 6 P.M.) or that guest is charged for the room. Group reservations may also be guaranteed, which results in the group agreeing to pay for any no-shows.

**history** Documented historical room performance of a group relative to the rooms contracted. History can show how an organization, a company, or an association has done over time.

**heat/light/power** h/l/p.

**hot** Descriptive term for the state in which a coaxial cable carries a live feed or when some AV device is in use.

**hotel controller** Person in charge of the financial reporting and cashflow management of a hotel.

**hotel location type** Classification by physical positioning relative to customers in the area and to their locales. A location type defines where the hotel is. The main location types are downtown, airport, resort, and suburban.

**hotel operational marketing** The methods, approaches, and collateral used in positioning and/or repositioning a hotel property to meet predetermined marketing goals as set out in the hotel's marketing plan. Operational marketing is also the way a marketer redirects the marketing effort to compensate for unforeseen challenges and/or opportunities that can arise by changes in market factors.

**hotel product type** Determines the service and amenity level as well as the target market. A product type defines how and for what the hotel is used. Product types are determined by service level and target markets.

**Hotel Sales and Marketing Association (HSMA)** A local grouping of hotel/motel managers and executives who get together to share ideas and network.

**hotel service level** Measured by the actual and perceived consideration a guest can reasonably expect to receive, based on the hotel's reputation as well as comparison with other product types.

**hotel size classification**

| Classification | Number of Sleeping Rooms |
|---|---|
| Small | 1–150 |
| Medium | 151–400 |
| Large | 401–1,500 |
| Mega | 1,501+ |

**house lights** Permanent lighting system in any function room.

**house sound** Permanent audio system in any function room.

**human marker** Aids rapport building by revealing traits and insights that are not readily apparent. Markers like body language and discourse level are vital to building rapport.

**hybrid markets** Combined target markets. Hybrid market classifications allow the marketer to the determine specific market segments within and among the main three hotel type market segments (standard, extended-stay, and all-suite).

**independent meeting planning firm (or individual)** Conducts searches and aids clients in deciding on and/or conducting meetings and conventions. In many instances, the hotel has no contact with the guests until they arrive.

**individual booking cycle** Time between when an individual reservation is made and when that reservation is due to arrive. The booking cycle can be anywhere from a few days to a few months.

**intermediary** Person or entity who acts as a liaison for a guest and the hotel.

**International Association of Travel Agents (IATA)** Internationally recognized body that certifies and regulates the travel agent industry.

**introduction/good-bye letter** Often called a transition letter, this letter documents the beginning or ending of a relationship.

**junior sales manager/"meetings manager"** Coordinates meetings and conferences of small to medium size. He or she is considered both a sales and a catering manager.

**lavaliere microphone** Small microphone that can be attached to a speaker to allow freedom of hand movement. It can be wireless or corded.

**LCD computer projector** Uses liquid crystal display (LCD) technology to project a computer's image onto a large screen without a projector.

**lead generation** Process undertaken by potential clients or the hotel to generate interest. This generation of interest creates tangible business opportunities called leads. Generating leads is the starting point from which all business originates at a hotel.

**level** Measurement of volume or intensity.

**limited-service hotels** Lack food and beverage outlets as well as meeting space.

**liquid crystal display (LCD) computer panel** Unique computer monitor that allows light to pass through it. Used with an overhead to display contents on a screen for a large audience.

**local catering** Hotel business with no associated group rooms. Specifically, local catering is business in which the function or meal is the primary focus. Some local catering may have sleeping rooms associated with it, but unless the main goal of the client is to book rooms, it is considered local catering.

**Lost Business Report (LBR)** Used to track the business that did not book at a hotel. Useful in covering trends and as a solicitation tool.

**lunch** Midday food function that can serve a full meal in the meeting room or in a separate room. Lunch menus can be similar to dinner menus, but slightly smaller. A roll-in lunch allows for the meal to be served while attendees conduct business. A sit-down lunch is more structured in that attendees must adjourn to another room. Lunches can be plated and served as a complete meal to attendees or as a buffet from which attendees serve themselves.

**major arrival or departure** Day when most group rooms arrive or depart.

**management by walking around (MBWA)** Management style characterized by visibility and accessibility.

**marker** Signal that allows the marketer to direct the marketing resources of a hotel in the most efficient and profitable ways.

**market share** Hotel's portion of the market relative to portions of the market taken by the competition. Market share analysis in the hotel industry factors in a hotel's size. A hotel's size dictates its potential market share. Therefore, hotel market share is further defined as the potential total market share relative to the actual market share.

**market segment** Portion of the actual or potential business pool at a hotel. Categorizing this business into segments that share characteristics is called market segmentation.

**marketing plan** Document put together by a hotel's marketing leaders to chart a course for the next year. This plan dictates any repositioning actions that must be taken by surveying competitive and market factors. It also summarizes the next year's marketing budget, advertising plan, and fiscal goals.

**meeting** Most frequent need for event space. Sometimes also referred to as a general session, the meeting is the most important event a group plans. The business conducted and topics addressed in these meetings generally bring the group to the hotel.

**meeting/function space** Used for any type of group function. A group function can be a meeting, a meal, a dance, an expositions, or any other gathering.

**Meeting Professionals International (MPI)** Perhaps the most recognized and well-run organization of its type in the country (and now the world), MPI is unique in its basic structure. In order for hotel salespeople to join, they must bring a meeting planner with them. This balance of planners and suppliers allows for equal influences and direction. MPI organizes national meetings, regional seminars, and even an informative newsletter.

**mixer** Audio device that combines multiple audio sources. It is often used to create a seamless recording level. A mixer must be used whenever sound is amplified or multiple microphones are used.

**modified American plan** Includes two meals, typically breakfast and dinner, and the room in the rate.

**monitor** Common term for a television monitor. It is used most often as a video playback viewer, but it can be used in many ways. The sizes are generally similar to home televisions. This term is sometimes used as jargon for an audio monitor.

**multimedia** Use of two or more AV devices in a presentation. Most often used to describe high-end and extravagant programs.

**National Association of Catering Executives (NACE)** An organization of hotel catering and convention service personnel who get together to share ideas and network.

**national sales office** Third-party lead generator available only to medium to large hotel chains. A national sales office (often abbreviated as NSO) is located in major cities like New York; Washington, DC; Chicago; and Los Angeles. NSOs are staffed with salespeople who actively seek business for their chains. The NSO acts like an extension of a hotel's sales team.

**no-show** Term used in transient rooms analysis to describe the number of guests with reservations who do not arrive on a given night.

**occupancy** Measurement of the rooms sold each night versus the rooms the hotel has available to sell. This percentage is viewed by the industry as one of the most important measurements of overall performance.

**office room** Area set aside for the meeting planner and his or her staff as a central point of operations. Large groups may require small meeting rooms to house all their materials, copiers, fax machines, and so on. The office is often held on a 24-hour basis.

**outlet/ancillary** An outlet is as a food and beverage point of sale. Restaurants, bars, lounges, room service, and other outlets can provide a hotel with significant revenue sources. Ancillary revenue sources are revenue sources outside of sleeping rooms or food and beverage. An ancillary revenue source can be a hotel's business center, golf course, tennis center, AV services, or gift shop. The revenue from outlets and ancillaries is generally tied to the number of guests in the hotel.

**overhead projector** Device by which light is sent through a directional lens and displayed in a forward direction. The overhead projector most often uses transparencies or LCD computer monitors as their presentation sources.

**overselling** Process by which a hotel sells more rooms than it has available on a given night.

**ownership actions** Acts or services performed by a salesperson to help ensure the success of a group. A salesperson can take ownership of a group by involving him- or herself in these actions.

**pan** Rotation of a camera around the viewing area. The goal often is to get a panoramic view.

**PBX** Acronym given to the hotel switchboard. All incoming calls are routed through this department. Guest faxes and messages are delivered from the PBX operators. The PBX department also manages the wireless inter-hotel communication via radios.

**pickup performance** Term used to define how well a group is doing with reservations relative to the number of contracted rooms.

**pinpont advertising** Process of using advertising media and other resources to reach targeted markets on a regional or national level.

**pipe and drape** Common term that describes portable dark draping that can be set up as a divider (useful in exhibits) or as a barrier to conceal something (rear screen).

**podium microphone** Microphone attached to a podium or lectern.

**Point of Sale (POS)** Cash registers in the outlets and ancillary areas where an exchange of goods or services occurs.

**positioning** Promoting a brand or product relative to the competition and how it is perceived by the consumer. In the hotel industry, positioning brings together the concepts of product types, location types, actual and traditional business mixes, service levels, and target markets.

**postcon** Postconvention meeting; a forum by which the relevant hotel staff meet with the contacts of a recently concluded function in order to review the bill and discuss what went well and what didn't.

**precon** Preconvention meeting; a forum by which the relevant hotel staff meet with the contacts of an upcoming function to make both parties fully aware of what is to come.

**preopening sales office** Generates community awareness and books business for the hotel prior to its opening.

**prime selling time** The specific hours during the day where the salespeople have the best opportunity to reach current and prospective clients. The optimal selling hours of any hotel may differ slightly based on their respective time zone location.

**Professional Convention Management Association (PCMA)** Similar to MPI, this national organization brings planners and suppliers together to share ideas and network.

**profit margin** Determined by comparing the sales revenue and costs incurred in providing a service or product. In hospitality, profit margins of each side of the success triangle can be derived from analyzing room cost and food cost.

**Property Management System (PMS)** Ties different operational departments together. Housekeeping, accounting, reservations and the other various departments are connected to the front desk.

**proposal** Communication sent to generate interest or outline client discussions.

**public address (PA) system** Portable audio speaker set up that is generally used in large areas or auditoriums. Useful when the house sound does not suffice.

**qualification** Process by which a salesperson learns the specific characteristics of a business opportunity. Qualification uncovers the who, what, where, when, and why attributes (5 *W*s) of a piece of business. Qualification of business is considered the first and one of the most important steps in hospitality sales.

**readerboards** Posted daily event sheets or scrolling television monitors telling meeting attendees where and when their functions are.

**rear screen** Style of light projection that uses a rear-generated light source. The nonreflective screen can be viewed from the front of the room. It is useful in that no AV device can be viewed from the audience, but it tends to take up a lot of function space. Often, pipe and drape are used to hide everything behind the rear screen.

**reception** Often a precursor to dinner, a reception is designed to promote mingling and communication among attendees in the evening. Hard and/or soft beverages may be served with light snacks. A formal reception may include a full bar and an assortment of hors d'oeuvres. Receptions can occur at any time of day in today's market.

**receptive customer** One who is more likely than the general population to be interested in a product or service due to personal interest or need. A receptive customer may feel he or she received a special return for his or her money if he or she perceives value in the product or service.

**registration space** Set up in front of the general session room, registration space is made up of one or more 6-foot tables and serves as a meeting check-in point. The meeting planner may staff this area to hand out conference materials, identification credentials, and other items needed by attendees.

**Religious Conference Management Association (RCMA)** Another nationally recognized organization that is focused on planning meetings and conventions for religious groups of all kinds. Their national meeting is a must for tapping into this large meeting potential.

**remote** Device used to activate an AV device from some distance. It can be attached via wire or it can be wireless. It is used often in slide projector and video presentations.

**request for proposal (RFP)** A formal request made by a client for a sales proposal from a hotel.

**reservations manager** Employed traditionally by large hotels as a day-to-day manager of the reservation agents engaged in transient sales.

**resident manager** Position that started for the manager who lived at the hotel (hence the term *resident*). Today, at large hotels, it is rare to find the resident manager residing at the hotel, but, because of the age-old responsibilities of coordinating the operational side of the room-related hotel functions, the title remains. Some hotels use the title "rooms division manager" in lieu of resident manager.

**revenue source** Result of a product or service a hotel makes available to guests for a price. The size and scope of these sources can differ greatly from hotel to hotel. Most hotels use three main revenue sources:

1. Sleeping rooms
2. Meeting/function space
3. Outlets/ancillaries

**rev-par** Revenue per available room. This analysis allows hotels of different sizes to compare the revenue generated by the sale of sleeping rooms. Rev-par divides the total sleeping room revenue generated for a predetermined time frame by the total number of hotel rooms. Rev-par goes beyond occupancy analysis because it factors in ADR.

**roadblock** Hidden goal that becomes a barrier to winning a sale.

**room availability** Number of sleeping rooms that are available for sale on any given night.

**room rental** Cost of function space. The cost of this space is not considered part of a meal or a meeting. It is often called a setup fee.

**room-to-space ratio** Number of overnight rooms needed by a business opportunity relative to the total amount of square feet the group needs for function space.

**sales manager** Working under the direction of a senior sales manager or the DOGS, this is the most prevalent position in hospitality sales.

**sales operations** Functions/roles/duties a salesperson may engage in before, during, and after a sale.

**sales team** Divided into two main parts that mirror the two main hotel revenue sources: room sales and catering sales.

**satellite downlink** The connection made to an orbiting communications satellite to link audio and video from other locations.

**seasonality** Term for the time of year when a special attraction is open or at its peak level.

**senior catering manager/catering manager/convention service manager** Primarily concerned with two things: the booking of local catering and the servicing of groups.

**senior sales manager** Handles major group accounts; sometimes called a national account manager.

**servicing** On-property coordination of the specifics of a group. Depending on the size of hotel, these specifics can be food and beverage related or rooms related.

**show rooms** Specially designated sleeping rooms that are unoccupied for display as part of the site inspection.

**site inspection** Used by potential clients to look at the facility under consideration.

**situational need periods** Unforeseen situations that may arise and disrupt the business cycle at a hotel.

**skirting** Using fabric or linen to wrap an AV cart or table to make it look more professional.

**sleeping room** Traditionally the main product of a hotel. A hotel's primary purpose is to provide accommodations. A sleeping room is one of these accommodation units. The price of each unit is the room rate.

**slide projector** Video device used to project one slide one at a time. Sometimes called a carousel projector because most slide projectors use the carousel tray to hold and advance the slides.

**sliding scale** Penalty clause in hotel contracts that adjusts to the number or scale of slippage in sleeping rooms or food/beverage revenue.

**slippage** Term used when analyzing the group room performance at a hotel. The difference between what is contracted for and what arrives.

**SMERF** Social, military, educational, religious, and fraternal market segments.

**Society of Government Meeting Professionals (SGMP)** A grouping of local hotel and meeting facility salespeople and various government meeting planners. A good group to work with if the government is a big local player or the hotel wants to focus on this market segment.

**solicitation** Process by which a salesperson seeks new business opportunities.

**space efficiency** Method by which a hotel's available space is allocated relative to other events in the hotel and upcoming functions. Optimizing the revenue potential of function space, while minimizing labor and other costs, is considered efficient space utilization.

**space intensity** Amount of function space used for an event or a group versus what is considered typical for the hotel.

**speaker phone** A "hands-free" phone.

**sphere of influence** Reach of a hotel's local marketing effort.

**spotlight** Can be part of the house lights in a permanent setup in a function room, or it can be portable. It allows light to be targeted on one person or object. Useful when a stage is in use.

**standing microphone** Microphone attached to a free-standing device that can be adjusted for height and angle.

**strobe** Rapidly blinking, high-intensity light. Often used in multimedia presentations to add visual impact.

**successful sales triangle** Three-sided relationship dictated by the selling of the three main revenue sources in a hotel. The room sales effort fills the sleeping rooms nightly. The catering sales effort endeavors to fill the meeting space. The combination of the two translates into sales in the outlets and ancillary revenue sources.

**surge protector** An electrical device that acts as a buffer between sensitive equipment and an electrical outlet.

**table microphone** Microphone attached to a small flexible stand that is mounted on a tabletop for those seated. Used in panel discussions.

**target market** Market segment(s) the hotel wants to penetrate. The target market can be tied to a product type or specifically designated by a marketer as a new focus.

**target rates** Minimum rate goals the group sales team must reach to achieve the predetermined revenue target.

**tentative** Term used to describe a business opportunity that has been qualified and has been determined by both the hotel and the client as viable.

**thank-you letter** Communication sent to show appreciation for business.

**third-party leads** Lead generation source coming to a hotel from an entity other than the client. A third party acts on the behalf of a client in the search of locations and facilities.

**throw** Measurement of projection distance.

**total hotel impact** Overall revenue contribution a group has to all three sides of the success triangle.

**traditional business mix** Pool of potential customers who are tied to a location or product type.

**traditional need periods** Occur at a hotel with regularity. The times of year when a hotel's business cycle traditionally drops.

**transient rooms** Rooms that originate as individual reservations.

**transient sales manager** Person primarily responsible for developing the nongroup room market at a hotel. Typically, the transient salesperson is the only proactive member of the transient sales team. He or she frequently approaches the local market to generate volume account agreements.

**travel agents** Primarily used for transient business travel. The travel agent coordinates many aspects of a traveler's trip, including hotel, airline, and ground transportation.

**turnover** Process by which a group salesperson makes the catering/convention services department aware of the details of a group.

**turn time** Time available between functions to change sets.

**video cassette recorder (VCR)** A VCR is used to record and playback video.

**VHS** Standard format all VCRs now use. The VHS system uses ½-inch videotape.

**video projection** Device used to project any VCR playback onto a screen. Often used when a standard monitor is not big enough to be seen by all in attendance.

**wedding specialist** Manager who handles the coordination and execution of weddings and wedding-related events.

**weekdays/weekends** Sunday through Thursday (weekdays) and Friday and Saturday (weekends). Classification of days of the week are shifted 1 day earlier.

**yield management** Management of the transient pricing strategy.

**zoom** The action of magnifying a subject over distance without moving or changing the actual camera or video source location.

# Index

Note: Page numbers with an *f* indicate figures; those with a *t* indicate tables.